009118

ᴎ 5399

D1486149

329540

THE COMMUNITY DEVELOPMENT PROCESS

The Rediscovery of Local Initiative

THE
COMMUNITY
DEVELOPMENT
PROCESS

The Rediscovery of Local Initiative

William W. Biddle

WITH THE COLLABORATION OF

Loureide J. Biddle

HOLT, RINEHART AND WINSTON, INC.

New York, Chicago, San Francisco, Toronto, London

To all who wish to work for a better future, and are
willing to begin on the local scene.

SOME ARE PROFESSIONALS:

To the educators who believe people can learn to become more
adequate persons as well as acquire knowledge.

To the scientifically trained who would use their skill as an instrument for bringing about favorable change.

To those planners who seek cooperation with citizens, in order to
make planning flexibly effective.

To the social workers who hope to stir the beneficiaries of welfare
services into the responsibility of self-help.

To religious workers whose faith is strong enough to allow other
people to discover the values that can be practiced.

To administrators who want to see initiative and dignity increase
in the persons they serve.

SOME ARE CITIZENS:

To those who are dissatisfied with popular predictions of despair
and would improve the fate of man by improving man himself.

preface

The idea that men might lift themselves into a good society takes on new life. Hopeful attitudes grow, in part, out of well-financed programs to eliminate ignorance, poverty, bad health, bad housing, and other social evils. But many of these proposals have a discouragingly familiar ring. Reformers have tried before to purchase a way into utopia. Hopefulness arises more out of the possibility that people can be encouraged to help create a better social order.

This book attempts to open a door upon the enormously difficult possibility that men may improve themselves. There is no certainty that this possibility is realizable. But there are hopeful leads to be followed. One of these grows out of experience with planned economic and social development in recent years. A second lead is found in new knowledge of human potentials for improvement coming from the social and especially the behavioral sciences. The two leads can be combined in a practical yet theoretical disciplining of the much discussed and much misunderstood field of community development.

For multitudes of citizens, a hope of self and social improvement seems unrealistic amid the fears, frustrations, and apathy of a disruptive age. Will the hope prevail or the apathy?

Governmental and private programs of improvement are launched, which depend for their implementation upon local committees that are assumed to exist or that will be created by proclamation. Certain writers and orators vaguely approve grass-roots participative organizations. Others more specifically endorse community development as the *sine qua non* of social progress.

This book makes the means of encouraging citizen initiative more specific by giving definition and content to the community development process. It describes methods by which great social improvements can be expedited by local citizens in a multitude of rediscovered and revitalized communities. The scientific knowledge is still incomplete; but, as this book points out, the beginnings of such a science can already be discerned.

The new emerging methodology of community development supports the conviction that social improvement does not occur until the people involved believe that improvement is possible. The people themselves must be sufficiently convinced to take the initiative. The fact that they may be mired in apathy does not preclude their growing into the self-confidence of responsibility. As people are brought to feel a sense of community and to adopt goals that serve their growing concept of community, the conviction that they are able to contribute to social improvement seems to increase in them.

Community development provides the small-scale social laboratory wherein the hope for a favorable future can be tested experimentally. Because it develops human beings, community development is an educational enterprise; but its methods disturb most traditional educators. Accustomed disciplines of teaching are displaced by disciplines from the behavioral sciences. Research—action research—is accented. The research methodology grows out of the unique experience of cooperating with people in a process of dynamic growth. Here a preliminary systematization of the discipline is given, offering a beginning for an applied social science of human improvement. The research thus far is largely nonquantitative, but, as the discipline matures, measurements as well as descriptions of processes may prove appropriate.

Although the methodology of disciplined community development derives from the behavioral sciences, it does not merely borrow from its parents. The field of community development begins to evolve its own rigorous discipline; it takes a form of its own, dictated not by precise, pure research but by respect for the persons who take part in it and for the discovered necessities of their developmental processes.

This book begins with an intimate view of the phenomenon

under consideration—human beings in process of self-chosen change. Specifically, it presents in case-study form the development process in two communities, a mining county in rural Appalachia and a deteriorating neighborhood in a northern industrial city. Concepts and commonly used terms are defined; a process of development is identified that can be used in groups small enough to permit attention to the growth of persons. The individually participative process is then related to the large-scale planning and complexity found in modern metropolitan living. The research design is outlined, and an attempt is made to clarify the relatedness of community development to various academic disciplines and helping professions. A preliminary identity is given the active community developer, who is essential to the process. Finally, appendixes give further information on community development, especially in the United States, and bibliographies list relevant literature in the social sciences and in world-wide community development.

The processes described in this book are needed by most programs instituted to create a better future. The Peace Corps has already realized the necessity of community development, as have other contributors to international social improvement. The same need in domestic areas is recognized by various programs under the Office of Economic Opportunity, such as VISTA (Volunteers in Service to America), Community Action Programs, the Job Corps, and Work Training and Retraining Activities. In time, other improvement programs will arise, and most of them will find indispensable the cultivation of people to assume local initiative.

Without adequate provision for community development, the construction of public facilities often fails to contribute to democratic social growth. Unless such provision is made, this failure will be repeated in urban renewal and rehabilitation, in area redevelopment, in highway construction, in subsidization of industry for needful regions, and in similar programs.

The local social forces on which federally financed programs depend stand in even greater need of the processes described in this book. Local governments can contribute to the growth of democracy as they press beyond political manipulation of social organizations toward the development of responsibility in their constituents. Social welfare agencies are called upon to seek out citizen initiative as well as to provide professional services for the needy. Planners, both urban and regional, will find in the community development process a means to democratize planning. Increasingly, churches will be called upon to cooperate across denominational lines to expedite the growth of people in community context. Civic enterprises and community relations councils that grow out of civil rights struggles all need to use the healing process by which community is created or recreated.

Responsibility for bringing the disciplines of social science to community development rests largely with academic institutions. They will find this book useful in meeting the obligation. Public schools, if they would, could become focal points in the community for antipoverty and society-building activities. But they must come to accept community development, sometimes relabeled "community education," as a feature of their work, in addition to the teaching of children.

Colleges and universities are the centers from which the assistance of social science can be made available to schools, nonacademic institutions, and government programs. The particular academic subdivisions that are likely to manifest interest in community development will vary among institutions: Interest may be evidenced by departments of sociology, anthropology, social psychology, or adult education; by schools of social work or of theology; by extension activities of large universities; or by special institutes for continuing education, urban affairs, human relations, public administration and planning, or even, in a few cases by those openly labeled community development.

Some, perhaps most, social scientists in universities will maintain that active social improvement is not their obligation. They will prefer to continue with teaching and with controlled campus-laboratory research. This book offers a challenge to such a limited concept of scientific responsibility. Experimentation for social improvement is under way and will go forward whether or not social scientists involve themselves in it. Such experimentation is more likely to produce a better society if it will give the scientists an opportunity to contribute their knowledge and skills to an emerging applied social science.

Equally importantly, social scientists who take part in experimentation for social improvement can expect to find their skepticism modified by an awareness of the beneficial changes that can occur in people. They may also find that optimism to experiment with man's future can be as respectable scientifically as descriptive gloom about his present.

New York City   W. W. B.
February 1965   L. J. B.

contents

THE COMMUNITY DEVELOPMENT PROCESS

The Rediscovery of Local Initiative

chapter 1

Introduction: A New Hope

Those who use the term "community development" (their number is legion) are enthusiastic for vague reasons. They are strongly in favor of "community" (whatever that may be). And they are equally in favor of "development" (as long as this moves toward their preferred objectives).

But the enthusiasts encounter difficulties when they become specific. They do not agree upon what "the community" is that they hope to develop. Their confusion reflects the fact that ordinary citizens have lost or are losing the sense of community, the experience of community. Whether the people live in older apartments or in new housing developments, in inner city slums or in unincorporated urban fringes, in affluent or in not-so-affluent suburbs, in smaller cities and towns or in sparsely settled areas, in trailers or in lodgings for transients, they find neighborly relationships difficult to maintain and less than satisfying.

The loss of community reality and participation jeopardizes many values of the democratic tradition. Those generous impulses that grow out of an awareness of a local common good are weakened. There is increasing conviction that one should be loyal, not to the common good, but to standards of dress, behavior, and belief that are set by people beyond local control or to large-scale associations that stress conformity to standards set by a distant headquarters, as in labor unions and professional organizations, or even in great

churches and political parties. Or one is merely lost in the amorphous anonymity of a huge population.

As a consequence, the ordinary citizen becomes less and less
articulate and makes fewer contributions to the decisions that shape
his own destiny or the collective destiny. The democratic experience, whereby the voice of the ordinary citizen at the local grass
roots has been heard in higher level decisions, is lost. So a method
of work that promises to increase the responsibility of the citizen,
is pertinent to the treatment of some of the malaise of our time.

Many authorities use the phrase "community development" as
a sort of magic incantation, a cure-all for ailing municipalities and
neighborhoods, and the residents therein. On examination it will
be discovered that these authorities have a vast variety of meanings
in mind. In their writings, they may give definitions of the phrase
and outline specific methods of operation. More characteristically,
they may leave the phrase undefined, on the tacit assumption that
other people will, "of course," agree with their unspoken objectives
and outline of work.

Much of the literature of community development is more ex-
pressive of the writer's enthusiasm to do good than of any discipline
of description and evaluation. Both the enthusiasm and the discipline are necessary if this field of work-with-people is even to approach a fulfillment of its promise. In the pages that follow, we
shall attempt to combine the two, leaning heavily upon the social
sciences for description and evaluation, but making as clear as possible the values served.

As to values, let it be stated immediately that development is
always normative. That is, it takes place in the midst of actions that
serve chosen goals. No scientist (social or any other kind), when
he takes part in development, can be content with description only.
He must approve actions and evaluate results in the light of some
scheme of values toward the attainment of which the development
is directed. The paradox for the scientist is that he will never describe man fully as long as he limits his attention to man-as-he-is.
He will need also to describe man-in-process-of-becoming. And
this latter task requires planned development that seeks chosen
goals.

What are the objectives of community development? They are
found in Judaeo-Christian teaching as it emerges in the democratic

tradition. An attempt to state these objectives fully will be found in Chapter 4. The social scientific justification for such normative thinking will be found in Chapter 12.

As to the methods of community development, there are many (often contradictory) outlines offered by different community developers, depending upon the objectives they accept. These methods will be discussed in Chapter 5 and, again, in Appendix I. Gradually, however, a general agreement on both objectives and methods is beginning to emerge from the welter of differences. Our presentations attempt to make explicit that emerging agreement, in order that it may be subjected to the discipline of social scientific thinking.

The emerging consensus clusters about a concept of the improvement of people, the underprivileged, the overprivileged, and all in between. Improvement is evaluated in terms of democratic skills, responsibility to serve a growing awareness of a common good, ethical sensitivity, and willingness to cooperate. All other improvements are judged good or bad by reference to what is happening to the people involved.

Most articulate authorities in the field are coming to accept such criteria. Most will accept also that such favorable development in persons is brought about, not so much by what is done to benefit these persons, as by the decisions for action that they make for themselves.

In order to expedite this development, a new kind of worker-with-people is called for. Does this mean that a new profession must be created or that the workers in already existing fields of endeavor must learn new skills? As a matter of practical actuality, the new worker remains identified with many traditional professions—teaching, social work, religious work, public health, planning, journalism, engineering and architecture, and even research work in a number of scientific disciplines. But community developers should not be hampered by any identification with any one profession. They must use scientific backgrounds that are not bounded by any one discipline, or even coalition of disciplines. While retaining their professional and academic connections, they seek to perfect research methods that grow out of a fresh examination of people who are changing purposively.

To get started on the task of bringing some order from the chaos of hope, we present two case studies. These tell of human beings in the process of contributing to the design and redesign of their environment. We have chosen projects in which we, the writers, were involved because an intimate familiarity with human processes is necessary for the conceptualization that follows.

chapter 2

A Rural Project [1]

Day County is located in the southern Appalachian mountains. It is in an economically depressed area that has been bypassed by much of modern life. The economic situation, dominated by an ailing coal industry, has steadily worsened since the end of the Second World War. As a consequence, the county has lost population at a rate that is among the highest in the state. Most of the residents who remain in the county face an uncertain future, both in standards of living and in attitudes.

The whole Appalachian region of which Day County is a part has been of concern to churches and philanthropic enterprises for generations. But the main achievements, until recently, have been the surveying of the area ("The place has been surveyed to death," said one prominent educator) and the partial alleviation of such acute needs as hunger, ill health, poor clothing, and shortage of formal education. Educational efforts have tended to drain the more promising young people out of the area, thus increasing the

---

[1] Fictitious names are used in the case studies presented in this and the next chapter. As community developers, we refer to ourselves in the third person. At the time these projects were under way, we often referred to the community development process as "community dynamics." The work was done under the auspices of the Program of Community Dynamics at Earlham College. Both case studies were financed by the Emil Schwarzhaupt Foundation.

difficulties for those who remain. Little has been done to help the
people find a viable way of living and thus cultivate the responsibility of self-help.

Mr. Fellows, head of a mission (consisting of an elementary
school, a two-year high school, a hospital, a small farm, and a
chapel), after working with Day County residents for thirteen
years, had become discouraged. The efforts of the mission had
failed to do more than increase the people's expectation of help.
The local people were unresponsive and had not learned how to
develop any initiative for their own improvement. Would it be possible, he asked, for a new approach to be made, using the methods
of community development?

The Environment of Living

Much has been written about the plight of the southern mountaineers. Those in Day County have much in common with people
in other areas, but they also have their own local and personal differences. Perhaps the key historic fact has been the isolation of the
region. Residents have been isolated from the changes that char-
acterize modern life, but they have also been isolated from each
other, living in the hollows, suspicious not only of outsiders, but
also of neighbors on the other side of the ridge.

The effects of isolation have been particularly noteworthy in the
churches of the area. These churches have been small, feeble, and
other-worldly, often not related to any national denominations.
They have often exhibited intense rivalry, each offering its own
exclusive interpretation of salvation. The term "Christian" is frequently used to designate members of the speaker's church; members of other churches are sometimes referred to as "unchristian"
(the latter term embracing also those obvious "sinners" who make
or drink bootleg whisky or who smoke and swear).

Living standards are low even among miners' families, for although the miner's daily rate of pay is high, his employment is
uncertain. Health and education services are substandard. A hospital built by the coalminers' union and public schools have begun
to improve these services. Yet many families are on relief or dependent upon philanthropy for the necessities of life.

Apart from small-scale farming, the chief means of livelihood has come from lumbering and coal mining. The construction of roads for both industries had been begun in the past, and even though both have diminished, the building of roads, to meet the demands of the motor age, has continued.

As the new roads have opened the area, the isolation has gradually broken down. Electricity has become more widely available; radios have introduced the advertising and commercial standards of the outside world. The old folk songs and stories, the native handcrafts and other indigenous and unique cultural expressions, are rapidly disappearing. Materially, the people are aspiring to come out into the confusion of the modern world. In habit and in attitude, they tend to live in an environment that is passing away.

Beginnings

In inaugurating a development project among the people in a depressed area, a community development worker immediately faces a serious problem. He hopes for an invitation to cooperation, a request for help in accomplishing some good thing that the citizens want. But people who are apathetic, suspicious of outsiders, and accustomed to charity, are not likely to extend such an invitation.

In this case, workers were found on the social science staff of a distant college. The director of community dynamics there had to be content with an invitation from Mr. Fellows. But it was necessary to differentiate the expediter's role from that ascribed to the mission and its personnel. It was necessary to create a friendly rapport with the citizens, a rapport that would not be influenced by their attitudes toward the mission. Faculty representatives from the college undertook to establish such a relationship.

Activity in Day County was to be initiated by faculty visits to the area and by student and faculty work camps beginning in the summer of 1957. The promise of student participation in the work camps and of their eagerness to work was to be used to encourage cooperative activity by the local citizens. But as it turned out, the work camps were not the key contributors to the community development process.

In a development project, it is important to be aware of the probable expectations of the participants, both at its beginning and during its course, when expectations change. The mission staff members, with Mr. Fellows as their spokesman, were seeking a method for increasing initiative among the local people, but they were skeptical about success. The faculty and students from the college wished to carry out an action research experiment in the development of those who learn to guide change in themselves.

The motivations of the local citizens cannot be stated so clearly. They must be inferred, initially, from the statements of those people who had been in contact with the local citizens, then from the reactions of the citizens as the project continued. That the people were dissatisfied with their lot was clear. That they had any desires which could be utilized for self-improvement was doubted by the missionaries, who had labored with the people over the years. Indeed, the missionaries insisted that the local people were hopelessly sunk in apathy.

A first task for the expediters of process, therefore, was to discover prosocial motivations that could be utilized for self-help development. This was a difficult assignment when those who knew the people so well were convinced that any desire for improvement was lacking.

History of a Process

In this human development project, genuine changes in the participants occurred within a short period of three years. There were improvements in self-perceptions, in motivations, and in conduct, and these improvements have lasted. The local encouragers of the process have taken responsibility for their indefinite continuation.

PRIOR TO 1956

Over the years, according to more than one staff member of the mission, the work had proved frustrating in terms of the people's response. The constituents served had come to expect that the churches and wealthy donors would continue to care for them. Indeed, it was pointed out that when a public road was constructed to the mission, the local residents who owned land along the right of way had resisted the improvement by raising the price of land sold to the county. The construction of the road had been delayed by this demand for individual profit.

The failure to elicit cooperation had been further corroborated by the outcome of two student work camps that a religious organization had conducted a few years earlier. These camps had constructed facilities at the mission and had improved the homes of some local residents. The mountaineers had accepted these services as their due, offering no helping hand, and often complaining that so little was done for them.

Mr. Fellows pointed out that the personnel of the mission tended to have a stultifying effect upon individuals and meetings. He was so convinced of the mission's tendency to dampen initiative that he proposed to stay away from the committees that were to be formed. He did not want the mission to take part in the activities of the development project. He held to this position—for himself —until there was a clear-cut demand for his presence.

Whether such a self- and mission-effacing attitude was as necessary as Mr. Fellows thought is debatable. Eventually, both he and the mission staff came actively into the enterprise. Perhaps they could have done so much sooner. Perhaps the people's attitudes toward the mission might have improved more rapidly.

1956

Mr. Fellows and the director of community dynamics met for the first time at the annual convention of the Council for the Southern Mountains, in February, 1956. Mr. Fellows' expression of his dissatisfaction with the methods and results of the mission invited experimentation with other methods. The director mentioned community development work with populations having some similarity to the southern mountaineers. He agreed to send to Mr. Fellows printed accounts of development projects that might have bearing upon the problems of the depressed area.

Thereafter, the two corresponded, discussing by mail the possibility of undertaking a demonstration project. At the invitation of Mr. Fellows the director and his wife made three trips to the mission during the course of the year. The first two were friendly, get-acquainted visits. The last marked the definite beginning of the project.

In the early fall of 1956, before the third visit, a definite commitment was made to undertake a three-year action research program. That limited period was to be used to discover whether enough progress could be made toward self-motivated growth to allow the process to continue on the initiative of the local participants.

The visit to launch the project was scheduled for early December. Early in November, Mr. Fellows wrote to express qualms about the proposed undertaking.

> . . . I have been feeling of late, very pessimistic about the kind of genuine community response which I think is essential in anything we undertake. I am sure that you felt last spring my strong concern in this regard and a real question in my mind whether our surrounding community could be expected to develop new attitudes and a more positive, healthy form of cooperation, with a fairly sizeable and long established institution like [our] school [mission]. There is a further question in my mind, even apart from the presence of the . . . school, whether our immediate community is not abnormal in the degree of its lethargy and indifference to opportunity and desire ever to help itself on any basis. This is a fearful thing to say. It is true that we have not tried all the approaches that could be made. At the same time, I am conscious of all that has been tried, not only since we came here in 1942, but even earlier, and one must keep one's eyes open to the indications that one sees almost daily. . . . —my question is still concerned with the attitudes of local people here. I am sure it is going to take a very fresh approach to overcome their present attitude toward outsiders coming in to offer something to them. I am not sure but what this new approach to have best chance of success, should not be kept free from any association in the minds of local people with such an institution as the [mission] school.

Two or three days later, the director of community dynamics replied:

> Your letter of November 6th was received with appreciation, but not with alarm. . . .
>
> It was valuable to have you outline the difficulties of the situation. I think these should be made as clear as possible before any project is undertaken. May I say, however, that these difficulties are the kind we take into consideration whenever we are planning a new project. We have run into the same lack of response before. In our thinking the problems merely present a challenge to work out the possible approach to overcome the difficulties.

Following this exchange of letters, the director of community dynamics and his wife spent two days at the mission. They conferred with the staff, but concentrated more upon talking with local residents who might assume responsibility in the project. Prior to visiting the homes of these local people, they asked Mr. Fellows to circulate the word that the visitors were kindly folk who were to be trusted. This generalized endorsement utilized positive attitudes toward the mission without identifying the visitors with it.

The purpose of the home visits was to discover any prosocial motivations that might become the basis for local decision making and action. The visitors started with the assumption that such motivations are present even among those who have had a long history of apathy. Thus they encouraged the people to talk about their problems and asked them for ideas as to what might be done cooperatively to improve local conditions. They asked also whether the local citizens would be willing to work with others and whether others would be willing to join in. Finally, they asked if there was any way for getting people together to start activity. As an inducement to cooperation, they promised that a group of students and faculty would be willing to come and help with whatever task was undertaken during the following summer.

Before their visit ended, the director and his wife had compiled a long list of proposals for the improvement of the area. These proposals were quite diverse: making homes and churches better, controlling floods, building better roads, finding new ways of making a living. Many were impractical; all were sincere. Some of the mission staff were surprised that such ideas came from these people. They had doubted that the people had any constructive ideas.

Several factors probably contributed to this early positive response: the endorsement by the head of the mission (whose judgment was trusted perhaps more than he realized); an attitude in the visitors that implied belief in the people's importance and capability; the judicious use of a husband-wife team, which made easy an approach to both sexes; a degree of local readiness that the mission staff had not previously discovered—because no attempt had been made to discover it. The question now was, would the people act upon their ideas?

The selection or formation of a local organization to expedite cooperation was a difficult matter. These mountain people had had little experience with, or loyalty to, a sense of community. Conversation with them led them to the conclusion that the most promising group with which to begin was the Parent-Teachers Association of the mission school. The chairman of this newly formed organization, Dorothy Drake, was a miner's wife. At the urging of others, she agreed to act also as chairman for a citizens' committee; she would call meetings and urge members to take responsibility.

Those who had given some indication of their interest accepted two obligations: to select some task (from among the numerous ideas already proposed or from any other) as a beginning activity, and to prepare for the reception of the student-faculty work camp that would help them on this task during the summer.

Two personalities were prominent at the beginning and during the next six months, Dorothy Drake, housewife, energetic, full of ideas, and Abner Peters, native of the area, college-educated, quiet but devoted, and recently chosen to be pastor of a small church.

1957

Over the years the mission had served a wide area with its hospital and school. For a community development project, however, a smaller area had to be selected as a focus of the activity. A geographic center for the activities was chosen by mission personnel in conference with the initial leaders of a committee. They chose the small settlement of Big Maple, about five miles from the mission and close to Abner Peters' small church. There, at the confluence of two creeks, were half a dozen homes, a store, a service station, a post office, two churches, and an empty building belonging to the mission. Families from several "hollers" by custom came to this small center for various services.

In January a citizen's group began to meet in Big Maple. The numbers were small, less than half a dozen. They met in homes and in the back room of the store. They kept in touch with community dynamics people by mail.

Toward the end of March, Abner Peters was able to write:

> ... Full cooperation and participation is assured. We agreed upon some possible committee members to be approached. B.B. of Big Maple will serve. *No* hesitation. Flood wall is of great interest and local industry, but in his words, "It will be worthwhile just to have some young people with high ideals to be with my boy." His long range evaluation of such activity was, "Even if we could not get everything accomplished we will have gotten together anyway." This just shows

that I have underestimated the people of our community. Other ideas flow fast and it will be good to have you come to help us in the program.

To this letter community dynamics people replied:

> Your letter . . . was most pleasing to us here. The response of B.B. (and perhaps others by now) must be very encouraging to you. . . . As for a project, we'll be ready to work on anything the committee decides is best.

As a result of discussion the committee chose as its first task the construction of flood walls to protect roads, bridges, and small fields from further devastation. Looking forward to the summer as an active work period, they found it necessary to make plans, to design walls with some help from local experts, to enlist neighbors who would haul stones to the site by mule and stoneboat, to purchase and assemble supplies of cement and tools. All this required activity by individuals and subcommittees.

In addition, the Citizen's Committee extended an invitation to the future work campers. They made preparations to care for these helpers during the period of work. They asked the mission for the use of an empty building, which had been used as a clinic some years back. They requested also the use of a stove, beds, and other equipment necessary for the proper care of the visitors. They even repaired the unused building, fixing the roof and stairs and cleaning up after the tenancy of rats and squirrels.

While these preparations were being made, there developed a crisis serious enough to threaten the whole enterprise and to provoke a hurried visit by the director of community dynamics. The members of the local committee, mostly men, had rejected the leadership of the feminine chairman, Mrs. Drake, and had begun to stay away from committee meetings.

The rejection seemed to grow out of the fact that Dorothy Drake expressed too many ideas, had too much energy, pushed people too much. These expressions of personality were especially inexcusable in a cultural setting in which women must not be too prominent. Further, the Drakes had recently laid a new sidewalk from the road to their front door and had planted a garden. The upshot was that the people concluded Dorothy Drake was "uppity." Finally, her husband, "the mister," ordered her to attend no more meetings. In sorrow, she complied.

The director of community dynamics and his wife, acting as an expediting team, discussed the failure with Mrs. Drake. She was encouraged to analyze the situation, as she saw it. She admitted that she had pushed the men too hard and even suggested how, by acting more diplomatically, she might have minimized the unfortunate results. She agreed, however, to help pass the chairmanship on to Abner Peters and so make possible the reorganization of the committee. After she had achieved some objectivity of judgment, she said to the wife of the director of community dynamics (after he had left), "He gives a body hope, doesn't he?"

Dorothy Drake represented an emergent leader upon whom the expediters had relied too heavily. As is often the case with people new to leadership, she took actions that, according to members of her group, were unwise. Still, it is possible that she might have learned from her unfortunate experience and emerged again as a leader, more seasoned and more successful, if her husband had not interfered with this possibility. Some time later, her husband retired and the family moved out of the county.

A few facts about Abner Peters, who now assumed the chairmanship, are important. As a native, he was acceptable to the local people. His college education was not a handicap, nor had his employment by the mission school, a short time before, interfered with his relations to the people. His selection as pastor of a little church in the nearby valley had come later. (He is an ordained minister.) He was known to be related to many persons in the region, including the new deposed former chairman, Mrs. Drake. These several assets, combined with a sense of humor, made him an excellent choice for the job of local community development encourager which he eventually accepted.

It is to be noted, however, that Mr. Peters chose to act initially in his role as the pastor of a church, rather than as an employee of the mission school. He was convinced that, coming from a small church that "belonged" to a local congregation, he would be acceptable to all. This conclusion seemed to be correct as time went on. As a pastor, he seemed to belong in the area. He was liked even by those who did not attend his church.

Despite organizational problems, the members of the committee and the people of the area took seriously their obligations to prepare for the activities of the summer. They had a place more or less ready for the students on their arrival, they had work materials on hand, and they had set aside time for their own labors. More significantly, perhaps, they had planned to hold a number of the committee meetings while the helpful visitors were present.

The work campers were received cordially. (A faculty member, with wife and four young children, helped.) The warmth of welcome was noteworthy, especially in view of some earlier unhappy experiences with outsiders. Perhaps the fact that local people planned for their coming, invited them, and prepared for their arrival, made a difference. Instead of being looked upon as good-hearted folk come to serve, these work campers were accepted as collaborators. The cordiality was probably an expression of the rapport already established by the husband and wife team. There was some evidence that the local citizens came to work, and later for recreation activities, to appear in a favorable light with the newcomers.

An additional factor operating to change self-perception and conduct, however, was the nature of the task undertaken. The construction of flood walls demands cooperation. A stream on the rampage is no respecter of anyone's property. Protection against its ravages must be obtained for the stream as a whole, not just for one householder. A wall to redirect flood waters must be designed for many properties, for public roads and buildings. Its completion necessitates the cooperative effort of numerous people. Those who had been separated by geography or religious rivalry found themselves coming together in a common cause that would benefit all who lived along the stream or in the valley. The presence of workers willing to work as directed by local decision helped to increase the cooperation that the task required. Several dangerous sections of the stream were protected by wall, the total length of which might have been about a hundred yards.

During the summer, work campers regularly attended the meetings of the Citizen's Committee. They were able to make suggestions and contribute to a developing sense of unity. But they avoided taking responsibility for the decisions that had to be made by the citizens. They contributed chiefly to the growing local conviction that the meetings and the committee were important.

While most of the committee's time was given to solving the problems involved in the building of flood walls, a beginning was made also in the setting up of playgrounds. The committee assumed the responsibility of purchasing the equipment for the playgrounds.

About this time, thought was also given to the selection of a name for the committee. It needed an identity, and a name would be a recognition of the importance of its work. Thus the committee now became "Big Maple Community Council."

At the end of the summer, with expressions of genuine regret on both sides, the work campers departed. There followed a period of slump in interest and activity. This phenomenon is often observed in community development enterprises, especially after great endeavors, and even after observable success. The flood wall had been constructed; the playgrounds were in operation. Citizens had enjoyed the visitors and cared for them. They could now relax in self-congratulation.

Abner Peters wisely did not urge the local people too much to resume activity. For they were looking forward to another summer and were thinking about the selection of other tasks to keep the group going. After two or three months of lessened vigor, they began to attend meetings again in gradually increasing numbers, and with a gradually increasing sense of responsibility.

1958

During the spring of 1958, there was a noticeable increase among members of the council of a sense of responsibility and of a sense of the importance of the work. Perhaps this was encouraged by the acquisition of letterhead stationery, a matter of pride, since it visibly affirmed the group's identity. More important, however, were the activities and the events that demonstrated the growing influence of the council.

Again and again the question of improving the roads had come into group discussions. At first the general opinion had been that local people could do nothing to influence the distant and impersonal bureaucracy that decided such matters. But gradually the question had been raised whether they might not draw attention to their local needs. After they had studied figures on tax collections and on allocations for roads, they concluded that the county had been neglected.

Finally, a petition asking for the construction of new roads and for the blacktopping of others was drawn up. Council members circulated this petition widely to obtain signatures and then conveyed it to the bureau of roads at the state capital. To the astonishment of some, the bureau responded with interest. Before the cold weather set in, machinery appeared, and the main road into the area was blacktopped.

It should be stated that the first successful petitioning did not solve the problem of road building for all time. The state crews discontinued work when the winter brought bad weather. To keep the state at work on the roads, the appeals had to be repeated from time to time. But the state's response to the appeals and petitions provided convincing evidence that these people, who had thought themselves powerless, could obtain the interested attention of important and powerful public officials.

Attention from the holders of power came in other ways as well. Representatives in the state legislature, and politicians of both parties, attended council meetings from time to time to ask what they could do to serve the area better. Business leaders from the county seat, becoming aware of the council, asked it to appoint representatives to confer with them and inquired how they might fit into further planning.

At the same time, the council began to discuss a wider array of topics. It sought to increase the service of the bookmobile. It began the consideration of the feasibility of various new economic activities, such as the making of cement blocks for home construction, the raising of sheep, and the preservation of berry crops. Abner Peters started a small bakery, which sold cakes to the stores in nearby towns. There was even an investigation into the possibility of using local clay for ceramic products.

Then, too, it was necessary for the council to plan for the activities of the following summer. Again, this included an invitation to the work campers and the preparation of the buildings in which they would stay, as well as the selection of tasks upon which all could work. It was decided that more work should be done on the playgrounds and, especially, on several church buildings that needed rehabilitation.

Throughout this period there was evidence of excessive dependence upon Abner Peters. He carried on the correspondence, wrote or edited the petitions, called the meetings, collected the study materials for the discussions, and assembled the proper materials and tools. Until other members of the council became more self-reliant, such dependence was perhaps necessary, but Abner was disturbed by it.

There was also some question whether there was not too much dependence upon the encouragement of work camps sent from a distant college. To make the development process more permanent, was not the encouragement of a nearby institution needed?

In order to prepare the personnel of the mission school to assume more of this responsibility, a number of steps were taken by the director of community dynamics. Letters constantly interpreted the philosophy and methodology of community development. Printed materials, books, and pamphlets were sent. Plans were made for both Mr. Fellows, and Mr. Peters to visit the college to become familiar with other community enterprises.

When summer arrived, a second work camp came as invited and as promised. But when the campers arrived, for the entire summer this year, Abner Peters was absent. He would use the summer months to obtain additional college training. When he had first made his plans, his absence looked like a calamity, but on reflection, and as matters worked out, his absence helped to diffuse the responsibility for leadership.

Mr. Fellows found it necessary to be absent at the time of the campers' arrival. During May he wrote:

> It will be good for Abner to have this opportunity. [Away at school] I am reluctant to have him away from the camp at any time. At the same time, it is possible that this might be just "what the doctor ordered" as a means of forcing more distribution of responsibility among others. . . . I have sometimes suspected that there is too much dependence on Abner and I hope the time is right for a little change in this picture.

In reply, the community dynamics expediters asked that substitutes be appointed for Mr. Peters and Mr. Fellows, so that the visitors could "look forward to hard work and good fellowship with the people." Abner Peters then emphasized to the council in a letter that "this is a people's project and that it would be as effective as the people make it." Another chairman, F. T., was chosen, and a secretary was elected to handle the great number of details. As the summer wore on, the spreading responsibility worked out satisfactorily, although at the beginning there were many occasions when people seemed lost and insisted that particular tasks had "always" been taken care of by Abner. But in his absence other leaders emerged.

Eventually, F. T. proved an effective chairman, and the members of the council made extra efforts to be friendly to the work campers. Indeed, it is possible that the visitors were closer to the people during this summer because, with both Mr. Peters and Mr. Fellows away, there was less tendency to make contacts through an intermediary.

The campers' group was smaller this year—four students and two faculty members. Again a professor brought his family. Cooperative labor for the summer included the painting of the various churches in the area, the excavation of basements for Sunday School rooms, and additional work on the playgrounds, floodwalls, and small bridges. Recreation activities, including some handcrafts, assumed more prominence. Social contacts with the people became a major responsibility for the campers. They visited with local families, both nearby and out in the "hollers." It is probable that these contacts added further to the local importance of the Community Council.

The efforts to rehabilitate and improve the churches were particularly noteworthy, since congregations that had lived in long-standing rivalry worked cooperatively in this activity. Teams made up of members from more than one church (or from no church) worked with the campers upon a single building. When the work was finished there, they all moved to the next church, all working for the benefit of the entire community. Through such cooperation, supplemented by the discussion and planning of the council, an experience and a concept of community was beginning to become real to these people.

About this time a distracting event threatened to interfere with the progress of the project. A graduate student appeared. A doctoral candidate in anthropology at a large university, he wished to collect data from local people for his thesis. He proposed to give personality tests (by paper and pencil response as well as by interview) to the people, and he asked that the good relationship that campers, mission staff, and other visitors had achieved, be used to make the testing possible. The community development workers

refused. Instead, they encouraged Abner Peters (who had returned) to help the graduate student find another population in another section of the mountain area.

In addition to the desire to avoid the confusion caused by mix-
ing two experimental procedures, there was another good reason
for the refusal to cooperate. The collecting of data for a monograph
is a scientific procedure of objective description; no responsibility
for the people involved is accepted, and no process of change is
contemplated. In the scientific method being followed in the community development project, the emphasis was upon a compassionate objectivity, which is concerned for the progress of people
toward a better life. The action research was dynamic; it rested
upon a warmth of friendship that, it was hoped, would induce the
people to take responsibility for their own improvement. To introduce an investigator who might be perceived as taking advantage of friendship would have been to violate the confidence local
people had placed in the expediters.

The graduate student was invited to attend council meetings as
an interested and interesting friend. But his testing was carried on
elsewhere.

With the return of Abner Peters in the fall, the Community
Council was in full swing of discussion and planning; its members
continued to take responsibility for many activities. It was possible
for an assistant on the community dynamics staff to summarize the
endeavor as follows:

> The activity . . . has been designed to accomplish certain objec-
tives.
> First, an effort has been made to raise the citizenship capacities of the
people of the mountain community . . . . Second, educational growth of
. . . students and faculty members has been sought. Third, in order to
better understand community change processes, research was undertaken into inter-personal interaction patterns and into county development possibilities.
> The first purpose was advanced by a process of personal and group
encouragement of . . . citizens. Encouragement was effected through
home visits, participation in regular community affairs, and the agency
of a newly formed Community Council. . . . For two summers faculty
members and students lived in the . . . community. There they worked
in cooperation with local residents in carrying out projects for the

benefit of the community. The project work was carried out by the Community Council with the encouragement and assistance, but not the direction of the students and faculty personnel. The . . . Community Council has continued functioning and . . . Community leaders are investigating the possibilities for small economic enterprises. . . .

With the fall the question of the ultimate withdrawal by community dynamics also began to be considered. The quesion of withdrawal must be faced by every helper of community processes when the local citizens have reached a point where further aid interferes with the achievement of greater responsibility. The question is especially pertinent when the help comes from afar and when on-the-scene institutions can be induced to carry on the work more effectively. The problem involves the transferring of functions and responsibilities from one set of encouragers to another.

At this stage the problem became a simple question, "Could the mission be encouraged to move beyond its historically induced reluctance, become officially more active in the Big Maple area, and look to making such work a regular part of its on-going program?" Early in October, the director of community dynamics wrote to Mr. Fellows:

> It seems to us that the time has now arrived for Abner Peters and you, and other people connected with the school, to be more free in taking initiative as citizens of the area. The old picture which people had of the school as a philanthropic institution, may be changed into a picture of an institution which allows certain individuals to live in the area and take part in its activity. Possibly this will be easier for Abner as a native of the area. . . .

In addition, Mr. Fellows himself was urged to take a more active role in the council now that nearby citizens had discovered their own initiative.

An unexpected event that occurred at this juncture was turned to good account. Abner Peters lost his position as pastor. His church had preserved a tenuous connection with a distant hierarchical office. This office, wishing to stress emphases that had no relationship to the problems of the community or the mountaineers, insisted upon sending a replacement to preach its doctrines. Rather than resist such pressures, the local congregation reluctantly let Mr. Peters go.

In October, Mr. Fellows wrote to the director of community dynamics:

> Although the news about Abner Peters sounds bad at first, I am not sure but what his new situation may be turned to advantage. As he is no longer connected with the church . . . then possibly he could bring himself up in the thinking of the people as a leader of the [Community] Council without the suspicion that he was trying to build up the strength of his own church. In this capacity he could speak as someone connected with the [mission] school.

With the memory of former failures still fresh, the mission was reluctant to become active, even at this stage. The presence of Abner Peters and his success as a leader who had inspired others to take leadership provided a means for overcoming this reluctance.

A differentiation needs to be made between the dependence, upon a person or an institution, in which initiative is pauperized, and the dependence in which the encouragement that can lead to growing responsibility is expected. The line between the two is often difficult to find, but it is important. Community dynamics was trying to help the mission personnel to achieve the latter. It seemed unlikely that mountaineer citizens would make further progress toward self-help unless some institution accepted systematic encouragement as a regular responsibility.

1959

In January, 1959, Mr. Fellows wrote:

> In an earlier letter last fall you mentioned your thought that the time might be coming for [the mission] to take a more active role, either as an institution, or through some of us on the staff here participating in the Council at Big Maple. On this one point I have not felt able to agree that the time had come for this. I am increasingly impressed with the apparent effect which the long continued program of the [mission] for the past forty-five years has had on the present generations in our community. Also, I have noted the experience we have had in recent years in attempts to get groups of citizens together for specific discussions. No matter which way we have come at it there has always been a smothering effect when [mission] staff members have come too largely into the picture. It seems very hard to overcome old associations, and I have felt it important to see that this time the community leaders

themselves establish a sound working relationship, even if we have to wait a long time.

This is where the recent Council meeting had such a gratifying result. I am exceedingly happy that this has happened just before Abner came to the college. It was very hard to lie low all last fall, and yet I felt that this was the wisest thing to do, particularly in view of the change in the pastoral situation in the Big Maple Church. I think we were right in allowing time for that situation to settle down, and for the people to overcome a certain embarrassment which I think they may have had in letting Abner go. I also think that they have a keener appreciation of Abner's potential, and are now convinced that he is still in the picture to help in any way that he can, without any reference to the pastoral situation.

Later in the same month, Abner Peters came for a ten-day visit to the program of community dynamics at the college. He was present at a number of other community endeavors, attended classes, and conferred with faculty members. During his visit the staff had an opportunity to interpret for him both the philosophy and the methods of community dynamics and to raise questions about changes in the functions and responsibilities of the council at Big Maple. He carried ideas back to the mission.

After the visit the expediters sent a letter to Mr. Fellows:

> Would it be possible to look upon a section within a convenient distance of [the mission] as an intensive demonstration-research-training area and make [the mission] the institutional organizing center for this work. I could see Abner handling the main local contact work and you mainly the money-raising and relationships with other agencies and educational institutions. . . .
>
> Your judgment on refraining from an over-active role with the people in Big Maple may be correct. I did suggest to Abner, however, that I thought you should be active to change their attitudes from one of expecting charity from [the mission] to one of expecting stimulation for self-help. We recommended that Abner seek to have you invited to attend meetings of the . . . Council. . . . Might not Abner and you seek to start one or two other similar groups of self-developing citizens in other nearby communities? . . .
>
> In making all these suggestions, I am aware of "the smothering effect when [mission] staff members have come too largely into the picture." We find this same effect out in [another state] also, but are working with the people there to change it. We believe you can do the same, but it

requires your taking positive actions to create new impressions to replace the old. These positive steps are part of the proposed new emphasis.

The positive steps were to act as a community dynamics encourager, instead of as a mere dispenser of charity or conductor of traditional religious services. As an encourager, the director of the mission might visit in homes, encourage the people to talk and to express ideas, and attend meetings as a participant and not as a director of discussion. He might also take part, from time to time, in the cooperative activity of painting a church or laying out a playground.

Meanwhile, the Community Council was meeting. Genuine interest was manifest, even though attendance might fluctuate widely, from four persons at one time to thirty at another. Of the first meeting of the year, Abner Peters wrote:

> The first meeting was held at the community center [the mission-owned building in Big Maple, which had housed the workcampers] for several reasons. The main one was to make the meeting more public than it had been. . . . The result . . . ten people were present and it was not long before people were exchanging ideas and I confess that a good many of them seemed like dreams too great to fulfill. In this meeting we discussed: Iron Ore, Coal By-products, Clay, Cement Products plant [Blocks], Guard rails on our roads, Bridges across the creek in at least two places. As an almost impossible afterthought these ideas came forth: Canning vegetables on a community basis, Casket making and a Mechanic shop. We went far enough to discuss Co-op financing and decided that it is the best way to finance a project. L. T. and I made a trip to [a town in a neighboring state] to observe the methods of manufacture of an aggregate for blocks and other products. We were a bit discouraged when we found it not at all a community project but one sponsored by a Pittsburgh firm.

After a later meeting, he wrote:

> We had an election. Mr. C. [principal of the mission school] refused the nomination and thought the people of the community should be in front. He is right. F. T. is the chairman or president and M. B. is vice chairman. I am still secretary. . . .

In this meeting little reference was made to the workcamp or the fact that the community dynamics program had anything to do with the foundation work of our council. I am sorry to say this. It seems that some people are ungrateful and yet there is a better side to it when we think there is reward in seeing the thing we had hoped for, and that is a clicking Community Council. As I see it, the people of the Council really think that they plan such big things that the young people who come in workcamps ... are ... not able to really be leaders in big decisions. ... The people are not really ungrateful as it appears but it is a way to hold prestige. The Community Dynamics program is really effective and is appreciated ... I know.

Abner Peters' apology for the council's failure to credit the outside expediters bespoke his as yet incomplete understanding of the purposes of those who originated the action research experiment. For the encouragers from community dynamics were well aware that as people gain confidence in their ability to study, discuss, and solve their own problems, they seek credit for their own initiative and contribution and often forget the help given by others. The credit given to themselves is, in part, an indication of their growing self-confidence.

Mr. Fellows, in a letter written shortly after the report from Abner Peters, indicated that he did understand the process better.

Now, Abner was a little regretful in reporting to me that the men themselves seem to show some feeling that they, themselves, have brought this all about, without much conscious thought or mention of the participation of [college] friends. I quickly and emphatically told Abner that according to my understanding of your basic principles, this is exactly the way you operated, and what you hoped would happen. Of course, we all like appreciation at the proper time and place, but in instances like this it is the last thing that we fuss about. It seems to me that this is a beautiful example of stimulating people to do something for themselves. ...

In addition to the discussion of the ideas mentioned by Abner Peters in his letter, the council was also giving attention to the obtaining of telephone service (inviting in a phone company executive to address a meeting) and a motel or hotel for visitors. Beginnings were made in the production of concrete building blocks and caskets. Some local residents began raising strawberries and reported to the council about the profits realized. The council as a whole joined in the active consideration of a public high school proposed for the area, a four-year school that would replace the two-year school at the mission. Other economic and public service interests continued in discussion that might eventually emerge in enterprises.

By the middle of March, Mr. Fellows was able to write:

> Still keeping in mind that there are hard knocks ahead, I feel that, without our realizing it before, the . . . project is one of your outstanding achievements, and perhaps one of your most rapid ones. . . . It seems to me that the Big Maple Council is well on the way to setting an example for other community councils which may be formed with even less stimulation from the outside. Of course, they should have what stimulation they need, but the example itself will be one element of importance. I hope that [the mission] in general, and Abner in particular, can continue their present roles, and expand them as and when necessary. If the good work continues, we will be in all the better position to prove the idea of making [the mission] a center for others interested in community development. In other words, we need first to develop our exhibits as well as our experience.
>
> Your last letter confirms what I had already quite well understood from your previous letter about your relationship here, and the need for considering previous commitments, and terminating with this year. It is hard to believe that three years have passed, and yet things have happened that I might not have looked for in thirteen years. I think you should feel that results thus far have fully repaid your effort and expense.

In May, Mr. Fellows was able to make a trip to the community dynamics office, as Abner Peters had done the preceding year. His stay afforded him the opportunity to observe and to discuss the methods and philosophy of the community dynamics staff.

That summer, the third of the experiment, a small delegation from the college was again in residence in the Day County area. This group should not be dignified by the name of work camp, since it consisted of one faculty member and one student. Both circulated among council members to give assurance of their continued interest, but they gave the major portion of their time to collecting data for descriptive research studies. The student, to obtain college credit, made a study of the economic resources of the area. The professor, although he visited in the homes of the council members, was more concerned to make contacts with businessmen, ministers, newspapermen, and public officials at the county seat. He was able to promote cordial relationships between local residents and the town dwellers who had heard of the work of the council.

In great contrast with the two preceding summers of cooperation with work campers, the council was not active throughout the summer. This lull, however, indicated no permanent diminishing of the members' interest. By fall, meetings had started again, with such renewed vigor that the promise of contagion for the idea began to work out. By the middle of November, Mr. Fellows was able to write:

It seems wonderfully appropriate to be able to tell you that new blossoms are already appearing. Abner Peters has been very quietly cultivating possibilities in the community around Cedar, where Dorothy Drake lives. Following certain likely leads with the right kind of encouragement, he is now rewarded with a seemingly spontaneous effort on the part of a good-sized group of men in that community to get together. They have had at least two meetings, and have organized themselves as another branch of the . . . Community Council. They are taking action on improvements in traffic conditions and community economic problems. They have made Abner secretary of their group, and they are exploring what their relationship with the Big Maple group should be. They have a meeting place in the old school house, and are making plans to make that more useable. This group seems to be meeting twice a month at this stage. All this is most gratifying, and well in advance of the schedule that I had permitted myself to hope for.

Meanwhile, the Big Maple group continues into its third year. I have been to most of the meetings since May, when they definitely expressed interest in my coming. They did not meet during the summer while Abner Peters was away. . . .

It is especially significant, I think, that the new council at Cedar is in the community of Dorothy Drake, and that her husband is one of the vocal members. Typically, no women are present, I understand. Still the seed was sown and growth takes its own local pattern.

During the same month, a report from Abner Peters corroborated Mr. Fellows' interpretation and gave an indication of his attitude for the present and future.

I just feel it would be of interest to you to know something of our activities. . . . At the top of this page you will notice there is a new unit in the organization and we have chosen to call it our #2 section of the same Council and that in itself gives us strength. Same Council doubly strong!

The first meeting at the Cedar school house was attended by 17 men and no women. Dorothy Drake's husband was there. I am also secretary for this group. This group has asked to have two meetings each month and these are held on the first and third Fridays at 7:00 P.M.

We are tussling with some of the same problems that are on the minds of the Big Maple group. The Big Maple group is trying to strike up a courtship between the two groups and have at least one meeting a month together and one meeting at their own unit level. My business is to keep as much out of the way as possible and rejoice at their, yea *our* development.

One man has already in his garage more than 1500 feet of suitable lumber to be used in the first three caskets to be made in the Cedar group. I was to try and help get the lumber dressed and when I got the arrangements made I stopped in to tell the man that I had carried out my part of the job. He listened a little and then surprised me with this —"I am ahead of you, for I have already had 1500 feet dressed and put in the basement."

Now because I have written in a hilarious manner doesn't mean that all our problems are solved but I am happy that there is some attempt being made to help ourselves.

Greet those I know, and the best to all of you for the inspiration you have brought me.

By the end of three years of the action research experiment, three notable and apparently permanent changes had come about:

1.   A vigorous Community Council was in operation in the Big Maple area. The group had made substantial progress upon certain problems of importance to them. Although the council had yet to solve the basic problems, especially the economic ones, it was facing them intelligently and making decisions pointed toward solutions. As a result, the members had gained in confidence and in the sense of responsibility upon which any initiative for self-help must rest. They were reaching out for cooperation with sources of help—business-men, planners, government agencies, educational institutions, and others. But the initiative remained with local citizens.

2.   The idea of self-help had begun to spread. A second community unit was in operation, and requests for help in forming councils in adjacent areas had been received.

3.   The mission had begun a reconsideration of its responsibilities. This was perhaps inevitable, since the hospital closed during the three-year period and because the school's functions may soon be taken over by public authority. The selection of new functions,

however, was not forced upon the mission, but was based upon a positive desire to provide services needed by the people of the area.

AFTER 1959

In March, 1960, after the expediting relationship had officially terminated, Mr. Fellows wrote to the president of the college. He expressed

> ... the appreciation which all of us very sincerely feel in connection with the splendid and very successful demonstration of Community Development principles, which was very skillfully undertaken by your staff and patiently carried out over a three year period.
>
> I have increasing confidence in the soundness of these principles because of the amazing growth of community awareness which has taken place before our eeys. You cannot appreciate as we do this contrast with the effort in past years of many workers in the area of community organization, with a rather consistent pattern of failure. The fresh approach of the [college] project and the soundness of the principles proposed have proved a definite turning point in our experience here, and I am sure will be of significance to many others in this area in years to come.
>
> We are most gratified that the work undertaken by your staff, with such competence and tact, is now being carried forward by the people themselves as though they had been solely responsible for this growth from the very beginning. Our highest hopes have been more than fulfilled.

And he wrote to the director of community dynamics:

> Meanwhile, we continue to be greatly encouraged by local developments here. Both Councils are still in operation, and the new one at Cedar is still meeting twice a month. They have developed some projects and are exploring others. I may have told you that there were inquiries from further out in the valley on the part of a missionary group. My only question there was whether they could get off to the right start without a thorough re-examination of old type missionary approaches. The potential is great, and I believe that if we are patient we will have some very spontaneous developments which could become available as guideposts for others.

By the fall of 1961, the two community councils were busily continuing their earlier activities and, at the same time, expanding their interests. The Big Maple Council's attention to road building was still obtaining results. There was also a study of suitable locations for schools, old and new, and of roads and bus routes to carry the children to the schools. Political interests were expressed as the council members studied and recommended policy relating to the purchase of voting machines and worked to remove the names of ineligible voters from registration lists. The council's campaign for local telephone service had also succeeded; the telephones were shortly to be installed in homes. The council was also actively dealing with the Rural Electrification Administration to obtain electricity for more families. The county agricultural agent, after becoming aware of the council, had asked to be invited to the meetings, and by attending them, he reached some people he had found inaccessible up to this time. Council members had proposed that they take up a collection to pay for stationery, stamps, and other expenses.

The Cedar Council was even more active than the Big Maple Council; it was meeting twice as often, and was involved in more projects. The flow of ideas had been prolific, and women had finally been included as regular members of the council, as had the teenagers. The greater activity at Cedar may have derived from the origination of the group, which had grown out of a spontaneous demand for it. The Cedar Council had not depended upon encouragement from outsiders; it had arisen in imitation of a group that had been thus started.

Most of the interests expressed in the Big Maple group were pursued in the Cedar Council as well, but they were studied, and resulted in action, sooner. One product of the work of the council is especially noteworthy: the emergent generosity of the people. Among those who contributed land, lumber, and money for the common good were some who, a few years before, had delayed the construction of the road to the mission because they had demanded excessive prices for their properties.

Other activities have been unique to the Cedar Council. Even before the council was formed, a community playground had been set up on property that had been donated specifically to start cooperative action. A roadside park, organized and maintained by the council, has been developed on another site obtained from the mission school. The state legislature has been persuaded to change the school attendance law to keep young people in school until age eighteen rather than sixteen. The teen-agers in the council took part in this discussion.

Numerous proposals for small-scale industries have been discussed by both councils, and beginnings have been made on some— the manufacture of concrete blocks (quite successful) and of caskets (less so), the investigation of the usefulness of local minerals, the raising of poultry and of vegetables (in greenhouses), and the manufacture of potato chips and cupcakes (both have been tried with moderate success). Thought has also been given to attracting tourists to the area.

In two small cities nearby, the chambers of commerce have become aware of the councils and have sought their cooperation. New industries are coming to these cities, and the interest in tourists has been increasing. A county industrial development association and a state planning program have asked that representatives from the councils be appointed.

Today, there is little evidence that the problems of the area have been solved, but there is abundant evidence that the people have changed their attitudes and have acquired the skills needed to work constructively toward the solution of their problems. There is, in short, evidence of progress and a promise of more to come.

Significance of the Project

Every community development project needs to be interpreted in terms of the particular population involved and of the problems it faces. From the point of view of the community development encourager, the outstanding problem with the people of Day County was the achievement of habits of initiative and cooperation for the common good; the problem was to move the people from attitudes of despair to those in which they realized their ability to help themselves. This change was to be sought by the people's working together to achieve new ways of living together.

The uniqueness for this population can be illustrated by contrasting community meetings among these people with community meetings elsewhere. In the councils formal parliamentary procedures are notable by their absence; important group problems are solved in extended conversations, not in debates or the enactment of motions. There are few speeches, and there are periods of silent pondering.

The meeting as a whole readily breaks up into informal "buzz sessions" and reassembles, all without formal procedure or announcement. Controversy occurs in personal conversation, but the whole group presses toward consensus, because there is much commitment to action for the common good.

The people are still in process of learning collective responsibility. With tactful help from Abner Peters, they may discover that formal procedures are more efficient. Or they may not. (May they also discover some improvements for themselves upon the processes of group decision-making and responsible action?)

If parliamentary procedures and debating skills are lacking, cooperation is not. The tendency is for large numbers of people to respond with volunteer labor upon the projects that have been chosen by the councils and planned by the subcommittees.

Some suggestions on the problem of leadership grow out of this experience. These can be examined at several different levels of competence. Many citizens who had not previously considered themselves leaders developed skill and gained confidence as chairmen of subcommittees, organizers of work episodes, circulators of petitions, and emissaries to make outside contacts and collect needed money or information. Top officers of the council emerged as leaders, some successful, some not, but all learning. These emergent leaders gained in dignity and competence by associating on a man-to-man basis with such established leaders as state legislators, businessmen from nearby cities, and state and corporation bureaucratic employees. Abner Peters developed into a leader of a different kind. He became a community development encourager, discovering new functions for his continuing work.

Role of the Community Development Workers

As is the case when several expediters are active, the impact upon the local situation and local people varied. Individual variations in the personalities, motivations, and understanding of the representatives from the college may have confused people at times. Nevertheless, an attempt was made to have all expediters follow an agreed-upon general philosophy. And the personalities of one couple, who acted as a team throughout, remained a permanent influence.

Changes were hoped for from people at two levels—from the citizens resident in the area and from the missionaries who had come to serve the people. The citizens came to regard themselves as responsible decision makers; the missionaries decided to adopt new attitudes and skills as resident community development encouragers.

Community development workers had to measure success, not by what they did, but by what the citizens and the missionaries did. In the case of citizens, the expediters did not seek to induce changes to specific behaviors, loyalties, or beliefs; they sought instead to promote the acceptance of responsibility for doing those things that the citizen choosers believed to be prosocial. In the case of missionaries, the expediters did seek a change to a specific attitude; they sought to persuade the missionaries to accept a role similar to that of the expediters—as encouragers of growth. In both cases reliance was placed upon the initiation and continuance of processes of self-chosen and self-persuaded growth. Individuals in process of development were expected to change themselves as a result of meaningful experiences.

Individual expediters, however, were far from colorless or uninfluential. They were free to ask opinions of others, and to give opinions in return. They were scrupulous to point out continually that no opinions thus expressed were authoritarian or final. All were points of view, or alternatives available for choosing, and there were many other opinions available from a variety of sources. A constant effort was made to increase respect for information and interpretations from well-educated and competent sources.

The individual encouragers sought friendly rapport with the people who became involved in the experimental process. Such rapport tended to cause friends to give thoughtful consideration to the opinions expressed, but not to accept them without critical thought. Indeed, there were occasions when the local residents differed with the expediters and even rejected their proposals outright. But these negative responses did not destroy the ties of friendship.

Those who changed accepted the various individual helpers as persons of good will, whose methods of encouragement led them to begin and to continue their own processes of development. Now the processes continue—even after the expediters have withdrawn, even after the local citizens (but not the missionaries) have forgotten to grant any credit to the outsiders

chapter 3

An Urban Project

The northern industrial city in which this urban project was located suffers many of the social ills normally ascribed to metropolitan life. Slum sections surround the main downtown office and shopping center, comfortable home sections lie at the edge of the municipality or in the suburbs, and in between are "transitional" areas, older residential neighborhoods that are giving way to the encroachment of commercial enterprises and of expanding slums.

There are several of these transitional neighborhoods, and they vary in the amount of obvious social decay. Urban blight is found both in the structures and in the lives of the residents. The usual city ailments increase as low-income families take over block after block—deteriorated dwellings, disease, delinquency, gang warfare, small stores, and "joints" that are "hangouts" for gambling, vice, and violence.

In general, the creeping urban blight seems to spread outward from the existing slums. Usually the deterioration is blamed upon the arrival of Negro families in a block. Many white people believe that the decay is caused more by race than by low incomes and the accompanying poor educational and cultural standards. There is a continuous flow of disadvantaged families into the city. A few are white, but most are Negro. They come first to the crowded slums, then gradually press out for more space in which to live.

There is an awareness of the pressure that threatens to spread the slums and lower the quality of life for the whole city. Some responsible people who have worked through churches and social welfare agencies have demanded the setting up of a Mayor's Committee on Human Relations. Others have tried to "hold the line" against any further encroachment by the supposed blight-producing families. It has been rumored (and believed by certain people) that real estate and financial interests will decide to open up one section of the city to Negroes, while other neighborhoods are held inviolate by devious methods.

According to believers in inevitability, the deteriorative sequence, once a neighborhood of the city has been opened to Negroes, follows a pattern: One colored family moves into a block, a panic ensues among the white residents, and "For Sale" signs appear on the block. The panic is made more frightful by the real estate dealers, who advise the property owners to sell at once before the prices drop still more. Soon, all the white families leave and the block is taken over by Negroes, who often fail to keep their homes and yards in order. Then, finding mortgage payments difficult, the Negroes subdivide the residences into substandard apartments, which they rent, thus overcrowding the premises, or use the property for stores or other small businesses. All the popularly condemned social pathologies grow as a result.

Some frightened people point to the neighborhoods where this deteriorative process has already taken place, to others where it is going on at the present time, and to still others that are threatened. They insist that the deterioration can be avoided by the exclusion of Negroes. And as a result they justify all kinds of discrimination. Or they yield to the "blockbusting" tactics of certain real estate dealers.

The community development workers sought a project in the city in hopes of finding an alternative to the deteriorative process. Would it be possible to save a threatened neighborhood, to see it become integrated, with a decent environment for both races, and to accomplish this with the methods of good will? Such idealistically motivated objectives could be reached only if the residents of a neighborhood chose to seek them, and by thus choosing, start a process of becoming kindlier, more competent citizens. Might a few residents be found in some local area who could be encouraged to make a beginning?

Beginnings

The initiative to start a project in a neighborhood of the city was
taken by the program of community dynamics of a college, located
some miles distant. In the spring of 1957, the director of the college
community program began to make inquiries about problem situations in the distant city. Initially, these inquiries were made in casual
conversations with persons who knew about the city and with knowledgeable residents. In addition to the raising of questions, the director left word that the college might be interested in starting a community development project in the city.

By late spring, contacts had been made with the secretary of the
Mayor's Committee on Race Relations and with the head of the
Council of Social Agencies. Both expressed approval of a project.
They suggested the names of other people and organizations to interview, and listed areas in the city that might possibly be of interest
to the college. The Hanson Neighborhood appeared on the lists of
both, along with the names of other locations, but at this stage there
was no choosing of a location. The expediter was waiting for a citizen response vigorous enough to start a process of growth.

The Council of Social Agencies proposed that the project be
inaugurated under its auspices. The Church Federation, the Chamber of Commerce, the Metropolitan Planning Commission, the Jewish and Catholic Community Relations groups, a Human Relations
Council (made up of church representatives and other people of
good will—but, unfortunately, then inactive), and the Mayor's Committee (lacking both employed personnel and a program of activities) were also mentioned as likely participants. Although these
organizations expressed a willingness to cooperate, none had suggestions for taking the necessary first steps on a neighborhood basis.
All seemed to look to the college program to propose ideas for a
beginning.

Early in June the Mayor's Committee invited the college representatives to attend its next meeting, late in September, to outline
the project. Meanwhile, in conversation, the representatives were
encouraging various people to discuss the possibility of a neighborhood project and mentioning the willingness of the college to cooperate. The purpose of these conversations was to seek contact with
the people at a grass-roots level, and so elicit an invitation to begin.

It was hoped that an awareness of the need and the availability of help might bring such a request from interested citizens in some neighborhood in the city.

Early in July the director of the college program received a letter from a resident of the Hanson Neighborhood. The writer, Mr. Henry, a Negro professional man who had lived in the area for many years, indicated genuine concern about the problems of a neighborhood "going through a period of radical change." In his concluding paragraph he said he had heard that the director was "interested in some work in community development" in the city and asked for an opportunity to "present some of the implications of this problem" in the hope that the director "might provide some advice and leadership." In the correspondence that followed, Mr. Henry and the director arranged a meeting for the evening of the day when the college representatives would meet with the Mayor's Committee.

At the meeting with the committee, the college representatives outlined their philosophy and methods of citizen self-help and mentioned the possibilities that might grow out of contacts in the Hanson area. The Mayor's Committee could offer no help beyond moral encouragement.

The meeting with Mr. Henry, however, proved much more fruitful. After analyzing the difficulties of the project, he agreed to call together a racially mixed group to discuss matters further. As a long-time resident in the neighborhood, he had acquaintances among both races, and he was known to them as a stable and responsible person.

The conversation with Mr. Henry, in his home, marked the true beginning of the project. A concerned husband and wife were involved as first participants. Although they were church members, they operated as individuals seeking practical expression for their religious convictions. It is probable that they, and the friends they invited, sought primarily to save the neighborhood, although the friends, too, were inspired by a general good will that sought practical expression.

The Environment of Living

The Hanson Neighborhood had long been a pleasant residential section for professional and middle-class families. For the most part, the homes had been individually owned; there were few rentals and no apartment houses. The residences had been well kept and were surrounded by gardens and well-trimmed lawns. But all this had begun to change for the worse.

There is evidence that the resident families had not felt a great loyalty to the neighborhood, although they had regarded it as a pleasant place to live and rear children. The adults, for the most part, worked in other parts of the city, belonged to city-wide clubs and churches, attended social events that were open to all city residents, and related their problems to city hall. The churches in the area (several Protestant and one Roman Catholic) were attractive, and even large, but most served members from outside the neighborhood. A university, located in a section farthest removed from the encroaching blight, also served constituencies from afar and looked upon itself as an institution more related to the city, and even to the state and nation, than to the neighborhood.

One public elementary school served the neighborhood. High school students traveled to a secondary school that serves wider territory. There was one neglected park, covering a city block, in which the children played among weeds and tin cans. The university campus, which would have been a desirable play space, was not available for this use. The authorities at the university were also reluctant to allow the people to use its facilities for local meetings, except when these were deemed to be intellectual or cultural activities of city-wide or area-wide interest. Neighborhood meeting places were scarce until the churches could be persuaded to make rooms or auditoriums available.

In this well-established neighborhood, there was no modern shopping center. Local grocery, drug, hardware, and service stores had accumulated around certain street intersections. Serious shopping, however, was done in downtown department stores.

Until the "invasion" of low-income families began, Hanson Neighborhood, although racially mixed for twenty years or more, had a relatively stable population made up of educated and professional people who had lived side-by-side in seeming harmony. Actually, however, Negroes and whites had been geographic, but not psychological or friendly, neighbors. They had lived near each other, but had made little attempt to mingle or to understand each other's problems. That friendship and understanding were missing was made clear during the course of the project.

The actual size of the neighborhood was difficult to determine, as is often the case in urban development projects. A western boundary was set by a river valley, a northern boundary by the university campus. An eastern limit seemed to be determined by a main traffic artery, although this was a matter of debate among the residents. (Some wished to include neighbors from across the busy street.) The southern boundary was even more a matter of dispute; the street chosen for delimitation had shifted as the lower income families advanced.

A decision on the size of the neighborhood was made by the citizens who became active participants in the project. Although they revised their conclusions from time to time as a result of experience, mainly by including small areas on the fringes, in general they concluded that the Hanson Neighborhood was about fourteen city blocks north and south and about ten blocks east and west.

Until the effect of the project was felt, the institutions located within the neighborhood responded to the deterioration with programs that served the institutions more than the people. The university continued its traditional teaching and research programs. From time to time, it purchased residential properties for campus expansion. Public school authorities had viewed with concern both the increase in the number of underprivileged children and the departure of families with more cultured background. But they had not adapted the curriculum to meet the needs of the newcomers, nor had they assumed more responsibility in the community. The churches continued to conduct worship services and to carry on routine activities for established congregations. They continued to try to serve families that were gradually moving away, and gave little heed to the new lower-class residents.

City-wide agencies, however, had begun to be concerned about the transitional areas. The Council of Social Agencies had begun research studies of urban blight—centered more upon the areas of greatest deterioration. Social settlements and neighborhood houses had made real progress in certain obvious slums. The Mayor's Committee on Race Relations had been appointed in 1956, but was hamstrung by lack of funds. It had grown out of concern expressed by the city Federation of (Protestant) Churches, by Roman Catholic offices, and by a Jewish society. A county-wide planning bureau, influenced by these city-wide religious groups, was also giving thought to master planning. But these organizations had failed to find ways to express their concern and to help the citizens become more competent to contend with their problems.

In the Hanson Neighborhood, tensions were mounting. White families were fleeing from block after block as the Negroes advanced. Nearby blocks were decorated with "for sale" signs. Real estate brokers were sending "scare" letters to the threatened homeowners. There had been some episodes of racial gang warfare, property defacement, and bombings, and anonymous letters and telephone calls promised even greater violence.

History of a Process

PRIOR TO 1957

According to verbal reports, attempts at interracial cooperation had been made by neighborhood Negroes in previous years. The churches and the university had been approached only to elicit responses indicating lack of interest. Indeed, some animosity against the university was expressed in the comments of Negroes, who had interpreted the rebuffs as an indication of racial prejudice.

Before any active work was undertaken, the director and staff of the college community dynamics program made an appointment to discuss the proposed project with the president of the university. He was friendly enough during the conversation, but his response was reserved. Staff members tried to interpret the contemplated activity to him as an opportunity for the university to serve the community, and to explain that the project would open up new vistas to the social sciences and give pertinence to religion. The president stated that, officially, the university could have no part in the project but that he would not stand in the way of any of his faculty who might give extracurricular time.

Throughout the project, members of the university's social science, philosophy, and religion faculties have been active; the university administration has never officially recognized the neighborhood activity. When the project became successful, however, the newspapers gave the credit to the university.

1957

The first meeting, which planned for the formation of a neighborhood council, came together at the personal invitation of Mr. Henry. Present at this meeting were three white couples and two Negro couples. The whites were Rev. and Mrs. Carter (he was assistant pastor of a downtown church, she a welfare worker—the meeting was held in their home), Professor and Mrs. Osborn, from the university, and Dr. and Mrs. Evans (he was a medical doctor, and she an active civic worker). The Negro couples were Mr. and Mrs. Joseph (he was a professional associate of Mr. Henry) and Mr. and Mrs. Henry. The membership of the preliminary group is noteworthy because, with the exception of Professor Osborn and Mrs. Evans, all lost participative interest in the eventual permanent citizens' organization. Their reasons for dropping out varied. Their contribution was to start a process that others have continued.

At the meeting, spokesmen for the college community program outlined the possibilities for a solution of the problems of a neighborhood in transition. The method suggested was cooperative study and action. Ideas were made explicit by citing the experience of other citizen groups. After discussing these ideas, the group decided to meet again a week later.

The second meeting of the group (again in the Carter home) was attended by a second white couple from the university faculty, Professor and Mrs. Edwards, and by a representative of the Council of Social Agencies. In the discussion it developed that local merchants were seeking to obtain the neglected neighborhood park as a parking lot. Aroused by the fear of losing the one local recreation space (which no one had bothered to utilize up to this time), the group agreed to accept this challenge as their first activity. They decided to petition the City Park Board to preserve the park and to develop it as play space for children. They decided to organize themselves immediately as the Hanson Neighborhood Citizen's Council.

As the second meeting was being arranged, dissension arose. It was prophetic of the conflicts to come. Mrs. Evans had invited a friend who worked for a prominent city newspaper. When she mentioned this invitation to the Henrys, over the phone, they vetoed the invitation. They insisted, first, that publicity was premature and, second, that reporters from Negro newspapers should be given equal consideration; the white newspapers should not be allowed to scoop the Negro publications. Considerable altercation occurred over this matter, but the invitation was withdrawn.

The third and fourth meetings of the group occurred in November and December. Despite misunderstandings, over eight hundred signatures were obtained on a petition to the Park Board. And committees on zoning, study materials (on urban problems), and park development became active. The group had decided to have co-chairmen, Mr. Henry as the Negro, Rev. Carter as the white. The spokesmen for the college program expressed doubt about this arrangement, but they did not insist upon its modification. By the December meeting, the Park Board had decided to keep the local park intact. Later, under persuasion, it appropriated funds to clean up the play space, to equip it, and to provide supervision for play.

During this period, Professor Osborn and Professor Edwards suggested ways to stop the panic selling of properties by white owners. They advanced such ideas as the organization of blocks and the education of white families, by personal contact and literature, to remain in the neighborhood. These suggestions were not picked up by Negro members, and no action followed.

Late in the year, the meetings began to be held in one of the Protestant churches; the move had been suggested by the assistant minister, whose interest and participation had been aroused. This minister, Rev. Ashton, was one of several new people (and couples) brought into the council by the success with the Park Board and by participants' growing sensitivity to the problems of the area.

1958

Toward the close of 1957 and running on into early 1958, an open conflict developed over the proposals for "block organization." The whites, spearheaded by the university professors, urged that some such organization of immediate neighbors be formed by the council. The Negro members resisted the proposals, at first silently, and gradually with open antagonism. The white members could not understand why their apparently innocent recommendation aroused such strong objections.

Only after months of patient inquiry by the community development encouragers was a meaningful explanation of the Negroes' reaction discovered. Some years before, it was finally learned, a white citizens' protective association had attempted to form "block organizations" for the purpose of "holding the line" against Negro home buyers. Though this association had been defunct for years, the Negroes had not forgotten. The whites, apparently, were totally unfamiliar with any such history. This difference in remembered experience might explain the confusion in emotional connotation. But great as was the conflict over the proposal, even greater conflicts of purpose were present, as subsequent events made clear.

During the early part of the year, monthly meetings were held regularly. In the March meeting, Professor Edwards was elected to replace Rev. Carter as co-chairman, for the latter's church obligations were taking him out of the city. An informal "steering committee" of Mr. Henry, Professor Edwards, and Professor Osborn began to come together outside regular meetings. In spite of these more intimate personal contacts, however, as the whites pushed for block-by-block action to educate householders, the Negroes' resistance increased. Professor Osborn announced that he would be dropping out by late fall to spend a sabbatical year away from the university.

Study activities broadened to include municipal ordinances and their enforcement, recreation and welfare activities of the Council of Social Agencies, and planning by public agencies. Reports from other cities were given scrutiny and discussion. Some work was done on a survey of the physical condition of the community. A large public meeting was planned for June, at which a prominent official of the County Planning Commission was to speak.

Early in June the open meeting was held. It was highly successful in terms of program interest and attendance. More than one hundred people of both races were present. They responded with enthusiasm to a presentation by the Executive Secretary of the County Planning Commission, and they became potential recruits for the neighborhood council.

Paradoxically, while such positive activity was going forward, the relations between the races were deteriorating. The co-chairmen tended to be identified as spokesmen for racial antagonisms. In the meetings of the council, but even more in phone calls and conversations in homes, misunderstanding was increasing. Some Negroes stated (to the college community development personnel) that they would be accused of "Uncle Tomism" by their own people if cooperation with white council members were interpreted as a means of keeping the whites in the neighborhood, thus making fewer decent dwellings available to Negroes. The whites professed themselves bewildered. Each side began to question the motives of the other, first in private conversation, and then in council meetings.

In the third week of June, after the large public meeting had taken place, the regular monthly business meeting of the council was held. In the absence of any community development helpers, the differences between the two races came to an open break; the factions became entangled in a heated argument. Because no conciliator was present to help resolve the conflict, the meeting broke up in anger. No further meetings were held, and none was planned. No committees met. Apparently, the Hanson Neighborhood Council was dead. The local participants could find no way to revive it.

Early in September, after a delay dictated partly by the necessities of the academic calendar and partly by a desire to allow heated tempers to cool off, the director of community dynamics and his wife met with the spokesmen for the two estranged factions. No attempt was made to call the antagonistic individuals together. Instead, the members of each faction were interviewed separately, in the hope of finding some way to bring the council back to life. The co-chairmen, apologetic for the events of the preceding June, offered to resign. Everyone consulted agreed that the work of the council was so important that it must continue. But no one was able to suggest a way to break the deadlock.

Finally, after some urging, the co-chairman who was scheduled to preside next, agreed to call another meeting—if the other co-chairman would attend. The purpose of the meeting would be to select new officers. Both of these agreements occurred in separate conversations, after the estranged individuals had had an opportunity to air their grievances to the conciliators and to express contrition for their conduct.

The reorganization meeting was held about the middle of October. The rival spokesmen were present with their supporters, but all were on guard against extreme statements. The Negroes called for a city-wide publicity campaign for "open occupancy." The whites again called for attention to the blocks in the neighborhood. No action was taken on either proposal. Instead, the officers' resignations were received and a nominating committee was appointed to report at the next meeting. A hitherto quiet Negro, Mr. Fox, called for a discussion and statement of the purpose of the group, a suggestion that was favorably received.

At the November meeting, the co-chairmanship arrangement was abandoned, and another faculty member, Professor McCall, was elected chairman. Professor McCall found it necessary to reconstitute the committees with new or reassigned persons.

1959

Professor McCall had accepted the chairmanship reluctantly, pointing out that he was not a resident of the neighborhood. Yet so great was his commitment to local improvement and to the stimulation of good will that he was prevailed upon to serve. (He later moved into the neighborhood.) His year-long tenure of office, in which he had to carry more than his share of the responsibility, was difficult. Not only was it necessary to rebuild the morale of the group after a factional fight, but he had to do the job largely single-handedly. The two previous chairmen felt they could not help. Professor Osborn left on his sabbatical year. Rev. Ashton, in whose church the council continued to meet, departed for another city, and no substitute pastor appeared to take his place in community responsibility.

The meetings of the council were still held monthly, but for some time the attendance was small. Gradually, new faces began to appear at the meetings, some to attend only once or twice, a few to become involved in the council's on-going activities. Negroes who interpreted white motivations more tolerantly became more prominent, and white people, in addition to the university faculty, began to come from the churches and from business groups. Certain of the quieter "old faithfuls" remained, notably the women who provided the refreshments and generated a sociable atmosphere at each meeting.

The committees that had been studying books and pamphlets began to bring their research findings into the meetings. Printed reports from other cities were presented and discussed. Motion pictures were shown. A professor of geography who had studied population movements within the city and the neighborhood presented his conclusions. All these materials called for exchange of opinions.

More immediate issues were also considered: How to make new

residents (of any race) feel welcome? How to educate to good neighborly behavior those who are new to city life? How to diminish the number of episodes of unpleasantness to newcomers? How to reduce the incidence of juvenile delinquency? Though a complete solution was found to none of these questions, study of them became vigorous. And attempts were made to solve them. The council became better known throughout the neighborhood. Contacts with neighbors became more frequent, and more invitations to join the association were extended. City ordinances on zoning were studied and attempts made to decrease the violations that caused the neighborhood to be a less pleasant place in which to live.

During this time, a decision was made to give publicity to the council's activities, being careful to send the stories to all newspapers for simultaneous publication. One Negro newspaper commented that now, finally, "the wraps have come off the supersecret Hanson Community Council." In general, however, the reactions were favorable.

More large-scale public meetings were held, bringing out fifty to eighty people at one time. Motion pictures, as well as prominent speakers, were used to encourage attendance. One member of the staff from the college community development program proposed that a research study be conducted to discover why persons attended meetings or became active. The research was approved by the most active participants; they aided the study in many ways, notably by giving personal interpretations in interviews.

Contact with various governmental bodies and privately-supported metropolitan agencies increased. Many supplied speakers or participants who took part in open discussions. By the end of the year, the Mayor's Committee on Race Relations was publicly describing the activity of the Hanson Council as an excellent example of neighborhood initiative in studying and meeting human relation problems. (Did they boast of the Hanson Council because they could claim no other achievement?) Shortly thereafter, the moribunnd city-wide Human Rights Council began to meet again. Representatives from the Hanson Neighborhood Council attended the meetings and advocated such ideas as general open occupancy for the entire metropolitan area. The Human Rights Council was urged to draw attention to the neglect of the Mayor's Committee and to request an appropriation from the city council, to pay the salary of an executive secretary. They also encouraged the Human Rights Council to make research studies of conflict situations.

During this same period, a subtle change took place in the attitudes of those most active in the neighborhood council. There had been a tendency, in discussions, to blame the real estate brokers as the villains who promoted and profited by neighborhood deterioration. (It was noted that such brokers were both Negro and white.) In several meetings, the community development encouragers suggested that perhaps real estate operators were also human; although some might be taking advantage of human misery, others might be willing to seek a better community life for everyone. On the basis of this encouragement, personal contacts were made with individual brokers, and some attempt was made to understand their point of view and to persuade a few to support integrated housing. Two or three real estate brokers became friendly.

Such a broadening of understanding and contact did not, however, diminish the vigor with which differences of opinion were presented in discussions. Indeed, an important permanent function for the Hanson Neighborhood Council was beginning to emerge, that of providing a local forum for the open examination of controversy preliminary to the attempt to influence municipal and private agencies. In the council comments upon differing points of view within both Negro and white groups were aired. It was possible to give some consideration, for example, to the long-rumored accusation that the university had attempted to halt the influx of Negroes by secretly purchasing properties that otherwise might be available to Negro purchasers. (It was concluded that though there might be some truth in the allegation, even the university could not be regarded as a monolithic enemy; the university, and various of its employees, the council decided, would also be responsive to appeals based upon rational and ethical considerations.)

During the latter half of the year, another election of officers took place. Mr. Quimby, an engineer employed by an industrial firm, was chosen chairman. He changed the personnel of several committees, bringing into active work a number of new members who had been attracted by the enlarged meeting. He laid down a policy of continuing neighborhood discussions, but he avoided adopting any program for the subdivision of the organization into block units

1960

By 1960 the composition of the group was beginning to change. Although university faculty members such as Professors McCall and Osborn (who had returned) were still prominent, they shared more and more of the responsibilities with other whites—church members, businessmen, and other residents of the neighborhood. The new Negro residents recruited by their friends also were becoming influential. Greater skill in cooperation developed as a result both of new personalities (white and colored) and of changed attitudes among the old-timers.

Intensive discussion in the business meetings, supplemented by larger general public gatherings, became characteristic of the council's operations. In the inner group, such matters as episodes of persecution were considered and alleviative steps agreed upon—friendly gestures were made to the aggrieved and counseling was addressed to the persecutors. A research on participation was authorized and pursued, questionnaires being prepared and mailed out to larger numbers. The larger meetings featured educative discussions, a history of the neighborhood, a panel of city officials and persons from the real estate board—with probing questions from the audience. The results of the research survey were released to a large public meeting.

The city-wide Human Relations Council became more active with the participation of the Hanson Neighborhood Council. In its announcement of a midyear meeting it stated:

> We are faced with a major problem of increasing racial tensions in many changing neighborhoods.—We will be discussing the organization of a volunteer group who will be available to do block to block work in these neighborhoods.

In the thinking of many citizens, the Hanson Neighborhood Council had become a prototype for neighborhood cooperative effort to alleviate racial tensions. White and Negro families were working together to preserve and improve an area where they might live in harmony. Attempts were being made to welcome newcomers and to educate them to standards of neighborliness. Episodes of persecution and violence were being held to a minimum, and when they occurred, the victim's hurt was treated. Schools and churches were successfully urged to develop programs to serve an integrated population. In the midst of the confusion of city life, citizens were actively studying the processes of change, reading widely on the problems, consulting experts, and making decisions directed toward the creation of integrated harmony. As a result, requests were coming from other sections of the city (from both Negroes and whites) for help to do likewise.

AFTER 1960

Following Mr. Quimby's leadership, Mr. Boles, a businessman, became chairman. He was succeeded by the pastor of a church, Mr. Stewart, in 1961 and 1962. Mr. Stewart represented an interesting reversal of usual church practice: his church was situated in an "unthreatened" neighborhood, but he chose to live in this area of conflict.

By 1961-1962, the paid membership of the council had increased to about three hundred. The Association had been incorporated to benefit from tax-exempt donations, and to each member was given a membership card, which stated that the purpose of the Association was "the establishment and maintenance of the ideal American Integrated Community." A regular newsletter (published more or less monthly) informed the members of meetings and other activities.

Since then, the group's relationship to the churches of the neighborhood has become more positive. Interest and participation are still on an individual basis. The council meets regularly in a large Protestant church. Although this church does not participate as an institution, many of its members are active. It is, however, currently accepting its first Negro member. Another Protestant church, deciding to remain in the area, bought a home for a manse and installed a new minister, who insisted he would be happy to live next to a parishioner who might be colored.

Two administrative devices have been developed to expedite the council's work, an executive committee and a breakdown of the neighborhood into ten smaller districts, each headed by a district chairman. The executive committee (composed of all officers, the committee chairman and last year's council chairman) is responsible for planning between meetings, and moves rapidly to contend with emergencies when they arise. The district chairmen keep informed about the families that may come or go, recruit members, report or emergencies and zoning violations, and promote harmonious relations. There are now numerous informal social events to welcome new families (more often for Negroes than for whites, an imbalance that some hope to correct).

One episode alone will illustrate how the alert council can move to counteract racial persecution. Two Negro families were moving into a block in which Negroes had not previously lived. During one night, unknown hoodlums painted swastikas and obscene words on the windows and stones of the two houses. The executive committee, when notified by the district chairman, acted immediately. It persuaded a professor at the university to excuse his class (on race relations) to scour away the defacement. Then, inspired by their own worthy endeavors, the students went on to interview restaurants about the employment of Negroes, reporting back to class on both activities. The executive committee spoke to the police and the mayor about the incident. The police are still searching for the culprits, but the mayor visited the scene of the damage and came forward with strong condemnation of such practices.

In another more recent episode, the council was not so active. One white householder erected upon his property an ugly sign that referred scurrilously to integrated housing. The executive committee conferred with police and the public prosecutor, but they could find no legal way to obtain the removal of the sign. The council could do no more than express public disapproval of the man's conduct. The offender was, however, isolated and shown to be out of step with the prevailing mood of the neighborhood. He was unable to obtain any following or lead an anti-integration opposition. The sign finally came down.

Quick action to handle and condemn unpleasantries has resulted in a reduction of such emergencies. An increase of personal social contacts has had the same result. According to council members, the atmosphere of the neighborhood has improved; the panic flight of whites has ceased; "For Sale" signs no longer appear with the threat or arrival of a Negro family. Some white families have moved into the area. Newspapers, radio, and television have given favorable coverage to the activities of the council, and even more important, they have advocated open occupancy and pointed to this neighborhood as proof that the idea of integration works well.

A new constitution and statement of purpose has been drawn up for the council. A recreation program for the public school is operating with a council member in charge. The school principal has become an active member of the Hanson Council. Delegates from the council have lobbied, with some success, for civil rights laws in the state legislature. With the encouragement of faculty members, a student human relations council has been formed on the university campus. The regular monthly meetings of the council cover a wide range of activities—banquets, motion pictures, lectures, discussions —on housing, employment, delinquency, city planning, political controversies, and so on.

A quotation from the Newsletter gives the on-going purpose of the Neighborhood Council:

> [Hanson Council] is, first of all, a neighborhood association. It seeks to do what all neighborhood associations do: To keep the quality of the neighborhood high, to develop a sense of community among the residents, to work together on any problems we face as residents of this area, to develop procedures for checking on zoning law violations, to assure the maintenance of proper municipal services, recreational facilities, etc. All these things we do, as any neighborhood association does, for the benefit of the residents of the area.
>
> [Hanson Council] is, in the second place, an interracial neighborhood association. In the context of a culture which does not, in most cases, treat all people as people, this gives added dimensions to our neighborhood association. As such an organization, we have importance to the city, and beyond that, to our whole society. We represent an experiment in living, the like of which exists only in a few other places in the country. We are, or at least we contain for an area of several blocks, an integrated residential area. We propose to show, as an example, that open occupancy is possible; does not lead to a racial ghetto; does not destroy property values, and does not lead to the deterioration of a neighborhood.

Significance of the Project

The importance of the Hanson Neighborhood Council lies less in its specific accomplishments (though these are important) than in continuations. It has become an apparently permanent study-action group on the local scene. The citizens who participate give a long-term commitment to thoughtful and ethical decision making on the complex and baffling problems of changing urban life.

Too often, community improvement is thought of as a single enterprise (or a set of enterprises) that is to be completed. A contrasting point of view is that of nonterminal process: Citizens address themselves to the alleviation of the endless problems that modern life presents. They make progress only to discover that additional difficulties have arisen, some of which are indeed caused by the changes they have helped to bring about. The citizens involved (their involvement increases and decreases from time to time as they move into and out of positions of responsibility) become more ethically competent contributors to the planned change.

Is it possible that certain people have greater abilities for initiating development projects and that others are more successful in continuation? Both are useful functions. As leadership and active participation rotate, it seems that the total process continues and that the impact upon persons and upon the neighborhood is cumulative.

Perhaps the democratic society of the future will require a multiplication of such continuing groups devoted to the discovery of ways to carry the humane teachings of religion into living. The Hanson Council could be an example for groups that search for solutions to problems upon the local as well as upon the wider social scene.

Members of the council are experimenting more with the assumptions of good will than with aspirations to power. They are appealing to themselves, to neighbors, to powerful decision makers, to planners, and to public officials in the hope that each may respond more often to the promptings of a Judaeo-Christian conscience. They are experimenting with cooperation and discovering the increased influence that arises from group action as contrasted with individual decision and action. They are becoming convinced that since they can affect the course of events, social controls within a democratic society can be shared. Perhaps democracy thrives not so much in the triumph of one faction (even a good one) over another, but in the sharing of controls and in the seeking after the welfare and increased responsibility of everyone.

The road to interracial cooperation has not been an easy one. That these were people of good will was demonstrated by their willingness to give time to community improvement on an interracial basis. But they often could not agree with each other upon ways to implement their generous impulses. Conflict was sometimes a result of misunderstanding, of semantic confusion. For words and phrases involved different experiential connotations to the two races. Thus "block organizations" or "to educate people to new attitudes" aroused different reactions and emotions among the people. Communication of meaning does not consist only of words spoken and heard. It is easy to ascribe bad motives to an opponent. Positive steps need to be taken to make kindly communication possible.

But there were profounder difficulties among these people of good will, some that grew out of basic differences of purpose. The break that threatened the continuation of the council after a year of operation exposed fundamental conflicts of purpose. As far as a sympathetic and sensitive observer could interpret, some Negroes in the group suffered from an unresolved ambivalence. What did they want most—decent homes or an integrated neighborhood? The first might call for a Negro takeover of the entire area and the departure of the white families; the second would call for the retention of some white families (50 percent? more? less?) who would become good neighbors to the newcomers.

Some white members may also have suffered from ambivalences. Did they most desire an integrated and pleasant neighborhood? Or did they wish most to protect an institution? Was the fear of deteriorating property and cultural values entirely exorcised? Did they differentiate between the fear of engulfment by Negro families and the fear of engulfment by families low on the economic and educational scales?

It cannot be said that ambivalences of purpose have been eliminated. But those (of both races) who join in discussion have learned to examine the ambivalences openly and to seek for decisions of good will on the immediate problems that arise.

Certain tentative conclusions can be drawn from the experience:

1. Often it is concluded that progress toward the solution of social problems cannot be made by ordinary citizens. Or it is stated that if citizens are depended upon to make the decisions, then the solutions of problems will be fatally delayed. The need, and the desire, to find quick solutions is used as a justification for much undemocratic procedure in communities.

In this project, despite major internal controversy, substantial progress was made in a short time. The park was saved and developed within the first year. By the end of the third year, a solid core of committed leaders had been established. By the fifth year, a large membership was involved, with social arrangements worked out for study and publicity and for meeting emergencies when they arise. People were committed to the building of a better neighborhood for everyone.

2. Often the impatient seek solutions to the problems of race relations, housing, delinquency, and so on, "once and for all." Such hopes are unrealistic in a world in turmoil. Citizens, as well as governments and churches and other agencies of good will, must learn to live with these problems, making progress toward solutions over the years. Those associated with the Hanson Council have accepted this responsibility.

3. The people's ability to deal with recurring problems increased. They achieved self-confidence as well as a belief in the practicality of their ideals. These gains apparently tended to permeate the neighborhood.

4. Many residents of the neighborhood did not participate in the group's activities. Others participated for a time and then dropped out. The reasons why were not always clear. If these nonparticipants are also to grow in competence, are some additional methods of appealing to them required?

5. It proved to be a mistake to ascribe a single point of view to all people of a certain category—whether that category was determined by race, occupation, economic level, or institutional connection. This mistake is all but universal in social controversy. In this project, people of particular classifications were found to differ widely. They changed their opinions under the impact of their experience together. The determination of which experiences contributed to the changes will require further research. Is it possible that the determining factor was the experiencing of friendliness to persons of another point of view when, together, all sought commonly held goals?

6. Although certain institutions (university, church, school, government, real estate board) refused to become involved in the improvement project, they were not therefore treated as enemies. Individual members of the institutions were invited to participate, and their participation tended to bring about the cooperation of the institutions, so that some even received (undeserved?) credit.

7. Finally, the neighborhood has been preserved as a pleasant place for family life—at least so far. It has even tended to become a model of integration for the rest of the city.

Role of the Community Development Workers

The persons from the college acted as collective expediters of processes that grew out of a local need. One couple and one college staff member, in his research, represented the continuing contact for three years. Thereafter, citizen participants assumed responsibility for further progress. Certain faculty couples from the city university gradually shifted roles to become encouragers and guides of process. In this function they acted, and still act, as individuals, not as representatives of the university.

The project illustrated the stages of indigenous growth. It is, nonetheless, unlikely that the process would have started or continued, at certain stages, without the encouragement of community development encouragers. Many citizens who grew in responsibility sufficiently to take over the project have forgotten the actions taken by the original expediters. This is evidence that the continuing process has become their own.

The original encouragers of the process pointed out the advantages of cooperation. They urged that the council's efforts be coordinated with many resources in government, social agencies, churches, and schools. They suggested the study of experiences from other cities. They recommended a broadening of the horizons of friendship. As a result, the council has spent more energy upon seeking allies than in attacking enemies.

The encouragers attended as many meetings as possible, sometimes remaining silent, sometimes joining the discussion as participants. They conferred also with individuals in conversations. Their task was to raise questions, present alternatives for group choosing, and sometimes to urge a choice with the understanding that this might be rejected or modified.

The method of encouragement left the decisions in the hands of the citizens. They were urged to grow in responsibility by study, thoughtful discussion, and learning from both wise and mistaken actions. The expediters tried to deter the members from making unwise decisions, as in the case of the biracial chairmanship, but the group members often had to learn from painful experience.

When the unfortunate effects of a bad decision or an insurmountable problem became too great, the expediters could call for sober reconsideration. Their role then became that of conciliators who exemplified a creative neutrality. They could be committed to none of the factions in conflict, but they could be, and were, deeply committed to the continuation of the process that might solve problems. In pursuing conciliation, certain members of the college staff found themselves condemned by both factions. This could have been caused by their lack of skills or by the traditional fate of the peacemaker, or by both. It then became possible for other members of the staff to repair the broken rapport and assure continuation of the process of growth.

In the complexities of modern city life, there are many factions (actual and potential), problems, and resources for the solution of problems. There is also a spreading malaise, a conviction that ordinary persons can do nothing to improve a deteriorating way of life. This defeatist attitude and conviction is to be found at every economic and social level. Perhaps the most important contribution of the encouragers was to give to some of the citizens in this city a hope that they could grow in ethical competence to influence the future.

Interpretation

Fundamental questions remain. Why did the people respond to the encouragement of the workers? Why did the citizens of Day County propose ideas for improvement and then work on those proposals when they had always before been apathetic? Why did the members of the Hanson Neighborhood change their attitudes to make wider cooperation possible? These are questions of concern to all who hope for improvement in people.

Tentative answers can be offered for guidance in further experiments. Possibly these people responded because

—they felt a need for improvement.
—they trusted a person (or persons) who represented some authority or wisdom, who yet was friendly and invited their ideas.

—they knew that he was aware of many of their failings, yet that he liked them, believed in their better impulses, and treated them as though he expected them to become better.

—the worker was reluctant to propose solutions to their problems, and offered these as ideas for examination, not as programs for adoption.

—the worker "worried" with them, seeking to help them expedite those activities which they had chosen as good.

—the worker was accepted as a friend who was "in favor of" whatever good actions they and he could agree upon.

Answers to the "why" of favorable response and change in people are to be found in the many subtleties of human relationships. The difficulty of finding explicit answers should not deter community development workers from further searching.

chapter 4

Intention and Outcome

Most community developers are optimistic about people. The belief in human potential for favorable growth is necessary to the process they hope to inspire. But despite their hopefulness, many may not realize the extent to which they have yielded to a popular cynicism, which is one of the sophisticated clichés of our time.

The attitudes that a worker with people has toward them contributes substantially to their development or lack of development. People respond to their perception of attitudes as these are expressed in gesture, word, and deed. If the worker acts as though he believes people are unworthy, not to be trusted, or selfishly motivated, his influence is not likely to awaken generous initiative. If he acts as though he believes people have constructive ideas (often despite evidence to the contrary) and potentialities for development beyond their present limitations, he is likely to prove more encouraging. The beliefs he holds about human beings and his intentions, stated or implied, are important to the outcome in people's lives.

What beliefs about people and consequent intentions guided the encouragers in the two case studies reported? Those operating assumptions that trusted the participants' ability to make ethically wise choices were selected.

If the basic intention of the encouragers was the observation of participant-guided growth, this expectation rested upon optimistic assumptions (general hypotheses) about the people involved. The community workers believed that the people were at least potentially capable of self-guidance. But the belief had to be genuine. It was not a mere verbal assurance that could be given or withdrawn. It had to represent a sustaining philosophy of life that gave warmth to the relationship between the encouragers and the citizens. Psychiatrists refer to this warmth of relationship as "rapport." Theologians call it "love." Whatever the term used, it is very real and very necessary in the starting and sustaining of a process of growth toward community responsibility.

Intentions (toward people) affect outcomes (in their lives).

Difficulties of Communication

Among the reasons why the literature of community development is so inadequate is the difficulty of communicating richly meaningful experience through the medium of words. The words can convey meaning only if the reader has passed through similar experiences. But if his point of view has been such as to limit his contacts with people to responses that support distrust, then the account will lack persuasiveness.

If the reader has known people only in situations that call for an acquiescent or even subservient behavior, he will scarcely be able to convince himself that such people can have original ideas, or initiative. If, because he has assumed them to be self-seeking, and they prove to be just that in situations where no other response is appropriate, then generous behavior will seem well-nigh impossible.

Community development processes, resting upon optimistic assumptions about people, tend to bring forth behavior that the wordly-wise doubt is possible. The reader may be called upon to understand and believe human responses that contradict his previous experiences and beliefs.

The reader is asked further to understand a method of influencing people that neither seeks to control them nor waits for them to ask for help; it is neither directive nor permissive. The first approach demands a prechosen response; the second abdicates responsibility. The method based on optimism about people's potential for development takes the initiative to awaken initiative in others. It seeks to help them discover their own abilities and good impulses, which they often have not realized they possessed.

Participants in the process of development are not urged to seek control over others, not even over those who have dominated them. They are urged rather to share ideas, points of view, and control, because even the power of figures of a community ought also to be afforded an opportunity to develop. Development for people of low status frequently means an increase in their influence. For those who already exercise control over others, it often means the humbling discovery that they are happier and more human when they share the decision making.

Further discomforts of understanding are asked of the reader—to realize that an important process has been going on, even though it was not housed in an impressive institutional headquarters, and did not make use of much technical equipment or illustrate high-sounding methods of procedure. Hopefully, a well-trained community developer has an institutional connection and knows about the equipment and techniques. But he reaches the people where they are, away from headquarters. And he holds the technical methods in abeyance while he concentrates upon the people and their perceived need for growth. He plays up the institution and introduces technical equipment and methods only when they will expedite the development process.

Operational Assumptions

Intention can be made explicit by listing the operational assumptions that we as community developers attempted to illustrate in the case studies.

1. Each person is valuable, unique, and capable of growth toward greater social sensitivity and responsibility.
    a. Each person has underdeveloped abilities in initiative, originality, and leadership. These qualities can be cultivated and strengthened.
    b. These abilities tend to emerge and grow stronger when people work together in small groups that serve the common (community) good.

    c. There will always be conflicts between persons and factions. Properly handled, the conflicts can be used creatively.

    d. Agreement can be reached on specific next steps of improvement, without destroying philosophic or religious differences.

    e. Although the people may express their differences freely, when they become responsible they often choose to refrain in order to further the interest of the whole group and of their idea of community.

    f. People will respond to an appeal to altruism as well as to an appeal to selfishness.

    g. These generous motivations may be used to form groups that serve an inclusive welfare of all people in a community.

    h. Groups are capable of growth toward self-direction when the members assume responsibility for group growth and for an inclusive local welfare.

2. Human beings and groups have both good and bad impulses.

    a. Under wise encouragement they can strengthen the better in themselves and help others to do likewise.

    b. When the people are free of coercive pressures, and can then examine a wide range of alternatives, they tend to choose the ethically better and the intelligently wiser course of action.

    c. There is satisfaction in serving the common welfare, even as in serving self-interest.

    d. A concept of the common good can grow out of group experience that serves the welfare of all in some local area. This sense of responsibility and belonging can be strengthened even for those to whom community is least meaningful.

3. Satisfaction and self-confidence gained from small accomplishments can lead to the contending with more and more difficult problems, in a process of continuing growth.

4. Within the broad role of community developer, there are several subroles to be chosen, depending upon the developer's judgment of the people's needs:

a. Encourager, friend, source of inspiration, and believer in the good in people.
b. Objective observer, analyst, truth seeker, and kindly commentator.
c. Participant in discussion, to clarify alternatives and the values these serve.
d. Participant in some actions—not all.
e. Process expert, adviser, conciliator, expediter of on-going development.
f. The prominence of the community developer is likely to be greater in the early stages, then taper off toward a termination date, but it may increase temporarily at any time.

Finally, in summary:

5. When community developers work on a friendly basis with people, in activities that serve the common good;
   When they persist patiently in this;
   When their actions affirm a belief in the good in people;
   When the process continues, even in the face of discouragement;
   Then people tend to develop themselves to become more ethically competent persons;
   Then they may become involved in a process of self-guided growth that continues indefinitely.

The list contains much more than the pious slogans to which "proper" people give lip service. It represents a compilation of the operating principles that were followed by the community developers, to the best of their abilities, in the two projects.

The list is meant to include the basic assumptions of developmental good will. It stands in contrast, for example, to the assumptions that people will move into action only to serve selfish interest or only to gain power. It places faith in the unrealized potentials for good to be found in even the least promising of human beings. But it tries to avoid straying off into a pollyanna cheerfulness. The encouragement of the community development process seeks to minimize the antisocial and strengthen the prosocial impulses that people discover when they search for a common good.

Hypotheses

Operational assumptions can be tested in the reality of the developmental process upon the local scene. They are hypotheses-in-action. Are they subject to scientific proof or disproof?

Hypotheses about human beings and the ways in which they may be expected to change may be classified in many ways. At one extreme is the generalized attitude of trust or distrust, of friendship or antagonism, and so on. Such attitudes (seldom stated in a form that can be tested) contribute importantly to human behavior.

In the middle of the scale are broad hypotheses (which may or may not be stated in words). Evidence to support or contradict such broad hypotheses can be accumulated over long periods of experience, especially if these have been reduced to a verbal statement and a record of development has been kept.

At the precise end of the scale of exactness are specific hypotheses, stated accurately and subject to proof or disproof in the limited time span of a traditional social scientific research.

The operational assumptions we have given are located from the general to the midpoint of the scale of exactness. They are stated in a form that allows an accumulation of experimental evidence to support or to contradict them. Developmental experiences will modify the generalized attitudes of the participants, and hopefully, might do something similar for a few nonparticipants who read about the experience. Toward the precise end of the scale, some of the assumptions could be restated more explicitly as specific hypotheses for short-time testing.

Many workers with human beings, including numerous social scientists, allow generalized attitudes and broad but unstated hypotheses to govern their contacts with people—because "everybody knows" about "human nature." These unexamined generalized attitudes and conclusions, in our age of disillusion, are more likely to be uncomplimentary than complimentary. One modest virtue we can claim, in stating our operational assumptions, is that we have tried to make more explicit our underlying attitudes and governing conclusions, so that these may be subjected to some critical testing in experience.

Intentions of Participants

What of the intentions of the people who entered into the two projects? They did not subscribe to, were not even aware of, our operating assumptions about them or about people in general—except as these were expressed in our behavior. The participants' intentions were probably more specific, although they had to be inferred from the responses to the problems that brought the people together in cooperative action. As their experience with the process continued, it was our hope (and intention) that the developing citizens would become more aware of our operational assumptions (and similar value judgments that might govern conduct).

Self-fulfilling Prophecies

Wise sociologists draw attention to self-fulfilling prophecies. In research upon human beings, a social scientist will predict the probable response people will make. This is refined into his hypothesis for experiment. His hypothesis will reflect his conscious or unconscious attitudes toward and assumptions about the people. Then he will set up a test, but so organize the experiment as to make easy or even inevitable a response of most people that will "prove" his prediction was correct. Pollers of opinion and makers of questionnaires have concluded that they are more likely to find a majority giving the "right" answer if the question is phrased to invite that answer. In certain community studies, the citizens will be asked "Who are the members of the power elite in this city?" or "List the powerful people who make the real decisions in this town." Responders will name the people they believe fit the description, thereby "proving" that the city or town is run by a powerful minority. But the scientific "finding" was implicit in the question that was asked.

If our hypotheses about people are carried into the treatment they receive, do these operational assumptions become self-fulfilling prophecies? If they do, so much the better. If we can prove that all kinds of people tend to become more ethically intelligent and responsible when dealt with in a manner that invites such development, then that is all we ask.

Re-examination of Operational Assumptions

What preliminary conclusions can be drawn from the two case studies?

1. Each person is valuable, unique, and capable of growth toward greater social sensitivity and responsibility.

This broad statement of faith is inherent in the democratic tradition. It affirms the possibility of encouraging growth. This statement is not subject to specific test. Experience noted under the subheads that follow might or might not corroborate the faith.

1a. Each person has underdeveloped abilities in initiative, originality, and leadership. These qualities can be cultivated and strengthened.

1b. These abilities tend to emerge and grow stronger when people work together in small groups that serve the common (community) good.

In both projects, local people emerged as leaders with initiative, originality, ideas of their own. These emergent leaders acquired the ability to carry some of their ideas into action, but not without episodes of fumbling and discouragement. The abilities appeared in certain participants, but not in all, and certainly not in all residents of the areas involved. On the other hand, leadership did emerge which had not been discernible before the projects began and which certain knowledgeable onlookers had predicted would not be found. And it emerged among some whom the community developers had not considered likely candidates.

A reasonable anticipation would seem to be that leadership ability can be expected to arise in community development projects when proper steps of encouragement are taken. It did in these two populations. Furthermore, when certain emergent leaders proved inadequate or had to step aside, other leaders developed out of and were refined by the process.

1c. There will always be conflicts between persons and factions. Properly handled, the conflicts can be used creatively.

> 1d. Agreement can be reached on specific next steps of improvement, without destroying philosophic or religious differences.

The first part of the first statement is another broad generality which is unprovable except as one reads history to predict the future. The second part of the statement is subject to test in group behavior that is focused upon a growing concept of the common good. The creativity was found in decisions for cooperative actions that led to greater group responsibility to continue to make problem-solving decisions.

The second statement points out that conflict can be resolved with mutual respect for differences. In both projects conflicts occurred. In both instances, after some struggle, the controversies were sufficiently resolved to allow the process to go on. The choosing of such cooperative activities as the building of the flood wall and the preserving of the park gave the participants the self-confidence to seek for further cooperation. The people found that they could plan more and more complex activities, yet could respect the fact that other participants belonged to religious faiths other than their own, to other races, to other political movements, or took opposing positions in matters under debate.

> 1e. Although the people may express their differences freely, when they become responsible they often choose to refrain in order to further the interest of the whole group and of their idea of community.

The experimental results are not too clear on this point. Some individuals in both projects came eventually to discipline themselves to serve the larger group and the community good. Others were unable to do so. Some who found such self-discipline irksome dropped out, but there were also other reasons for their discontinuing participation. Some others who found self-discipline difficult were asked by the groups as a whole, or by responsible individuals, to give greater heed to the common purpose than to their own eloquence.

An interesting example of the learning of self-discipline is found in the urban project, in the meetings that followed the factional split. It was apparently clear to responsible participants that the overfree expression of antagonisms had destroyed the group, at least temporarily. In re-establishing the council, those who felt the greatest responsibility held their tongues and drew attention to the challenges that lay before the reconstituted association. Since that time, those who hold first loyalty to the group's service to its neighborhood have determined the atmosphere of the meetings.

1f. People will respond to an appeal to altruism as well as an appeal to selfishness.

1g. These generous motivations may be used to form groups that serve an inclusive welfare of all people in a community.

Here the empirical evidence is much clearer. In both situations, invitations to start group activities were couched in terms of service to all the people in an area—to the folks who live around here (in the mountains), to the people of "our" neighborhood (in the city). The responses of those who were to become participants were given as proposed services to the people in yet-to-be defined areas (in both instances). One could argue that selfish impulses were still present. (They always are. Which of us is motivated by pure altruism?) But as far as the community developers and the responding future participants were concerned, the conscious motivation was service to some concept of the general good.

When a beginning generous motivation was sought among the rural, mountain people, their response opened up a new experience of initiative. These people had long been the recipients of charity, but had been largely unaware of the self-help that cooperation for a wider good would make possible. Altruistic motivation became the key to development.

1h. Groups are capable of growth toward self-direction when the members assume responsibility for group growth and for an inclusive local welfare.

This assumption draws attention to the development of the group in addition to the development of the individuals who comprise it. (The group progress is viewed as being more than the sum of the

individual parts—following the thinking of Gestalt psychologists.[1])
The evidence is clear that the central groups in both projects
achieved a stability and responsibility, in spite of changes in personnel and rotation of leadership. In fact, both were sufficiently
successful to call for imitation on the part of nearby people who
wished to form similar self-directing groups.

In totality, the subheads 1a through 1h seem to offer experience
that supports faith in human potential for development, both as
individuals and as community-serving small groups. One can infer
from all this that each person is capable of prosocial growth and
therefore is valuable and unique.

2.   Human beings and groups have both good and bad impulses.
     2a.   Under wise encouragement they can strengthen the
           better in themselves and help others to do likewise.

As given, the assumption presupposes that standards of good and
bad exist. It does not presuppose that the members of a group will
agree with one another or with the community developer. But human beings, and the group, as they mature in responsibility, will
arrive at ethical judgments about proposed actions.

Again and again in group discussions, moral considerations were
matters of controversy. The participants (including the community
developers) were aware that doubtful and antisocial impulses were
being expressed (at least by other people) as well as the prosocial.
In the normal process of making a decision, acting on that decision,
and criticizing both the decision and the action, the prosocial suggestions that could be put into action, and that seemed feasible,
tended to prevail. It was possible for the community developers to
raise questions, to inquire about the principles that a proposed
decision was to serve, to suggest other alternatives for consideration and trial. Out of the participants' own experience and increasing sensitivity, the more cooperative and kindly impulses tended
to be strengthened. The rural people decided to become friends
and to work together with the members of churches that they had

---

[1] See Peter F. Drucker, *Landmarks of Tomorrow* (New York: Harper and
Row, 1957), Chap. 1. Kurt Lewin, *Field Theory in Social Science,* Dorwin
Cartwright, ed. (New York: Harper and Row, 1951), Chap. 4.

originally condemned. The city people came to accept some real estate dealers they had originally attacked as enemies.

    2b. When the people are free of coercive pressures, and can then examine a wide range of alternatives, they tend to choose the ethically better and the intelligently wiser course of action.

    2c. There is satisfaction in serving the common welfare, even as in serving self-interest.

The first assumption is given as an assurance by psychotherapist Carl R. Rogers, who has had many years of clinical practice with disturbed people.[2] He was able to remove many of the pressures of hectic living in the quieter atmosphere of his client-centered counseling. The problem for the community developer was to achieve a comparable freedom from pressures upon individuals in groups that met to contend with local controversies.

Often the participants came to group meetings to act as obvious spokesmen for their churches, race (or fraction of a race), occupational classification, geographic area, or total community. They reflected a coercion from the faction for which they spoke and, as a consequence, they found difficult an examination of the merits of proposals before the groups. How, then, to reduce the sense of coercion?

Various initiatives were open to the community developer: He could seek to multiply the alternatives, from which the group could choose, beyond the usual opposed pair presented by contending factions. He could appeal to the unity of the group or of the total community. He could work to create an atmosphere of friendliness and confidence in persons, despite their vigorous differences of opinion. He could urge individuals to express their points of view openly but kindly to strengthen the unity of the group. Such steps require of the community developer a skill in human relations, a flexibility in varying the approach as needed, and a firm belief in the ultimate good intentions of those to be helped.

When these steps had reduced the pressures upon group members, there was a tendency for a more intelligently ethical choice

---

[2] Carl R. Rogers, "A Therapist's View of the Good Life," *Humanist,* No. 5 (1957), pp. 299–300.

to be made spontaneously. The community worker then had to accept the choice as a better one from the point of view of the participant choosers, not necessarily from his point of view. The choice was more likely to be made in the form of a consensus of the meeting, after much discussion and criticism of previous action, than in the form of a majority vote.

The choice, once made and acted upon, carried its own reward. Seldom was there self-congratulation or a pious sense of righteousness. Instead, the participants expressed quiet satisfaction at a good decision and at a job well done. And then they often inquired, "What do we do next?"

2d. A concept of the common good can grow out of group experience that serves the welfare of all in some local area. This sense of responsibility and belonging can be strengthened even for those to whom community is least meaningful.

In the rural project, there was little sense of any community at the beginning of the work. People were more identified with the "holler" in which they lived, and were suspicious of people up the stream or over the ridge. During the years of the project they clearly gained a sense of community larger than the loyalty to the "holler" that preceded it. Apparently, this consciousness grew out of cooperative planning and work together. It has extended also to contacts with cities some distance away in the county and with state offices and functions as well. A sense of their own dignity to meet with these other people and their identifications was a part of the growth achieved.

In the urban project, the older residents of the area already had an identification with the neighborhood (although its limits were ill defined). Newcomers had little or none; some even were new to city dwelling and to the proper behavior expected of good city neighbors. As far as we could determine, the sense of neighborhood became more sharply defined for the old-timers, with an increasing loyalty that held them and induced some to move back into the area. For the newcomers, a sense of neighborhood loyalty tended to grow, aided by committees of welcome, attendance at meetings, hearing about the activities of the neighborhood council and perhaps other such events.

3. Satisfaction and self-confidence gained from small accomplishments can lead to the undertaking of more and more difficult problems, in a process of continuing growth.

Both projects depended upon immediate activities to establish the groups and to start the process. In one, it was the construction of a flood wall. This moved on rapidly to include such additional interests as the construction of playgrounds for children and the rehabilitation of churches. In the other, it was the saving of a park. This was followed by efforts to provide equipment and supervision for the park, then by steps to survey the neighborhood to see who needed recreation and other social welfare services. In both instances, the immediate first activity was accepted as the initial step in a long-range improvement purpose.

This operational assumption, and the supporting experience, stand in contrast to those community development formulas that call for a self-survey as the necessary first recommended step.[3] In both projects, such self-surveys came later, and continue to be conducted in an on-going process. But when we encouraged local people to follow the logic of their own good motivations, they proceeded through immediate, simple activities to other more complex interests (with greater opportunity for controversy).

Although these two groups of people moved from simpler to more complex activities, there is no guarantee that such well-modulated progress will always occur. May not inexperienced groups choose an early activity that is so far beyond their present capabilities that it threatens to halt the process in immediate failure? Yes, the ups and downs of human learning experience suggest the need for warning, as well as for encouragement. This necessity makes the function of the community developer doubly important.

4. Within the broad role of community developer, there are several subroles to be chosen, depending upon the developer's judgment of the people's needs:
   4a. Encourager, friend
   4b. Objective observer, analyst
   4c. Participant in discussion

---

[3] Richard W. Poston, *Democracy Is You* (New York: Harper and Row, 1953).

    4d.   Participant in some action

    4e.   Process expert, adviser

    4f.   Flexible adjuster to varying needs for prominence

To expedite the process for both projects, community developers took all these subroles at one time or another. Since there were several persons fulfilling the broad role, it was possible to ask different persons to carry different subroles from time to time. But the chief community encourager himself had to emphasize one contribution to process at a time, then be prepared to shift emphasis as the need changed.

From the outset, the community developers let it be known that they hoped the process would have no termination, but that their contact with it, and with the people involved, would. These encouragers planned to stay with the projects for approximately three years (an arbitrary time span decided upon for reasons other than awareness of process). But in that time they hoped the process would have gained a sufficient momentum of its own. Their changing subroles were related to this expectation.

The summary assumption follows (Number 5) with emphasis upon patient belief in the good in people, which is expressed in action over a period that includes discouragements. Then, it is assumed, they tend to develop themselves into more ethically competent persons as a result of their involvement in the self-guided process. In general, this is a summary of the events that took place in the two projects. The people involved did improve themselves while working upon the task of improving their concept of their community.

Such projects give support to a belief in the dignity of man. But the support given is much more than a verbal proclamation; community development activity seeks to make that dignity real. It seeks to enhance and utilize that dignity, so that it can be rediscovered and strengthened even in the impersonal modern world.

These case studies (and other accounts of community development projects) present empirical evidence to support a belief in man's improvability. This belief stands in contrast to many philosophies of gloom—theological, scientific, and governmental. There is this difference, however: The optimism growing out of community development experience is a dynamic one, directed toward the realization of favorable potential in man, not resting upon a cheerful assertion. Community development seeks to strengthen the dignified ethical motivation of man in the face of his present inadequacies and antisocial motivations.

Every community developer knows about antisocial motives in man. He contends with them daily, in his contacts with other people—and in himself. The optimism about man's dignity and probability of growth is achieved in actual experience of facing and overcoming evil. In contending with and transcending antisocial impulses in dozens of decisions, actions, and evaluations, he observes people improving. There is, as yet, no known limit to the growth that may occur.

Tentative Generalizations

Out of these case studies, but also out of familiarity with many programs of community development, it becomes possible to formulate some tentative generalizations. These are offered as preliminary to an outline of a typical community development process.

The process seems to depend upon the formation of a community-serving small group—or the utilization of one already in existence. It frequently starts with a single group, but may proliferate into subassociations of many similar groups. But the intimate relationship of participants in small groups is important for the development of personal competence.

An encourager who takes responsibility (frequently professionally employed) is usually necessary for the activation of the process.

The encourager can influence growth toward self-direction; he cannot direct it. The learning of self-direction is learner-motivated. There are many other influences affecting the learning of citizens. The community developer's is but one of many.

The number of people from any population who become actively involved in a community project will be small at any one time. Those who give time to the planning and to the making of responsible decisions will usually be less than 5 percent of the total residents of an area, at any one time. The number participating in the planned activity will be larger (in work periods, in circulation of petitions, in parades or mass meetings, and so on). The number whose lives will be affected by the activities or by the changes in the community will be even larger. Over a period of several years, the number who have had responsible experience will increase, if steps are taken to rotate individuals into and out of office within the small groups.

Some people never become active participants. Some become active for a time and then drop out, with little or no evidence of favorable development—even though the process continues.

The development of persons, groups, and communities seldom occurs smoothly. It comes in the midst of heartache, worry, disappointment, and at irregular rates of progress. Human achievement is uneven. There are periods of enthusiasm and discouragement, activity and apathy, as the process moves on.

In a free-flowing process of community development, there is little of the crusade of all righteous people, on one side, against the forces of evil, all bad, on the other. Instead, people of good will are seen to be human, ambivalent, suffering from mixed motives, and developing by irregular increments of learning.

On the other hand, the process often works in the midst of controversy within the group and within the wider community. At best, it becomes a means for helping people to conciliate controversy by honestly facing the issues in contention.

Though the process starts with a few people and continues through the actions of small groups, it is holistic. That is, it seeks a local wholeness that includes all people, all factions.

Leaders can be expected to emerge from almost any population when the skill of the community developer is great enough.

Democratic responsibility and initiative are more readily acquired in the active meeting and solving of problems together than in verbal learning alone. Interpretive discussion can speed this learning from experience.

Learning is reciprocal between the citizen participant and the community developer.

The major skills for the community developer grow out of a friendship that encourages self-respect and self-confidence. Friendship means several things—a lack of domination, a willingness to suffer with the group, and to work cooperatively on the activities chosen by the group, and a willingness to share ideas in the expectation that these will be examined on their merits, not on the prestige of the suggester.

Progress occurs most rapidly when a collaborative effort invites the work of all institutions, agencies, class levels, and helping professions. The community approach seeks to be locally all-inclusive, focusing the efforts of many contributions upon the problem of human development, seeking no aggrandizement of any one individual or agency or faction or association.

Guides for Process

We present these tentative generalizations as broad hypotheses to be checked against further experience, our own and other investigators'. We offer them as guides for the outline of process that we shall present.

There is a need for much more experience with the development of people on the local scene. There is a need for more enterprises of this kind, to be set up carefully and recorded as events occur. There is a need for a greater awareness of the processes through which these enterprises go and for an understanding of how development can work in the complicated contemporary world.

chapter 5

Definitions

When one collects the multiplying literature about community and community development, one encounters a great confusion. We give definitions here in order to make clear what it is we are discussing. We are seeking, moreover, to define the concepts that we believe are basic to the many varieties of community development practice.

Differentiations

Community service is not the same thing as community development. Universities, churches, libraries, and so on, may offer such services as lectures, concerts, tutoring, research, and advice, but these admirable helps to citizens and organizations are not community development. As we use the term, community development is an indigenous process of growth that uses these and other helps.

Community development is something other than social action in support of some reform. The participants in development may exert militant pressure to bring about changes. But these episodes, if they occur, contribute to a larger process of development.

In much thinking (and in a number of books [1]) community

---

[1] A good example is Ward Hunt Goodenough, *Cooperation in Change: An Anthropological Approach to Community Development* (New York: Russell Sage Foundation, 1963).

development is identified as an activity addressed to underdeveloped peoples overseas. Its purpose then is to bring these disadvantaged people "up" to "our" level of advancement. In the pages that follow we seek to describe methods that are useful for people both abroad and in the United States. Our main emphasis, is however, upon domestic development and redevelopment, where it is more difficult to determine which changes move "up" to "higher" levels.

Then there are those who identify community development as a rural phenomenon only. We apply it to both rural and urban people, but we are especially concerned to apply it to metropolitan life. For this is where most Americans are to be found.

We have no desire to reduce the rich variety found in the numerous programs of community development. But we do ask that these approaches to planned local change be subject to research —that their objectives be stated and their effectiveness evaluated.

COMMUNITY

Sociological definitions of community tend to be structural. They refer to such entities as a town meeting, a self-contained rural hamlet, a planned settlement, a trade area, a neighborhood, an entire city, a "social system," a metropolitan complex. There are others. Each structural concept can be useful. But controversy among the users of the term can be hot.

Only when the definition is shifted to a functional concept (realistically based upon the citizens' awareness of community) is a common basis found to underlie the structural varieties. As we shall use it, *community is whatever sense of the local common good citizens can be helped to achieve.*[2] This perception of community is an achievement, not something given by reason of geographic residence. It is not fixed; it changes as a result of experience or purposeful effort. It may even shift according to the problem that catches the attention of the citizens. Hopefully, it expands from a small accumulation of people to a larger group with a larger responsibility.

---

[2] Compare this statement with the following: "By way of definition the local society and its institutions with which residents identify themselves is the community." Wayland J. Hayes, "The Problem of Community Intelligence," *International Review of Community Development*, No. 10 (1962), p. 153.

Any selection of an area in which to begin a community development activity is more arbitrary today than it was when citizens lived within a fixed and self-contained social system. Flexibility demands the use of a city block, a school district, an area bounded by superhighways, the parish of a church or several parishes, or any other geographic area within which the residents feel that they belong and within which they may seek the common good.

COMMUNITY DEVELOPMENT

Many definitions of community development, often tacit, stress the externals. Mention is made of the tangible (and easily publicized) achievements—the schools or hospitals or swimming pools that have been constructed, the building that serves as headquarters for activities, the meetings held and attendance recorded, the speeches made, the episodes of cooperative work, the petitions circulated and signed, the steps taken to bring influence to bear upon authority.

But more is involved than the monuments created, the triumphs achieved, or the events observed, whether colorful or dull. All these are external evidences of processes occurring within peoples' lives. Basically, *community development is a social process by which human beings can become more competent to live with and gain some control over local aspects of a frustrating and changing world.* It is a group method for expediting personality growth, which can occur when geographic neighbors work together to serve their growing concept of the good of all. It involves cooperative study, group decisions, collective action, and joint evaluation that leads to continuing action. It calls for the utilization of all helping professions and agencies (from local to international), that can assist in problem solving. But personality growth through group responsibility for the local common good is the focus.[3]

---

[3] Compare the following definitions (there are many others with minor variations):

"Community Development is a process of social action in which the people of a community organize themselves for planning and action; define their common and individual needs and problems; ... execute these plans with a maximum of reliance upon community resources; and supplement these resources when necessary with services and materials from governmental and non-governmental agencies outside the community." International Coopera-

The emphasis shifts from improvement of facilities, of economic life, and even of public opinion that supports community atmospheres, important as these are, to improvement in people. But the personal betterment is brought about in the midst of social action that serves a growing awareness of community need.

PROCESS

Process is one of the words freely used by community developers that is understood in a variety of ways. The word may refer to a series of stages or activities through which individuals are expected to pass automatically. Physical growth, from infancy to adulthood, is one example; the supposedly inevitable deterioration of a neighborhood is often assumed to be a similar automatic process.

The word "process" may refer to a procedure, set up by some wise person, to which other persons are expected to conform. An industrial methodology, such as the construction of an automobile on the assembly line, might be an example of this interpretation. Similarly, local or distant decision makers may prescribe a series of steps by which ordinary citizens may order a telephone installed or may apply for unemployment benefits.

As we shall use the word, *process refers to a progression of events that is planned by the participants to serve goals they progressively choose. The events point to changes in a group and in individuals that can be termed growth in social sensitivity and competence.* The essence of process does not consist in any fixed succession of events (these may vary widely from group to group and from one time to another) but in the growth that occurs within individuals, within groups, and within the communities they serve. The process is one that is motivated by participant choosing. Even if it has been initiated by a paid encourager, it has not genuinely

---

tion Administration, *Community Development Review,* No. 3 (December 1956), p. 1.

"The community development process is, in essence, a planned and organized effort to assist individuals to acquire the attitudes, skills and concepts required for their democratic participation in the effective solution of as wide a range of community improvement problems as possible in an order of priority determined by their increasing levels of competence." J. D. Mezirow, "Community Development as an Educational Process," *Community Development.* National Training Laboratories Selected Reading Series, No. 4 (1961), p. 16.

started until the participants themselves begin to assume the responsibility to direct and keep it going.[4]

Process will be more specifically defined later by outlining the typical stages through which it often seems to move in service to community need.[5]

ROLES

Conceivably, community development may arise through the efforts of volunteer local citizens. In fact, some examples of such indigenous initiative have been described.[6] But most often the process seems to require the attention of employed initiators. In an age of accelerated change and increasing problems, even the "do it yourself" task of citizen self-development requires encouragement from those who are specially qualified.

In the community development process that depends upon trained encouragers, there are several classifications of persons involved. For the moment, we are not talking about individual contributions, but about the part the encouragers play in contributing to the process. Each fits into a role. We shall define *role* in two ways: It is *both the part in the process that the individual perceives himself as playing and the part others perceive him as playing.* This can be made more specific by naming and discussing several persons who contribute to the process. There is the employed instigator, the institutional administrator who employs him,[7] the supplier

---

[4] Compare the following:

". . . One of the problems of considering community development as a subject . . . is that its very title can be confusing. It does not comprehend every aspect of the overall development of communities but only those aspects of that development which are due to certain defined processes. In other words community development is not co-terminous with the development of communities but is only a part . . . . As Mr. Zahir Ahmed, formerly of the U.N. Bureau of Social Affairs, has well written . . . : 'When we use the word process we think of a progression of changes when the people themselves make decisions about matters of common concern: from some co-operation to a larger method of co-operation. Emphasis is on what happens to people socially and psychologically.' . . ." Peter du Sautoy and Ross D. Waller, "Community Development and Adult Education in Urban Areas," *International Review of Community Development,* No. 8 (1961), p. 36.

[5] In Chaps. 6 and 7.

[6] Elmore McKee, *The People Act* (New York: Harper and Row, 1955).

[7] Although we use the grammatically correct pronoun, we wish to emphasize that the instigator is a "she" as often as a "he," which is as it should be. For good community development, both sexes should be active.

of funds (through contributions or taxes), and the community resident (who may be participative or opposed to the process or somewhere in between).

About the employed instigator of the process, we will have much to say. In fact, the entire book is devoted, in large part, to his role and responsibility. He may be a university extension teacher, a church worker, a social welfare worker, a public health worker, a technical assistance specialist from either a privately supported agency or a government bureau, and so on. The people with whom he is to work will probably have a preconceived role to ascribe to him before he appears. This role will depend in part upon their attitudes toward the employing institution. And he will find himself tending to accept this prejudgment of himself. On the other hand, however, he will find that he is able, within limits, to choose the kind of impact he will have upon people and to have some influence over the intentions they ascribe to him. This conscious choice of his own intentions is most important in the role of the encourager of this social process.

A book on community development could have been written from the point of view of any of the roles—the instigator, the institutional administrator, the supplier of funds, the community residents. While it is the progress of the citizen participants that justifies the process, we are focusing attention upon the community developer. We will attempt to make explicit certain attitudes and skills he needs.

The Community Developer

Responsibility for the process usually rests upon one person or upon several. What is a descriptive name for the person or role? We call him "the encourager" (of indigenous participant growth).

Many names have been advanced by the spokesmen for community development. We have come to prefer "encourager" rather than many others (some of which we have used in the past) as we seek to avoid certain implied meanings. "Teacher" implies the determination to instruct. "Change Agent" may suggest a prior decision on the changes to be brought about. "Catalyst" implies no change in the worker who brings about development in the participants. "Consultant" suggests the expert who supplies the "correct" answers. "Village Level Worker" seems to limit the process to rural environments. "Urban Agent" limits it to cities. "Helper" is vague. "Stimulator" may imply prodding of the unwilling. "Enabler" is better; but we believe "encourager" is clearer. We shall use as synonymous with this, such terms as "community developer" and "nucleus level worker."

Every time a community development encourager begins to work with the people in a locality, he initiates a process among those people—or he joins one already under way. Although every local process is unique, certain stages common to nearly every process, and through which it may pass, may be discerned. A process that becomes vital to the participants achieves a momentum of its own, which is directed by an increasing responsibility on the part of the people involved. It follows a logic of its own. The professional encourager may start it, or join it; he may keep it going through periods of crisis; he may have some influence upon it; but as time goes on, it is less and less his project. He finds that he has been responsible for initiating a growth of initiative in others. He has been party to a process of participant-guided learning of the habits of responsibility, of applied intelligence, and of ethical sensitivity. The indigenous process he has started, or helped to implement, is one of growth in democratic competence.

Great skill is required of the community developer to strike a proper balance between his initiative and that of local participants —a balance that gives the maximum encouragement for participants in the process to achieve a momentum of their own. The balance of initiative shifts from time to time throughout the process. The encourager's initiative is usually greatest in the early stages, and then tapers off as the local citizens gain in confidence and competence. But his initiative may increase, then decrease again, and may take a variety of forms, if the process bogs down. His decision to speak up or to remain silent, to offer guidance or to let people find their own way, depends upon his sensitivity to their needs, but even more upon an awareness of the process and of the encouragement needed to maintain its vigor.

Only gradually have community developers become aware of the basic process that their diverse efforts have barely begun to make clear. When they have increased their awareness of details and sequences, when they have learned more from careful research, when they have built up their skills to encourage the process in people, when they have made it the central focus of their encouragement, then they will give social scientific identity to their field.

SELF-CONSCIOUS COMMUNITY DEVELOPERS

Those community developers whose enthusiasm or circumstances of employment have convinced them that they have been pioneering a new field have been overeager to produce training handbooks. These handbooks have been addressed both to citizens and to future professionals who were to learn the new skills. They have represented either a codification of the unique experience of the individual writer or of the institution that employs him. Each handbook has tended to reflect the biases of employment, the personal philosophy of the writer, and the peculiarities of operation that grew out of the particular population served. The writers' defense of their outlines has tended to divert attention from the finding of common ground in their experience, or more important, from identifying and studying the process that occurred among the citizens. (The authors of this book have also contributed in the past to the handbooks and to the confusion.)

Such an emphasis upon instruction has been understandable when the community developers have been connected with an educational institution. Because the compulsion to teach has usually proved more powerful than the desire to conduct research, the new field has been regarded as an opportunity for instruction in the application of old knowledge, not as an opportunity for the discovery of the new. Some community developers have found themselves an adjunct to older academic departments, such as sociology, anthropology, education, or adult education. Still others have found their work attached to extenison education, where the necessity for tuition payments or for reports on the number of students has interefered with the developer's sensitivity to people or to the processes by which they could develop.

USERS OF THE TOOL

Workers in established helping professions, who look upon community development as a tool, suffer from their own insensitivity to process. If community development is a newly popular means for catching public attention, why not use it to gain acceptance of needed health programs? Why not use it to spread social welfare services? Why not use it to give new vitality to adult education? Why not introduce it into the planning process, into the new housing projects, and into programs of industrial development that may result from planning? And so on.

It would be unwise to respond to these queries negatively, for all these requests for help should receive a ready cooperation. Two difficulties arise, however. Community development is not ready to give positive answers until its exponents have described more clearly exactly what it is that this new field can do. This awareness will grow out of the discovery and description of basic processes. Then these exponents must ask the related fields which request help to understand that the method which seeks self-development of people is central. Their ability to help is therefore not just a "gimmick" to be used to serve objectives which may contradict the independent growth of persons.

In the chapters on relatedness,[8] we attempt to suggest some ways in which community development may prove most useful to these related professional fields. The suggestions stem from an awareness of the new field as an independent contributor to human growth.

The Domestic Prototype

As we have said, much of the good descriptive literature on community development is concerned with overseas programs. A novice reader may be dismayed to discover that a book advertised as a significant contribution to the literature of community development deals with village life in the Philippines or with the structure of government bureaus in Pakistan. He should not be surprised. Such particularity merely illustrates, again, the way in which the exponents of the new field focus upon their own work.

There are reasons, however, for giving most attention to community development in America. First, the authors are more familiar with domestic programs. Second, it is possible that process can be more clearly seen when attention is not distracted by bizarre details of a "picturesque" culture. But most important of all, the need for clarification of development possibilities is greater among

---

[8] Chaps. 12, 13, 14, and 15.

advanced peoples who have no charts for development into unprecedented change.

CONTRASTS

Programs overseas are more likely to be called community development; programs at home may be designated under many other labels. Does this difference arise because the less developed nations often have fewer agencies and organized services devoted to helping people? The greater domestic array of services available through many helping professions makes the discovery of process more difficult. Americans seem to be more ready to give financial support to development for foreigners than to development (so labeled) for themselves. This may be partly the arrogance of the privileged. But it may also be a recognition that many services at home are already helping people in need.

Most overseas programs are (typically) conducted as an arm of government. This is usually true even when major financial help may come from the U.S. government, from American philanthropic foundations, or even in some cases from church missions. As a consequence, the community development awareness of process may be dimmed by the need to support the party in power, its leader, or the prevailing "ideology." Thus community development may be seen primarily as a contribution to national unity and to the accomplishment of reforms chosen by the leadership (for example, a movement to increase the practice of scientific agriculture or to increase the product of industry—frequently government owned). Despite subservience to government, however, the vitality of the encouraged process frequently becomes strong enough to produce local citizens of independent judgment.

Typically, United States programs are nongovernmental. When the federal government provides funds, as in agricultural extension, area redevelopment, and urban renewal, it usually tries to assure local participation by sharing much control with states, state universities, cities, counties, or local committees. That local control is difficult to achieve testifies not so much to federal dictation as to the difficulty of stirring community responsibility through the methods written into law.

Some nongovernmental programs become antigovernmental. Chamber of commerce, corporation, and some neighborhood initiative programs have as an avowed purpose the building up of citizens strong enough to oppose the government, local, state, or federal.

OTHER DOMESTIC CHARACTERISTICS

A few other characteristics that influence process for domestic community developers may be mentioned—if it is understood that no complete listing is intended. The problems people face are those of an urban and industrial society, with numerous elements and points of view left over from an agricultural and rural past. The apathy frequently encountered is of a type that grows out of a statistically affluent society, interlaced with areas of persistent poverty. People are on the move geographically and upwardly mobile to higher social and economic levels. Welfare services provided by the federal government are on the increase (against much opposition) but are less comprehensive than in most European countries of comparable socioeconomic levels. There is room for more local initiative in seeking additional services, or in controlling the services that are available, and in creating a local atmosphere compatible with private enterprise.

These are some of the characteristics of community development in America that a wise domestic encourager will keep in mind. He will be mindful also of the multitudinous agencies, corporations, governmental bodies, civic associations, churches, committees to promote or to oppose, clubs and fraternal organizations, and other groups, some permanent and some temporary, that are part of the American community scene. He will remember that many of these carry on their activities in isolation from one another. Many or all of them will be attempting to influence community opinion and action. They may be allies or opponents depending upon how they perceive the encourager's efforts.

The multiplicity of organizations and propaganda pressures (and these increase as urbanization, industrialization, and mass communications media increase) means an increase in controversy. The American community developer cannot expect to live a quiet life in which he pursues some generally accepted goals of civic improvement (handbooks to the contrary). He must expect to help people work their way through racial conflicts, disputes between the privileged and the underprivileged, between tenants and landlords, between citizens and "city hall," and so on.

These, then, are a few of the confusions in the midst of which we will now hope to discover a basic process of community development.

chapter 6

The Basic Nucleus

Both in concept and in the reality of the citizen's experience, a process is something other than a formula. Most "how to" handbooks on community development offer formulas, recipes that give steps to be taken in a prescribed sequence. An outline of process, on the contrary, presents a method for seeking, a method by which citizen participants may evolve their own formulas. The outline provides a modifiable pattern to guide the seekers, so that their efforts contribute to self-development.

The encouragement of initiative does not occur on an unplanned basis. If the achievement of responsible freedom is to be expedited, the expediting follows a design that invites participation, an outline that depends upon the flexibility of group choosing.

The first expediting recommendation has to do with the group of people that discovers the process, organizes it, and makes it work. This social entity we shall refer to as a *nucleus*. This is the group that thinks out the steps to be taken, plans the actions, and reflects upon events to learn from them. In sociological language, it becomes a "primary group," a face-to-face association of friends who interact with each other frequently and over a long period of time. It is a group characterized by an intimacy of association and a warmth of mutual support.

A nucleus is a small group of serious-minded citizens from some locality who meet the conditions listed on the following page.

Few enough in number to come to know each other well and to trust each other despite disagreements.

Concerned enough about human problems in the area to do something to make life more worth while for all their neighbors.

Conscious of standards of right and wrong against which problems and success in alleviating difficulties will be measured.

Membership in a nucleus is voluntary and (this is the ideal, usually approached gradually) open to all who will give time to meetings, to study, to discussion, to planning, and to criticism of ideas, actions, and themselves. The nucleus seeks to serve a hope for local improvement, addressed to a first, local concept of all-inclusiveness. A nucleus gives voice to a beginning aspiration for the common good.

It is not possible to designate in advance the size of the area within which a nucleus may be expected to arise. A decision on geographic area will be made tentatively by a community developer as he invites conscientious persons to confer together. That decision will be modified by the citizens as they work together, and the area will probably be redefined with experience.

Since a nucleus often starts among neighbors, it can be expected to speak primarily for the limited geographic area from which it comes. Then other nuclei may arise in similar localities throughout a region or metropolitan complex. And many of these together may be expected to give a total voice to any neighborhood. A beginning with local nuclei contrasts with the traditional community organization approach, which starts with the existing organizations in an area and tries to work down to citizen participation.

Community development methods rest upon whatever local area a small face-to-face nucleus can serve. They may be financed and planned by a city-wide or even larger organization. But community development itself relies upon processes that build up from or utilize and strengthen community-serving small group experience.

The definition of community that we have given ("whatever sense of the common good people can achieve") is functionally related to the utilization of the nucleus. Through experience with an active nucleus, citizens who have lost the sense of community begin to rediscover it as they work together for a common good. Initially, their concept of community is likely to be narrowly defined. Geographically, it may be a small area, a city block or a part of a neighborhood. Socially, it may be limited to people of similar kind or similar purpose. A basic nucleus may produce a concept of community in which a certain group opposes its adversaries. But even this concept is a beginning.

A more comprehensive concept of community is one objective of the process. This is the sense of a larger community, which, hopefully, will develop in the discussions and actions of a small nucleus. And a community developer will encourage discussion that moves toward this larger, and enlarging, experience. As will be seen, the nucleus process normally moves in this direction.

A Flow Outline for a Nucleus

From scrutiny of numerous case studies of community development processes, it becomes apparent that there is a characteristic flow of events by which a responsible nucleus comes into being or grows from an existing organization. First, we will present an outline of a pattern of flow that we have seen develop within a number of contrasting populations—and which we have discerned in the writings of other community developers. Then we will amplify the outline, presenting details that will put firm flesh upon the bare bones of process.

BASIC NUCLEUS
An Outline for the Flow of Process

Major Stages	*Detailed Events*
Exploratory	*History*—Preliminary study for the community developer.
	Present Events—Information to guide the encourager.
	Invitation—Issued by some local person or organization.
	Introduction—Of the encourager to the people.
	Informal Conversations—Responsibility of the encourager.

Organizational

Problem—Of interest to local citizens.

Informal Meetings—Of interested citizens.

Structure—Set up by the citizens who are to work on the problem.

Commitment—By the citizens, to continue working on such problems.

Discussional Training—Using an outside resource. Mav be repeated many times.

Discussional

Definitions—Of the problem, setting limits for discussion.

Alternatives—Varieties of solutions to the problem.

Study—Of the advantages and the disadvantages of the proposed solutions.

Value Basis—Principles to guide the evaluation of alternatives.

Decision—Selection of a proposed action to solve the problem.

Action

Work Project—That carries the decision into action.

Reporting—On the work done and on its effectiveness.

Analysis—In discussions.

Evaluation—Critical judgment upon the work done.

New Projects

Repeat—Discussion and action on new or redefined problems.

Outside Contacts—With the agencies and the people of power in the larger community.

Controversy Increase—New problems increase in size and amount of conflict involved.

Pressure Action (?)—Controversy may call for pressure upon the "powers that be."

Need for Coalition—Contacts with outside "powers" call for working with other nucleus groups.

Continuation

Permanent Nucleus—Commitment changes to indefinite continuation of the nucleus.

Withdrawal—By the community developer.

Problems of Increasing Complexity—Undertaken by the nucleus.

Increasing Responsibility—To deal with more complex problems.

The process as given (or some approximation of it) may be expected to occur in the formation of several other groups nearby. The several nuclei may then coalesce. We have given the details of a process for one nucleus only.

A Basic Process

EXPLORATORY PHASE

History.   Every community developer arrives upon a local scene in midst of processes that were going on before he appeared and that will continue after he leaves. He may influence those processes —favorably, we hope. But he dare not ignore them. He should inform himself about the background of the population of the area —about the conflicts, the frustrations, and triumphs, about the hopes and fears of the people he hopes to encourage.

Present Events.   He needs to be aware of events that have taken place a short time before, are taking place when he arrives, and are about to take place in the near future. These are all important in relationship to the next item:

Invitation.   In view of processes already in progress, it is important that an encourager come upon a local scene only as a result of a bona fide invitation to make his help available. Characteristically, this request comes from some organization, committee, or small group that is discontented with present conditions. The difficulty, however, is that if the community developer waits in his office for an invitation, it probably will never come. He often finds it necessary to speak to friends who will speak to friends, who will let it be known that help is available for those who would like to seek for social improvement. The art of inviting an invitation is difficult to outline in the abstract, but tact obviously is required. The encourager must be available without being overeager or obnoxious.

Introduction to People.   When the encourager does come upon the local scene, he is likely to be introduced as a representative of some employing agency or program. Inevitably, he will find that he is handicapped by his identification with the organization. The people with whom he hopes to work will have predetermined attitudes toward social workers, church employees, government "bureaucrats," public health workers, adult educators, or social science researchers. And he, whatever his good intentions, will find it necessary to overcome some of the prejudices about himself formed as a result of his identification with the organization that pays his salary. The manner of his introduction is an important means of minimizing the prejudged conclusions about his purposes.

Informal conversation is a chief means for establishing the encourager as a person as well as an organization employee. Such an informal exchange with individuals occurs most often in homes or in other places where people feel "at home." Motivations that may have been mistakenly attributed to him can be changed gradually by simple friendliness as the encourager listens to other people's conversation and shares in their worries. There is an art of creative listening and sympathizing. There is also an art of raising questions that invite the other person to talk about those things that are dear to him. Especially important is the skill that enables the other person to make articulate the concerns, fears, and frustrations that make life difficult for him.

There is a purpose in inviting the local residents to talk freely. It is to discover whether there may be some hope for the future, some idea for improvement, which could become basis for cooperative work together. Often the question may be asked, briefly, gently, and tactfully, whether there is some proposed action within the scope of the speaker's ability and his neighbor's that might provide a beginning for active development.

Conversation starts with simple human sharing. It proceeds toward the discovery of ideas for cooperative self-help. Before it arrives at positive suggestions, however, it may go through long periods of suspicion, irrelevant comments, complaints about life, and the blaming of "enemies." But throughout it all, the encourager explores patiently for the ideas that might bring forth an initiative for people to work together. The exploration may require hours, days, weeks—even months, depending upon the attitudes of the people, upon the extent of their suspicions, and upon the skill of the encourager. He is seeking something more difficult to elicit than people's agreement with his ideas. He is seeking their ideas, which they may think are unworthy or impractical. But if he is patient enough and believes in the latent creativity of people, sooner or later usable ideas will begin to emerge.

ORGANIZATIONAL PHASE

If a community developer is flexible enough to recognize a concern that is sometimes more meaningful to the people than to himself, he soon begins to discern in the many conversations common factors of interest that may lead to cooperative action. Several people will indicate that there is some problem upon which they are willing to work and that they see some way of starting to make progress upon it. This, then, is the *Problem* for a beginning.

A point of realism needs to be made clear for a beginning. The number willing to work at the problem may seem distressingly small at first—especially to any citizens and community developers who believe that "bigger" is synonymous with "better." Though dozens of individuals may express an interest in the problem for a beginning, those willing to give time to meeting, discussing, and planning may be no more than two or three—at first. These two or three, or hopefully five or six, represent the beginnings for a nucleus. They become the means for involving others in cooperation. They are the few whose activity becomes contagious.

The few who will give time come together periodically to exchange thoughts about the problem under consideration. They carry into the more or less regular meetings of an informal group the concerns they have expressed in individual conversations. They invite their friends to join them, but they also begin to seek the interest and, if possible, the attendance of neighbors beyond the circle of immediate friendship—even though these neighbors may have differing points of view.

During such a period of *Informal Meetings,* an attempt is made to focus the area of interest under consideration. Just what is it the group is talking about? What considerations should be excluded, at least at the beginning? Such focusing, to which the community developer contributes by judicious questioning, tends to determine who will and who will not feel comfortable in the group that is moving toward becoming a nucleus.

Adoption of a *Structure.*   As a result of the informal meetings, a demand frequently arises that the group be organized in a way that will facilitate the work upon the proposed improvement. Although the immediate purpose of the organization may be the accomplishment of this specific improvement, the encourager can help the participants set up a structure that will give form to the permanent nucleus-in-the-making.

Exactly how formal the structure for a nucleus should be is disputed. Some developers believe that a constitution and by-laws, together with a slate of officers and an array of subcommittees, are necessary; others hold to the conviction that a minimum of a chairman, vice-chairman, and secretary-treasurer will suffice, with subcommittees to be chosen only when needed. We slightly prefer the less formal structure, since the enthusiasm for the task will then appear larger than the organizational structure. We believe, however, that on this, as on other points, the convictions of the participants should be respected.

Is it necessary to form a new organization, or can one already in existence be utilized? Again, the local situation and the convictions of the participants must be considered. If an already constituted committee of a church, or of a chamber of commerce, or of a League of Women Voters is to become the nucleus, some changes usually will have to be recommended, if only to open membership to all persons willing to work on the problem at hand. If a large organizational entity is used, such as a county-wide council of the Agricultural Extension Service, then smaller subnuclei may be recommended, because a county usually is too large an area for a local sense of neighborly wholeness. Again, we slightly prefer a new group for an active local nucleus, but we do not insist upon this choice when the participants prefer some association with which they are already connected.

When a structure has been agreed upon, and the group is ready to move ahead, it is important that a *Commitment* be agreed upon. Work upon planned improvement is not to be undertaken lightly. The agreement to work together for some time is often given open expression as a to-be-published statement of purpose. This can be adopted in a form that can be circulated to potential new members or to newspapers, if any are interested. This statement is, of course, subject to later modification as the group progresses. But its immediate value consists in the participants' pledging themselves to a defined purpose.

Commitment, however, calls for something far deeper than a statement drawn up to inform the curious. The spoken, typed, or printed words of purpose must come from a genuine determination to continue a search for the all-inclusive better that is undeterred by either failure or success. This determination must come from within each member of the group, in his fundamental motivation. The process, through both the exploratory and the organizational phases, will almost always produce a few local participants who will give a genuine commitment to their concept of the common good.

As a result, the participants in the nucleus can be helped to become sufficiently conscious of process to discuss the steps through which they have already moved. These steps can be criticized, and if the encourager's activities are called in question, so much the better for friendly objectivity. He is then freer to challenge some of their decisions. Then the participants can examine the next steps of process, such as those presented in this outline, and can adopt or modify them.

Informal *Discussional Training* is desirable toward the close of the organizational phase. The arrangements for this experience are usually made by the encourager at the request of the participants who are becoming conscious of their membership in a nucleus. A university faculty member, or some other qualified but sympathetic outsider, may be invited to act as resource discussant. Such training may be used to launch the nucleus, but it is an experience that can be repeated again and again, depending upon the changing needs of the group.

Training may also include help on record keeping. The community developer can show that he has kept a narrative record of encounters with people, events, and meetings. Then the training may persuade some participants to do likewise, all accounts to be put together to provide feedback for further decisions and actions of the process.

An additional purpose is to increase the participants' objectivity about themselves and their own growth. Such record keeping constitutes a beginning of research attitudes and skill. The readiness of the participants to move into such objectification varies widely from one nucleus to another.

Basic to the process is the willingness of the participants to search for workable answers to problems. Participants can be encouraged to realize that the willingness to search can be transformed into the increasing refinement of research. Skill for such work can increase for ordinary citizens from humble beginnings. The first record keeping is practical—to help in guiding the process. The deeper research comes later.

Any insistence upon a single first activity too narrowly restricts the possibilities by which a nucleus can come into being. Gaining a knowledge of "our community" by a survey, for example, is one out of thousands of first activities that might expedite the process. But it serves only one of many possible problems that can be used to develop the sense of loyalty to a group. Some immediate local concern is a better beginning point for a grass-roots nucleus. A survey is more suitable for a larger nucleus.

DISCUSSIONAL PHASE

Perhaps it will be contended that by the end of the organizational phase, much discussion has already taken place. This is correct. Then why a separate discussional phase? Because to make exchanges among nucleus members and between the nucleus and the larger community creative, much more is to be learned. This learning occurs in the period of extensive study and planning that is urged on by discussional exchange.

Few people are skilled in the art of creative discussion. Some are skilled in presenting a point of view as a monologue. Others are habitually quiescent; they may lack comprehension, they may be indifferent, they may fear to articulate their inner disagreement, they may be a spluttering and ineffective opposition. Most people find it difficult to address attention to the merit or lack of merit in an idea, preferring to react rather to persons liked or disliked or to reinforce their prejudices in a verbal exchange. Many conclude that a disagreement is an introduction to enmity rather than an opportunity for broadened understanding. The discussional skills upon which a successful nucleus must depend, have to be learned.

An early step in learning the art of effective discussion is taken when the group concentrates its attention upon the problem that brought it into being. Nucleus members are encouraged to narrow their interest further by choosing some aspect of the problem upon which they can realistically hope to make a beginning. The group must, through self-discipline, exclude certain related considerations and postpone them for later consideration. This specific *Definition* of the problem has a purpose. That purpose is to lead up in discussion to a decision for an action of improvement. A successful action can be expected to increase the group's confidence in its ability to undertake the postponed problems, and many others. Thus the group matures in competence. But the group, to concentrate upon relevant issues, usually discovers that self-discipline is necessary.

While there is an excluding of less relevant considerations, there is a deliberate seeking of a wider inclusiveness of possible solutions. The art of discussion is further cultivated by listing and examining as many alternative ways of solving a problem as the group can discover or create. A nucleus can be encouraged to examine numerous *Alternatives* before moving to a decision.

Most people, unaccustomed to creative discussion, and to the study and thought that lie behind it, are prone to exhibit the "one correct solution" syndrome. They find themselves yielding too readily to persons with a pat answer, to demagogues, or to the parroters of formulas. They stifle discussion in their own group by seeking only one alternative for serious consideration. Discussion is then limited to the pros and the cons of this alternative. This stultifying division can be avoided when the number of live alternatives is increased, so that group members find it easier to conclude that no one answer is the correct and final solution; all suggestions have limitations; some may have advantages that outweigh the limitations better than others.

The attitude sought in nucleus participants is not the wild enthusiasm of the crusader, but the quiet conviction that develops in the thoughtful comparison of many points of view. A richness of discussion, and even the possible creation of their own unique solution, can result from the examining of as many alternatives as make sense to discussants.

By encouraging the examination of numerous alternatives, on the way to a decision, the encouragers facilitate the participants' learning of skills that allow them to differ on issues while remaining friendly to the persons who differ. Within a nucleus group, the individuals who favor several competing solutions to a problem can be accepted as persons. This recognition of friendliness in their opponents can then be extended beyond the nucleus to other people in the wider community.

Another important learning can have its beginning at this point, the tendency to make decisions on the basis of consciously accepted standards of value. When the alternatives are being compared and criticized, the encourager can draw attention to the standards by which the goodness or badness of proposed solutions are to be judged. He does this, not by preachment, but by asking questions about ultimate objectives. He draws attention to standards of value in the conviction that, although people's judgments may be low on any ethical scale, these judgments may be improved with experience and further discussion. People thus begin to develop a *Value Basis* for choosing.

Some community developers insist that time be set aside for at this stage the formal acquisition of group skills. And they have recommended various techniques and experiences to increase the people's competence in discussion leadership and participation, in parliamentary procedure, in sensitivity to other people's feelings, and the like. Any of these [1] may contribute to individual and group development as long as they remain secondary to the process. This is an additional occasion for discussional training.

The termination of the separate discussional stage is marked by a *Decision* to take some steps designed to contribute to the solution of the problem. But discussion continues and increases in effectiveness, indefinitely.

ACTION PHASE

Action follows decision. The specific activities in which people participate may range from muscle-stretching labor to desk work. Tasks may include cleaning up the neighborhood, the making of surveys, the circulating of petitions, writing or visiting those in authority, or going into the "direct action" of public protest. The important element is that the people involved shall take part in a *Work Project* that they have helped to plan. For people low in self-confidence and prone to blame others for their ills, some small enterprise that requires little outside help is a good first project. The more complicated activities, which require dealings with the powerful, can come later.

The action may occur on a single busy day, may involve one weekend or several, or may run on for months. But it has a termi-

---

[1] We mention and evaluate some of these techniques in Chapter 16.

nation. It is followed by a *Report* to the nucleus as to what happened and how effective it was judged to be. (Such reporting is part of the research design.) This statement from several participants leads to an *Analysis* of the Action. And when the groundwork has been laid in previous discussion, an *Evaluation* can be expected to begin spontaneously. Such a judgment upon their own efforts will normally refer back to the standards of value that the people have already made articulate. But the evaluation can also be expected gradually to modify standards, in preparation for the next action project. The chief function for the encourager is to expedite the process by the questions he asks.

Experience with nuclei drawn from many contrasting populations leads to the conclusion that people will often prove quite vigorous in self-criticism. In fact, they will often judge themselves and their own collective effort more harshly than any encourager would dare. He sometimes finds himself in the position of softening the condemnation, especially if certain individuals react overly defensively. Nonetheless, the self-evaluation that follows a period of activity should be regarded as an essential part of the action. It is the means by which nucleus members learn from experience. As a result, people begin to revise their practical value systems.

NEW PROJECTS PHASE

After the first (usually simple) project, the nucleus tends to move on to other interests and problems of increasing complexity. It builds upon the self-confidence acquired in the first achievement, even though this has been self-criticized. For each project that follows, the nucleus tends to *Repeat* the previous two stages of the process, the discussional and action phases. The greater complexity of the problem is matched by the growing self-confidence and skill of the nucleus.

There tends to be an increase in *Outside Contacts* with power figures in the wider community and with the structures of authority. Because of their increasing self-dignity, the nucleus members find that they can meet important people, man to man. These members may be inferior in wealth, social status, education, or in authority to command, but they come to stand upon their human dignity to discuss issues, even though their requests may be refused.

Another contact outside the nucleus is that with agencies set up to serve the wider community. These social welfare or public service agencies will often welcome approaches from a nucleus, all the more because they have difficulty in reaching the more normal people before their problems have become overwhelming.

In the progression to more complex problems, it is not surprising to discover that the nucleus becomes more and more aware of *Controversy Increase*. Contacts with authority may prove abortive. Officials may prove bureaucratically rigid; they may respond with an impolite rejection or with a polite "run-around." It may become necessary to exert some pressure to gain the attention and response required to make progress upon a problem.

There is always the possibility of *Pressure Action* if the milder approaches to authority prove ineffective. Although some advocates of community action make conflict with "city hall" or with landlords, with real estate brokers or with other holders of privileged status, the sole basis for the development process, our own belief is that citizen participants should not be predetermined into conflict, lest their opportunities for cooperative development be curtailed. The nucleus should go as far as it can on the assumptions of good will, then move on to newspaper denunciations or demonstrations against the recalcitrant only when the cooperative steps have proven futile. In this way the decision to apply pressure is made by nucleus members, not by the community developer in advance. Then the citizens are in a position to learn from their action, as they evaluate it. Because they have already shown their good will, they can convincingly undertake cooperative negotiations when the representatives of authority are ready.

As any single nucleus matures to responsibility, it will often find it wise to make common cause with nearby nuclei that are willing to work upon similar problems. A *Coalition* of nuclei becomes a logical next step. This is especially necessary in dealing with the great and confusing problems of a complex society.

CONTINUATION PHASE

If the process of nucleus growth has been healthy, it should produce an on-going group that will continue indefinitely. This continuation can be anticipated despite changes from time to time in the membership and in the leadership. In fact, it is wise to state in the organization phase that an on-going life for the nucleus is anticipated and that the rotation of membership and officership is part of the expected pattern.

As the nucleus gains in self-confidence and takes on a life of its own, the need for outside encouragement diminishes. This means that the community developer should anticipate *Withdrawal,* the time and rapidity being matters of judgment, his own as well as that of nucleus leaders who no longer rely so much upon him.

Withdrawal may refer to a variety of changing relationships. It may mean the encourager attends fewer and fewer meetings and speaks up less and less often. It may mean complete disengagement, except for friendly visits and letters. It may call for the selection and training of an indigenous leader, or several, who can learn to take over community development responsibilities. It may result in professional community developers being on call to help again when the on-going nucleus encounters new crises. Experience with continuing nuclei is not extensive enough yet to offer a definitive statement. Perhaps the continuing relationship will always need to be adapted to local need.

Every continuing nucleus can expect to achieve an *Increasing Responsibility* to contend with problem after problem of *Increasing Complexity.* Since these more complex problems can be solved only by the involvement of many community and state and national organizations and forces, each nucleus can expect to relate to numerous established institutions of expanding community concept. Public schools, health institutions, police departments, housing authorities, social welfare agencies, representatives of national programs, all these and many others will be called upon to help meet the needs discovered by the nuclei.

LARGER COMMUNITY

The growing awareness of a wider community tends to lead toward a social entity that serves the larger concept. This entity, the need for which often emerges spontaneously out of broadening responsibility, we shall call a *Larger Nucleus.*

Sometimes a basic nucleus continuing into greater problems, and relating itself to many institutions, becomes a larger nucleus. It then tends to create subnuclei (district committees in our urban case study; companion nuclei in our rural case study). Any of these subgroups may become independent.

Sometimes several nuclei in one local area will coalesce to form a larger nucleus. We present a flow chart showing how this coalition may arise, fitting it into the latter stages of the basic nucleus process. Note that the independent nuclei continue, even while they benefit by their relationship to the larger nucleus.

The larger nucleus, in the best practice, is an expediter of process for the constituent nuclei. (We discuss this relationship in detail in the next chapter.) Service to a larger nucleus provides one way for a community developer to continue help to the constituent nuclei after his withdrawal.

Some nuclei continue, yet never do advance to the larger nucleus structure. These are not to be condemned; they also contribute to development.

FLOW CHART

From Several Nuclei to Larger Nucleus

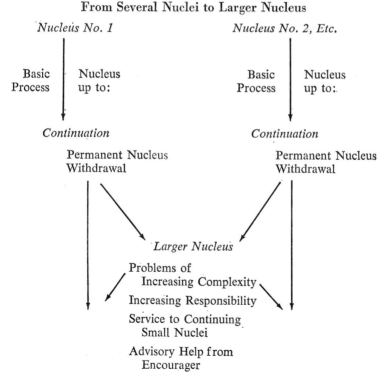

Nucleus No. 1   *Nucleus No. 2, Etc.*

Basic | Nucleus   Basic | Nucleus
Process | up to: Process | up to:

Continuation   *Continuation*

Permanent Nucleus   Permanent Nucleus
Withdrawal   Withdrawal

Larger Nucleus

Problems of
  Increasing Complexity
Increasing Responsibility
Service to Continuing
  Small Nuclei
Advisory Help from
  Encourager

VARIATIONS

From time to time, throughout the process, negative events may occur that will cause it to move with much less smoothness than the foregoing analysis might imply. These untoward events are not listed as part of the process because they do not always occur, and if they do appear, the time of their arrival is seldom predictable.

Apathy. The first response of the people, even at the time of the conversational introduction, is likely to be apathetic, or even resistant. Every community developer (and those whom he encourages) has had doors slammed in his face—or even worse, experienced the polite acquiescence that means indifference. Such resistance to the encouragement of initiative is accepted as one of the hazards of the process. It may occur at many points along the way. An encourager tries to avoid becoming hurt or upset, tries to understand the causes, seeks other ways of approaching people, and places reliance upon working through the few who will respond —hoping to evoke the cooperation of the apathetic later when something active is happening.

Group Catharsis. If there has been a long history of frustration and injustice (and there frequently has), episodes of bitter complaint may arise in discussion, either in small groups or in nucleus meetings. Such a catharsis of pent-up emotions can occur in the early days of nucleus formation, or later, in connection with the study of problems, or later still, at a time when nuclei of differing backgrounds come together in a larger nucleus.

An encourager is wise to be undisturbed by such episodes. A "blowing off of emotional steam" can be healthy for both the individual and the group, provided it does not become habitual. It is wise also to reassure any participants who may be offended that the speakers are exaggerating and will "cool off" after they have had their say. Sometimes it becomes necessary to urge the cathartic speakers to move on into constructive contributions, if they are enjoying their negative comments too much and too long. The problem is not to stop catharsis, but to move beyond it, lest its continuance threaten the growth of individuals and of the group.

Frequently, cathartic outbursts consist of no more than the blaming of someone else for one's own problems. Though there may be truth in the accusations, to dwell upon them is to paralyze one's own initiative for self-help. The encourager may acknowledge some truth in the allegations, but then move on to take the steps that will allow the people to move forward to correct the injustice.

Slump. The vigor of activity in a nucleus varies from time to time. The pace is uneven, and participation increases and decreases. One episode, however, may discourage the unwary encourager who does not anticipate it. This is the slump, when all activity ceases for weeks or months. A cessation of activity may occur at certain seasons of the year, in summer for certain populations, around Christmas and New Year's for others. But most alarming is the slump that comes after a successful project.

Actually, such a cessation of activity does not necessarily mean a loss of interest or a failing commitment. It may mean that the people are tired, especially after a job well done. It is best not to push them into a sense of guilt for negligence. It is better to keep the contacts of friendship, to continue to ask gentle questions, and to wait for energy to return and for a new idea to galvanize people into renewed activity. An encourager searches for another problem, often in conversation, that will renew the process.

Loss of Participants. In the course of the process, good people may either drop out be forced out of the nucleus. The community developer does all he can to make the unhappy feel more comfortable. He enlists the help of other nucleus members. But for a few, he may have to admit that he and the others have failed, often for reasons beyond their control. Then he regretfully sees the drop-outs go and hopes that a rotation of membership will produce new responsible participants. No process can serve everyone. No community developer is successful with all people.

The loss of good participants can be accepted with a sad equanimity when the people involved in the process can redefine their concepts of leadership. Certain writers use the term "natural leader." They seem to imply that certain especially talented persons must be used on the community scene, and that no others are qualified. In avoiding this statically limiting implication, the term "emergent leader" is more realistically descriptive. Though certain already existent leaders (not necessarily natural) took the original initiative, they can be replaced by emergent leaders whose abilities are brought forward by the process. And though an encourager regrets his inability to help some who leave, the process goes on to serve others who become active.

Disintegration of Nucleus.   As was apparent in the two case studies, any nucleus may reach a point where it disintegrates. This unhappy termination of process is more likely to occur in the earlier stages when loyalty to the nucleus has not been firmly established. It can grow out of poor leadership, unwise decisions, or factionalism. An alert encourager tries to be sensitive to the negative forces that might weaken the group or break it up. But even the most sensitive may misinterpret significant warning signals.

When a nucleus, or a potential nucleus, does disintegrate, all is not necessarily lost. An analysis of what went wrong—or even better, of what "I" did that was wrong, may open possibilities for correction. An encourager may then expect to take a much greater amount of initiative, for a while, acting as a conciliator, or as a mollifying bandager of the wounds inflicted by misunderstanding.

Throughout the process, the encourager will be wise to realize that development often is painful before it is triumphant. It moves at varying accelerations and with reversals. The community encourager needs a sense of humor that yields an imperturbability to try again. He is fortunate if he is blessed with an imagination that invents new ways to approach people, ways that will not violate their emerging self-image of dignity.

Warnings

No outline of a process should be accepted as final, not even ours. The steps given in the flow of events may occur in other sequences; some may be skipped altogether; others may occur simultaneously. Furthermore, the flow has been stated in a generalized form applicable to many brands of community development. Seldom will any actual nucleus experience all the details in the sequence given. But every step we have given has been taken by some nucleus with which we are familiar.

An encourager is the key to the process, until such time as the nucleus members take over—and even then he may be on call for consultative help. He must find himself making decisions that depend upon delicate judgments. Should he interfere when untrained leaders are making mistakes? Or should he wait until they ask for help? When should he recommend periods of training for the participants? Should he bring educational or other study materials? Or should he encourage people to find these for themselves? Should he try to delay action until the people have studied enough, have planned well, and have adopted an action and a research design? Should he display his own wisdom? When and how much? He will always have ample opportunity to make wrong decisions.

The process that frees, calls for the encouragement of responsibility. There is no sure formula by which such encouragement can provide guaranteed results. The developer of persons in a community setting proves faithful to process by adjusting his sensitivity to the people's changing needs for encouragement.

chapter 7

The Larger Nucleus

Much community development work (especially that which receives wide attention) does not start with a small, face-to-face nucleus. It starts with an "umbrella" organization that serves some concept of wider community. Effort is directed toward the formation of a community council that will serve a "social system," a town, a neighborhood, a suburb, or a city. The community developers choose an area that seems to them (not necessarily to the inhabitants) to be a community.

Such an umbrella council is a larger nucleus, in our terminology. Though it may not be built up from smaller nuclei, it can utilize elements of the basic nucleus process in some aspects of its formation. It can utilize the process in a flow of encouragement to many related nuclei.

A larger nucleus is more a representative body than a primary group. It has often been called a community or neighborhood council, supposedly representative of the many organizations that are active in the chosen area. Too often, such councils fail to give adequate encouragement for the inarticulate to be heard, since they are likely to give major prominence to "natural" rather than to "emergent" leaders. They are likely to contribute little to the development of persons. Unless they accept responsibility for encouragement through the basic nucleus process, they are poor larger nuclei.

Furthermore, a neighborhood or community council is often prone to speak for some special interest—a political organization, a chamber of commerce, a church federation, a housing administration, an area redevelopment program, or a human relations enterprise to help the underprivileged. There are numerous possibilities. Frequently, the spokesmen for the special interest will assume that their council is the spokesman for total community interest.

We do not condemn the enthusiasms of community developers who pursue special interests in this way. We admire the zeal and the effort, even when the various programs may be in conflict with each other. These separated efforts are to be understood as part of the pluralism that characterizes a free society.

Each special-interest community council serves the aspirations of some minority. (And ours is a nation of minorities. And each wider community is made up of minorites.) The sense of a wider community is often achieved by bringing together the aspirations of several minorities.

The process by which a council that starts with a special interest can bring together the seeking by minorities, we shall call the larger nucleus process. We present a flow chart of a typical sequence, by which multiple interests can be recognized to add up to a totality of an all-inclusive community—one that utilizes basic nuclei to develop people (page 110).

Broadening Special Interest

As in the case of the basic nucleus, we are assuming the presence of an encourager. He is even more important for the expediting of the larger nucleus process. Spontaneous citizen initiative seldom results in the creation of basic nuclei that serve subpopulations. We are assuming, moreover, (and this is usually true) that the encourager endorses the special-interest enthusiasm of the citizen initiators who pay his salary.

Although there are many enthusiasms that may lead to the organization of a community council, there is one particular contrast in point of view among the initiators that makes sympathy between developers difficult. This is the consciousness of serving the needs of the underprivileged versus serving the needs of the privileged.

LARGER NUCLEUS PROCESS

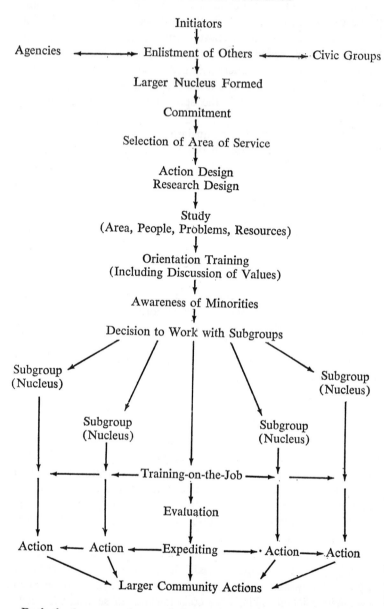

Both the larger nucleus and the smaller nuclei continue.

THE UNDERPRIVILEGED

Early community development, growing out of do-gooder impulses, was focused upon helping the underprivileged. There was, and still is, a justification for concentrating attention upon people of low social status. For their need for improvement has been obvious, even dramatic. Since they are often aware of their needs, they may prove more responsive than the comfortable and the complacent.

Much early work stressed those activities that disadvantaged people could carry on through their own efforts. Emphasis was placed upon go-it-alone projects or upon projects involving the cooperation only of other underprivileged persons. This emphasis was in keeping with the hope that even the least of these could develop in initiative. Genuine progress has been, and still is, reported from the work of numerous community projects that stress self-help among the seemingly helpless.

Soon, however, it becomes apparent that the underprivileged can go only so far in lifting themselves by their own bootstraps. They must relate themselves to various external sources of help that are found in the local larger community and in the nation as a whole. The persons or organizations that can help are often classified as strangers or as enemies—as the to-be-feared representatives of privilege. Nonetheless, their cooperation can be sought and often obtained, even to the point of having individuals of privilege become members of community councils that serve the needs of the underprivileged.

Many holders of privilege and power, however, will not cooperate; some even resist the attempts of the disadvantaged to advance themselves. When this happens (and sometimes even before it happens), the community developers who serve the less privileged people see their task as conflict between the "have-nots" and the "haves," between the "disinherited" and the "establishment." Sympathy for the underdog then leads to the identification of community development with the struggle against entrenched (and often evil) power. It becomes, in the thinking of some, a means for producing the change that will bring opportunity to the oppressed. Then community development stresses combative independence.

But such identification dichotomizes a larger community. It reduces the many minorities upon a local scene to the unreality of a two-way antagonism. Because it oversimplifies the variety of neighborly life, because it closes the door upon possible helpful allies, it does a disservice even to the disadvantaged people it is supposed to help. Community developers who work with the underdog often identify so much with their "clients" that they lose the objectivity to make a compassionate process of growth possible. Too easily they conceive of themselves as spokesmen for or defenders of the victims of discrimination. Taking pride in this identification, they find more satisfaction in recounting the woes of their clients, than in encouraging the disadvantaged to become self-respecting participants in cooperative improvement.

When the National Council of Churches set up a "migrant ministry" to serve itinerant agricultural workers (along with several denominational offices), they found themselves carrying on development in many communities. They could not bring any permanent benefit to these disadvantaged workers until they persuaded local communities to accept responsibility. They soon encountered opposition—from farm employers, from local municipal officials, and even from some local church members. Yet within each community might be found congregations in which the privileged were prominent. Might development be encouraged to serve both sides of the two-way split of privilege? A "dual approach" was worked out, setting up community councils that included representatives from both sides of the railroad track. Such an approach represented substantial progress toward cooperative development for all. But it still left thinking in an oversimplified dichotomy.

When the dwellers in the deteriorating sections of large cities have been encouraged into community organizations, they have often been urged to fight such "representatives of privilege" as real estate brokers, landlords, housing authorities, and city planners. As a result, some of the oppressed folk have "saved their neighborhood" and gained such advantages as property ownership and beautification of the neighborhood. Then the former victims of oppression have sought to defend their gains by excluding others from their improved neighborhood. The oppressed, gaining some privilege, have often become the oppressors. Such a reversal of roles may be expected when community controversy has been over-simplified into combat between two opposed enemy camps. Each side is put into an irreconcilable position that makes difficult any achievement of ethical sensitivity. Then continuing development is hampered.

Even the appeal for a dual approach, admittedly broader, is not broad enough. The all-inclusive community calls for a multiple approach. The two-way division is more reminiscent of the Marxian class struggle than of the reality of American pluralism.

REPRESENTATIVES OF PRIVILEGE(?)

Community development has more recently been taken up by the alleged representatives of privilege. In numbers engaged, in budget, in output of printed material, they are more active than the encouragers of development for people at the lower levels. This does not mean that these community developers are defenders of the *status quo*. In most of their literature, they also urge changes, not usually those that would benefit the disinherited, but those that would improve the business climate, bring better government, and improve public facilities. They express also an awareness that they speak for a minority that seeks popular support and often gets into controversy.

Several large business corporations carry on community development work. Certain electric utility companies have departments that work with local community councils in the areas they serve. So do some chain-store supermarkets. The General Electric Company has a Community and Business Relations Service. Several other companies make contributions to community development enterprises or award prizes for progress shown. Among these are Sears Roebuck; American Motors; and The National Paint, Varnish and Lacquer Association, which supports the National Paint Up, Fix Up, Clean Up Bureau. The corporations mentioned are illustrative only.

Philanthropic foundations contribute money but do not usually carry on programs. Notably, the Ford Foundation has granted millions of dollars to community development, both overseas and in the United States. Other philanthropies are generous on a smaller scale. The decision to make grants is seldom governed by the sales policy of the parent corporation. The "philanthropoids" (foundation administrators) pride themselves on their resistance to any such controls.

The Chamber of Commerce of the United States publishes an excellent series of pamphlets on community development, stressing economic growth, but inviting cooperation from many other interests. The National Junior Chamber of Commerce produces useful handbooks describing how a community council may be set up. All these materials pay respect to the concept of process, but they do not carry the flow of possible events down to the basic nucleus level.

There are many programs that seek community improvement (and sometimes the improvement of people) by the recruitment of industries for towns and small cities. These programs may recommend the formation of groups that approximate larger nuclei. Some of these programs are found in state capitals; some are associated with state universities. Related to such economic interest is the work of agricultural extension, also administered through state universities. This service has turned strongly toward county councils (or sometimes councils covering several counties). Much of the work of area redevelopment is promoted through agricultural extension.

In certain state governments, there are offices for general community development (not always so labeled). Most of these offices are committed to the formation of local community councils with handbook materials or personal guidance. Similar services are available from a number of universities. Sometimes these operate under their own name, but more often through adult education, or extension work, or the school of business or of social work.

To the naive, the influence of all such community work might seem to represent support for the "establishment." In actuality, the impact of these numerous programs is extremely varied, ranging from support for existing ways of life to changes of many kinds. The logic of development calls for change. The moment those in control of things support development, they run the risk of bringing about changes they had not anticipated. The process must always allow for unexpected results. Most of these promoters of process realize (openly or tacitly) that they may open a Pandora's box, but they are willing to take the risk. Many who serve the privileged make verbal reference to the disadvantaged, because they, too, are part of any total community. Their greatest weakness is that most of them start and stop with community councils, and so seldom carry the process down to the lives of ordinary people.

REPRESENTATIVES OF "GOOD CAUSES"

A third variety of special interest is that which seeks support for traditional and less controversial "good causes" as a focus for a community council. In most instances, the worthy purpose served is far older than the use of the community development process. The latter has come to the attention of the promoters of good works in such a way as to cause them to vacillate between loyalty to the cause and loyalty to the process.

In some cities a council of social agencies has become a larger nucleus serving an all-inclusive concept of community. Though this council may have originated in money-raising necessity or as a clearinghouse for family casework, its members may have become sensitive to the needs of all residents in the area served. They may have gone beyond the pursuit of recognition for their profession to become concerned about the people, all the people, not just those unfortunates who apply to an agency for help.

It should be said in all honesty, however, that the number of those who have reached this stage of emancipation is not great. Most councils of social agencies illustrate still the "agency approach" rather than the all-inclusive human approach of community development.

In much the same spirit, community developers that serve public health needs may or may not realize the possibilities of process in their work. Their special interest of good health for everyone often is a major concern for most larger nuclei. But if good health becomes the single overpowering objective, then the specific health proposal overshadows the benefit to be gained by encouraging people to choose to work for the achievement of that goal.

A local council of churches can start a larger nucleus process, if it will welcome all churches, Catholic, Jewish, and Protestant, and all agencies of good will that are represented in the area to be served. A human relations council set up to better relations between racial, national, and denominational groups can serve, if it is willing to give attention to other problems also. We do not question the merit of the special interest. Instead, we recommend that the worthiness of the cause be used as an introduction to a process that develops people.

It is among the supporters of a specific but limited concept of the community good that an encourager will seek for *Initiators* of a larger nucleus process. Though only a few prove responsive, some enthusiasts for a special interest can be persuaded to broaden their objectives. They move toward a concept of all-inclusive community by calling for the participation of other individuals to grow beyond their special goals. An attempt is made to recruit representatives from all significant *Civic Groups,* churches, *Agencies* that serve people, local government, educational institutions, and so on. Single potentially responsible individuals can often be discovered. They are more likely to prove active than the officially designated representatives of organizations.

As a result of the attempts to include other interests, a *Larger Nucleus* can be *Formed*. This larger nucleus then becomes the operating entity that sets up development processes that serve the all-inclusive community. It tries to maintain a balance between the numerous special interests and between the desire to work alone and the impulse to put pressure upon authority. Since it represents the wider community, it is in a position to establish relationships with experts, planners, educators, social scientists, researchers, in behalf of the several nuclei through which it will later work.

The formation of the larger nucleus is consummated in a *Commitment* of a core of active participants to accept responsibility and to work together during the months and years of adjusting, balancing, encouraging (and even discouraging) that can be anticipated. There will probably be a fringe of less determined and less actively interested members. But a core of the committed is necessary.

Moving toward Action

A first step after the formation of the larger nucleus is the *Selection of an Area of Service*. With the progressive disappearance of traditional structures and sense of community in modern life, the conscious designation of a beginning area of responsibility becomes important. In both metropolitan and rural areas, the boundaries of the wider community must often be selected somewhat arbitrarily at first. But selected they must be, or the efforts of improvement and development will not be focused enough to promise success. Once the boundaries are chosen, the larger nucleus must be prepared to modify them as the people respond, or fail to respond. This is one of the adjustments to be made and remade on the basis of experience.

About the same time, the larger nucleus becomes a chooser of an *Action Design* and a *Research Design*. The action design is a more sophisticated form of the awareness of process that members of a basic nucleus are asked to understand and adopt. Some such outline as we have presented in our larger nucleus flow chart is a good starting point for discussion and modification.

The research design is more difficult. It is covered in detail in the next chapter. Usually a larger nucleus process can be started at a higher level of educational achievement and civic experience than is possible for a basic nucleus. The larger nucleus is in a better position to authorize a research design and to set it up to serve the needs of the constituent nuclei.

A beginning is made on research by the *Study* that the larger nucleus undertakes. Such a study calls for an assembling of all pertinent data concerning the chosen area of service. Much of this information is already available in the files of existing agencies— police departments, social welfare organizations, school authorities, census bureaus, churches, and so on. A survey to collect additional information may be necessary, in the judgment of the larger nucleus. Or it may be made later. Or it may be made and then repeated again and again to keep the data up to date. But the more important task calls for the organizing and interpreting of the information that is available, so that the small nuclei can come to a central headquarters and obtain the data that will make their discussions realistic.

Throughout all these steps, the community developer has been active as encourager, guide, and asker of stimulating questions. He now has an additional obligation, the providing of some *Orientation Training* for the members of the larger nucleus. He may provide such orientation to the task himself, or he may call upon educators from nearby universities or upon other experts who can divest themselves of academic compulsions and rigidities.

Most educators for community development note that two varieties of training are necessary: [1] orientation to a philosophy that interprets people and how they can be expected to grow; and on-the-job training, which puts the orientation into practice. The first, of necessity, includes many questions of the humane values that should govern the decisions of those who are responsible for a program of local development. The second will be dealt with later.[2]

As the members of the larger nucleus take seriously the humane values discussed in the orientation, and as they study their chosen area of service, they become *Aware of Minorities* among their neighbors. They discover that their wider community is made up of many groupings and factions. They begin to conclude that numerous programs and projects are necessary to expedite the development of the people there.

MICRONEIGHBORHOODS AND SUBGROUPS

Every large community presents a multiple complexity of many groupings into which the people classify themselves. One such self-categorization is found in microneighborhoods. This term, as used by a number of sociologists, refers to racial, national, linguistic, or cultural enclaves of people. As examples, one thinks of those settlements of Negroes, American Indians, Mexicans, Puerto Ricans, or southern mountaineers now found in sections of a northern city. Included also may be accumulations of some folk who will fade into the general population in a generation or so, the Irish, the Scandinavians, the Italians, and even some poverty-stricken migrants from other states, the "Okies," and "Arkies" of Steinbeck's *Grapes of Wrath.*

The term "microneighborhood" can be extended to include other self-classifications. Sometimes these are distinguished by age: children, teen-agers, young married people, the retired, and the aging. Sometimes occupation is important: the unemployed (no occupation), blue-collar workers, and white-collar workers; or more definitively, doctors, lawyers, ministers, businessmen, organized laborers. Within any of these there may be differentiations by

---

[1] T. R. Batten, *Training for Community Development* (London: Oxford University Press, 1962).
[2] In Chap. 15, "Relation to Education."

sex. And often there is need for attention to some who are especially handicapped: delinquents, the blind, school dropouts, and so on.

These are some of the spontaneous subgroupings within which people in a larger community will feel at ease. These are the microneighborhoods to which a larger nucleus will turn its attention as it seeks to expedite the development of all the residents of an area.

One other kind of self-classified subgrouping needs to be mentioned. This is made up of the people, not yet aware of each other, who will come together when a particular problem under consideration interests them. A discussion of a school problem will tend to attract parents of school-age youngsters. A discussion of police protection, recreational facilities, or musical and artistic interests will each interest its own group of responders. Often such broad interests will cut across ethnic distinctions or other microneighborhood separations. Such varieties in interest and response discourage some community developers who look no further than an umbrella community council. The varieties appear as an opportunity for the encouragers who plan to move through a council to the formation and utilization of smaller nuclei.

Microneighborhoods and subgroupings may be expected in any area that a larger nucleus chooses to serve, and new subgroupings may be expected to arise as various community-serving interests are given attention. An awareness of the total community can be approached by working with minorities, but in nuclei that make decisions which seek to serve the total community interest.

It should be assumed that the minorities are not fixed or permanent subgroupings. They will shift. Though they are citizen-chosen, and many are traditional alignments, we have avoided referring to them as "natural," lest there be any implication of permanence. Many influences of modern life call for reclassification of human groupings. Among the prosocial influences could be the basic nucleus experience that points thinking toward an emerging concept of all-inclusive community.

Not only do the members of a larger nucleus become aware of the local subgroupings of humanity; many of them can be encouraged to interest themselves in a particular minority. As the study of the area continues, particular members can be encouraged to volunteer to give time to the minorities of their special concern.

The larger nucleus as a whole makes the *Decision to Work with Subgroups,* but the expediting work is done by the individual members. "Work with" means that the member, following the process given in the preceding chapter, forms (or utilizes) a basic nucleus from the area minority. Various participants in the larger nucleus become volunteer community developers who meet with the nuclei that arise from minorities.

Clearly, the designation "encourager" is now extended beyond the professionally employed to include amateurs, those who make a living from other employment. And clearly, these nonprofessionals require *On-the-Job Training,* to supplement the orientation they have already received. This practical day-by-day training is possible in meetings, where the members report their successes and failures with the nuclei. But it is carried on also by the professionally employed encourager in his personal contacts.

Some persons may fear that putting this responsibility for process in the hands of amateurs is unwise. Experience with larger nucleus process indicates, however, that in most localities promising candidates for such training can be found. With adequate encouragement and training, some of these amateurs work more successfully in the intimacy of the primary group than do paid professionals.

Another element of process has been implied: Only a limited number of minorities can be served at any time. A selection must be made. If commendable development is to occur, the work has to be intensive. With increasing competence the number may gradually be increased. And the need for intensive encouragement for a particular subgroup may diminish with time. The decisions on number and intensity are made by the larger nucleus as a whole.

The amateur encouragers report back to the larger nucleus to keep it up to date on progress and disappointment. They carry to the council meetings recommendations for projects, or *Actions,* of two kinds: those within the ability of a nucleus (which may need little help) and those that require broad community cooperation. The larger nucleus becomes a clearinghouse for ideas coming from the several smaller groups. It makes possible comprehensive programs that carry worthy proposals into action, and seeks to iron out differences between the nuclei when they arise. The proof of the success of the larger nucleus is found in the vitality of its relationship with the several people-level nuclei. It starts out to be a parent to these grass-roots groups. It succeeds when it becomes a servant to them.

Accepting Responsibility

All this maturation in responsibility represents a challenge to an encourager. In response to his friendly influence, a larger nucleus may become a forum for examining the diverse consciences of the larger community. It can search for unifying programs of public service. It can become a local focus for the seekers after a common good. In a time of fundamental change, every municipality, every neighborhood, every city, needs a focal point for the organization of the forces of intelligent good will.

MAINTAINING INDEPENDENCE

Whenever any nucleus group begins to have influence, it faces dangers and must guard against temptations. (This is true whether the group is small or large, but it is especially true of the larger group.) Political organizations, in or out of power, may seek to "take it over" or to use it. People ambitious for attention, votes, personal advancement, or jobs may seek the support of a group known to have the common good as an objective. Doubtful causes may seek the group's endorsement in order to "prove" their noble intentions. But independence is even more difficult to maintain when a genuine good cause—world peace, civil rights, the raising of money for a hospital, and the like—attempts to use the reputation of the larger nucleus to accomplish its own purposes.

If a larger nucleus is to fulfill its role over the years, it cannot allow itself to become a rubber stamp. The avoidance of political identification is most necessary. Members who run for public office or become active in campaigns should resign from prominent positions in the group; they must act as individuals, not as spokesmen for the nucleus. (The League of Women Voters has followed a similar policy for years.) It is important to avoid any identification with government, or with any branch or subdivision thereof.

People ambitious for their own advantage or for that of a special interest are always present. Many are adept at disguising selfishness in the high-sounding language of the community good. The nucleus had best be wary until discussion has brought into the open the special interest and the alternatives to it.

Does this mean that a larger nucleus is advised to abandon action in a surfeit of words, that it will never give vigorous support to good causes? Not at all. It does mean that the group will be wise to limit its support to those causes it has studied and chosen as its own. If those causes happen to coincide with a campaign inaugurated by others, this is good. Even better, if the larger nucleus discovers and initiates its own enthusiasms, it more clearly demonstrates its independence. In either case, the problem for the nucleus is to be sure that the choosing follows thorough and intelligent consideration of the action, so that citizens at large will tend to respect the group's self-moving integrity.

Respect for this integrity grows, in part, out of public awareness that the group has discovered unmet human needs and has independently adopted proposals to meet them. The recommendations are made to government, to school authorities, to social welfare institutions, to hospitals, that these and other operating agencies modify their programs or undertake new ones. If no existing agency will accept the responsibility, it may sometimes be necessary to create a new one. The larger nucleus can help to bring the new agency into being by suggesting how it is to be organized, who should be on the board of trustees, and so on. Never, however, should the nucleus itself become an operating or property-administering agency. It can remain effective only when it avoids becoming entrapped in institutional management. It must maintain its freedom to speak for the unmet needs, for the points at which human development is being frustrated.

CONTROL OF PUBLICITY

Processes of favorable development may be hampered or even stopped short by an injudicious use of publicity. Sometimes complimentary news stories are sought by the community developer in the hope of "proving" that he is doing a good job. Sometimes they are sought by the members of the larger nucleus in the hope of drawing attention to their commendable efforts (or to themselves?).

As rapidly as a larger nucleus assumes responsibility for the development process, it should control publicity, to insure that the publicity expedites the growth of people. But even this control does not give assurance that public mention will always be positive. In an age that measures merit by the frequency and the favorableness of news coverage, the temptation to glory in a sensational description of the group's activities is great. A first obligation for an encourager is to discipline himself lest he yield to the temptation. A second obligation is to help a larger nucleus learn the self-discipline that serves a development process.

By way of illustration, we present three newspaper clippings [3] that, in sequence, tell a story of what not to do. We have removed identifying names, since we have no desire to point a finger at anyone. We have compassion for the community developer involved, since we have made similar mistakes ourselves.

News Item, April 4

The Peace Corps in its first meeting with Taos representatives proposed a bold dynamic approach to the problems that face Taos County. At the meeting held Wednesday ... Dr. _____ outlined the aims of the organization and showed how Taos by working, aiding, helping, and planning with the Peace Corps could bring jobs, industry, and progress to Taos.

Present at the meeting were the staff of the Peace Corps in Taos, headed by Dr. _____ and representatives of Taos civic and service groups. Also in attendance were the heads of such groups as the Soil Conservation Service, Rural Area Development, as well as city and county officials.

A steering committee of 14 members was elected to function as a bridge between the Peace Corps and the varied city and county organizations. . . .

News Item, April 11

A community development program for Taos will be launched April 18 with a mass meeting at the high school. Peace Corps trainees stationed in Taos will assist and observe the "operation bootstrap" designed to help small towns help themselves by recognizing and solving their problems. . . .

It's hoped to have 1,500 residents from within Taos school district at the meeting. There'll be plenty of publicity for Taos at the mass meeting—cameramen from CBS, NBC, Movietone News and U.S. Information Agency have been invited. . . .

---

[3] From the *Taos News,* New Mexico, on the dates given, 1963

Community development will see Taos citizens probe social and economic problems, seek solutions for such physical problems as juvenile delinquency, schools, water, sanitation, unemployment. It will seek to bring together all segments of the town into one body capable of taking cohesive action. Problems and solutions are expected to be brought out and defined at subsequent committee meetings, similar to "town hall" meetings held long ago.

News Item, April 18

Efforts to hold a mass community development meeting in Taos April 18 have folded. . . .

At a meeting Thursday night several of the directors of the CD Steering Committee looking at the problem of half-hearted local interest, decided to cancel the April 18 meeting and start laying ground work for an educational campaign to explain just what community development is. . . .

Peace Corps CD officials said: "Further community development efforts are postponed until such time as the citizens of Taos show a genuine and obvious interest and enthusiasm in a self-help program in conjunction with the Peace Corps' CD training program."

Publicity can be a servant to development, but only when those who use it are committed to process. The development of people that can occur in a community is not likely to prove permanent unless a responsible group plans for growth of conviction, ethical responsibility, and competence in the lives of individual citizens. This personal growth is quiet and unspectacular. It can be hampered by an announcement that it is about to occur. Even a statement that it has occurred or is going on must be made with caution. Better to allow those who grow to discover the favorable change in themselves. Better to allow those who plan and choose the process on the local scene to control the publicity that serves the process of growth.

Mass meetings and parades are among the poorer ways to start a process of community development. They may, however, be used later. After a solid achievement, such public events may recruit interest and participation. Newspaper stories can encourage process when written with understanding for people's hopes and frustrations. The same is true for television or motion picture coverage. The people involved, and their growing feeling of competence—

these are the determining factors. Human beings and their development are central. Publicity should serve them. An encourager can help a larger nucleus discipline itself to carry responsibility for helpful publicity.

The Voice of Emerging Community

The process we have been describing can make a larger nucleus a voice for an emerging wider community. It encourages many contributions from the constituent nuclei, coordinates and interprets the contributions, and helps the nuclei to grow beyond the particularities of minority loyalties.

What about the community councils that fail to move on into the process of development through basic nuclei? Characteristically, these councils continue to be spokesmen for special-interest concepts of community; they qualify poorly as larger nuclei. Nonetheless, they often do contribute importantly to community improvement, and some become (almost accidentally) encouragers of individual development.

Though we recommend a process by which a community council may become more clearly a larger nucleus, we are not condemning those that fail. Actually, even those councils that stop short in process serve useful ends. They would be more valuable, however, if their enthusiasm made widely available the experiences that open up to everyone the search for community.

Is there a danger that a larger nucleus may become arrogant, enjoying the power to speak for the community good? Yes. Human beings who seek after righteousness are prone to self-righteousness. But the temptation can be minimized by two factors that are essential to the process: First, because the larger nucleus is a coordinator of many contradictory voices it is seldom able to speak for a unified point of view. Second, the larger nucleus remains effective and influential only so long as it does not become identified as a source of power. Part of the task for the encourager is to convince the larger nucleus that there is persuasiveness in a commitment to the common good. This works best when the nucleus does not possess the strength to control others. But first the encourager must convince himself that such persuasiveness is preferable to power.

The task described is not easy, either for the members of a larger nucleus or for the community developers. It is always difficult to move from the promotion of a special interest to the search for the community good. Even more difficult is to keep seeking for the experiences that develop people, despite failure and rebuff. Most difficult and painful of all is to eschew the delights of power in favor of trying to be right—and never quite making it.

chapter 8

Research Design

The concepts of "nucleus" and "larger nucleus" are heuristic; that is, they make research possible. Certain new research opportunities become available.

There is first a distinction to be made between community research and community development research. The former is more likely to be descriptive of present conditions in local situations and social structures. It too readily allows the implication that the existing condition (frequently bad) is inevitable. Usually such findings contribute to a pessimism about man and his improvability.

The latter is descriptive of change, a becoming. Being dynamic in reference, it is more likely to support an optimism. This is true even when the change reported is abortive or produces unfavorable results. There is always the hope, stated or implied, that results may be better next time.

A second differentiation is an emphasis upon utility. Community development research has a practical purpose, that is, to help people solve problems. This immediate utility means that data and records become feedback which people can use in discussing their development. Feedback in this meaning refers to information that nucleus participants use to guide decisions on further process.

That the research is useful to those who guide the process does not mean that it can make no contribution to basic social science. Important findings about human beings are possible in the research, even in the midst of its practical applications. In fact, some basic conclusions about human potential can be researched only in the midst of programs of conscious improvement.

A research design is called for, which is an integral part of the process of development. This design falls within the concept of action research. The outline we present gives one example of this discipline, a research compatible with the search for community. In our definition, *action research is an on-going study of a social process and its results to date, which is carried on as part of the process. The accumulating findings are used to guide and correct the decisions of the continuing process. Participants contribute to research in the manner that their increasing ability will allow. Contribution to scientific generalization may be sought by qualified participants, as well as practical answers to problems.*[1]

Although a research design involving citizen decision makers may seem to lack technical nicety, it falls within the scope of social scientific discipline. As action research, the design calls for the participation of many people involved, each according to his ability, each with the expectation that the process will tend to improve that ability.

The social psychologist Kurt Lewin introduced the concept of action research. In the quotation that follows, Lewin [2] makes reference to the solution of practical problems in the contexts of both the human situation and social scientific law.

> In the last year and a half I have had occasion to have contact with a great variety of organizations, institutions, and individuals who came for help in the field of group relations. . . .

---

[1] We make explicit the standard definition, which is: *"Action research:* use of scientific research principles for the study of actions that are aimed at a comprehensive goal. Generally, the research is done by some of the participants in the program of action. In action research the activities studied are undertaken in the hope of achieving certain useful results, and the research is designed to effect improvement in the on-going process, not merely in some future process. In pure experiment, by contrast, activities are prescribed primarily to obtain data that may be analyzed for scientific or technological generalization. When, however, practical programs of action are modified in such fashion as to facilitate research analysis, the distinction is one of degree." Ava C. English and Horace B. English, *A Comprehensive Dictionary of Psychological and Psychoanalytical Terms* (New York: Longmans, 1958), p. 9.

[2] Kurt Lewin, *Resolving Social Conflict* (New York: Harper and Row, 1948), Chap. 13.

If this amount of serious good-will could be transformed into organized, efficient action, there would be no danger for intergroup relations in the United States. But exactly here lies the difficulty. These eager people feel themselves to be in the fog. They feel in the fog on three counts: 1. What is the present situation? 2. What are the dangers? 3. And most important of all, what shall we do? . . .

Research that produces nothing but books will not suffice. . . .

It is important to understand clearly that social research concerns itself with two rather different types of questions, namely the study of general laws of group life and the diagnosis of a specific situation.

Problems of general laws deal with the relation between possible conditions and possible results. They are expressed in 'if so' propositions. The knowledge of laws can serve as guidance for the achievement of certain objectives under certain conditions. To act correctly, it does not suffice, however, if the engineer or the surgeon knows the general laws of physics or physiology. He has to know too the specific character of the situation at hand. This character is determined by a scientific fact-finding called diagnosis. For any field of action both types of scientific research are needed. . . .

At least of equal importance to the content of the research on intergroup relations is its proper place within social life. When, where, and by whom should social research be done? . . .

Rational social management, therefore, proceeds in a spiral of steps each of which is composed of a circle of planning, action, and fact-finding about the result of the action. . . .

This and similar experiences have convinced me that we should consider action, research, and training as a triangle that should be kept together for the sake of any of its corners. . . .

It seems to be crucial for the progress of social science that the practitioner understand that through social sciences and only through them can he hope to gain the power necessary to do a good job. . . .

The research is democratized. No longer is it conceived of as a separate area of skill open only to a technically trained elite. It is a shared responsibility in which social scientist, citizen, and encourager (practitioner) of process are co-experimenters. Various aspects of the total task may be divided among the three. There are different levels of technical exactness, but co-experimentation achieves a mutal respect for the contribution of each.

With contributions by the three in mind, it is important to make a distinction between two kinds of research. The first is external to the process. This is particularly available to the traditional social and behavioral science disciplines. It has to do with the collecting of objective data about the process and its progress, with no necessity for the researcher to become a participant. And it need not involve action research.

The second is internal to the process and must be action research. Scientists may be part of this dynamic research, provided they are willing themselves to become participants in process. Conclusions are reached by scientists and citizens, both for feedback to guide the process, and for basic findings. It is best when the findings are agreed upon in collaborative discussion between the two.

An encourager finds himself in the intermediary position, between citizen and scientist, mediating understanding for both external and internal research. It is important that scientists be kept from reducing people to objects under observation. It is equally important that citizens gain respect for scientists while coming to accept them as friends. The achievement of interrelationship is an obligation for the encourager.

The total research, however, remains in the hands of the citizen group that sets up both action and research design. These citizens consult with and accept guidance from the encourager and the technical advisors. But the ultimate responsibility is theirs. This responsibility must remain in participant hands, because involvement in the process is voluntary. The development that occurs is chosen by those who benefit from it.[3]

Our consideration of research design will cover both the external and internal varieties, but we will place greater stress upon the internal—which calls for action research. The reasons for this choice are simple. First, the external variety is already well covered in existing books.[4] In order to expedite action research, it is important to increase the responsibility of the citizen participants. This is part of their development. It is important to bring their skills up to a level that will make cooperation with the scientific researchers more likely. But it is also important to bring some self-

---

[3] For a detailed presentation of the co-experimenter relationship in overseas development projects, see Samuel P. Hayes, Jr., *Measuring the Results of Development Projects* (UNESCO, 1959). See especially "Step Three, Collecting Data—Before, During, and After."

[4] See App. II, "Bibliographies," Social Scientific Theory and Background.

discipline of humbleness to social scientists to make their association with citizens productive.

Responsible Authorization

The citizen group that authorizes the research, and participates in its continuance and utilization, is usually a larger nucleus. (Occasionally an exceptional smaller nucleus may serve.) This nucleus designs the research to fit into and expedite the action, providing for responsibilities that can be carried by the encourager, by the citizens willing to take part, and by the social scientists who will fit their skill into process. These several responsibilities may be assigned early, or they may be authorized as events continue. But it is well that a general over-all design be adopted early, so that it becomes an integral part of the process.

In the *Research Design* that we present on the next page we have tried to indicate its integral relatedness to the flow charts already given. The left-hand column repeats some of the action design for the larger nucleus—in abbreviated form. The central and right-hand columns show two streams of research, Data and Process, which are part of the total, relating these by arrows to the Flow of Action. The design is meant to be inclusive. As a practical matter, most citizen groups will not set up the entire research design, at least, not in the detail given. They will select those items that are most pertinent to their beginning interest and (hopefully) add others as the process continues.

Once a general design has been authorized, the serious work of research can begin. An early responsibility for citizens is to confer with the encourager, with the social scientists, and with other resource persons to make articulate the objectives by which the results are to be evaluated. At the point of *Commitment,* some specific problems are chosen, together with a statement of how progress in solving these probems is to be assessed. This provides the beginning criteria by which the group can judge its success or failure. These criteria are subject to later re-examination by the group.

A beginning statement of criteria can be made articulate in the *Orientation Period*. Another statement of the values sought can be made at this time through an examination of the operational as-

RESEARCH DESIGN

Flow of Action		*Flow of Research*
Commitment		
↓		
Selection of Area		
↓		
Action Design Research Design	→ Decision to Authorize Research	
		↓
		Study
		↓
↓		
Orientation	*Process Research* Record of Process up to Commitment	*Data Research* Assembly of Existing Information Survey (if needed)
↓	↓	↓
Decision ←	Base Line for Process ←	A Beginning Base Line
↓	↓	↓
Actions	Recording of Meetings, Events, Decisions, Evaluations	A Data Assembling Bureau
↓	↓	↓
Evaluation	Process Analysis	An Interpretation of Data
		↓
		Continuation of Assembly and Interpretation
↓	↓	↓
New Decisions	Continuing Recording and Summary	Data to Show Progress (or its lack)
↓		
New Actions		
↓	↓	↓
New Evaluation	Eventual Narrative (to be published?)	Continuing
↓	↓	
Continuing	Continuing	

sumptions (general hypotheses) about people, about "our" community. An effort can be made to refine some of these to specific hypotheses for testing. Although the first efforts to state testable hypotheses will probably not prove very fruitful, the time spent in discussion is well used. It is worth while on at least two counts: the members of the group are sensitized to the concept of broad hypotheses and in the process, can be expected to sharpen their thinking; the social scientists who are present are guided in their selection of specific hypotheses for their work.

There is a normal flow that goes on in such discussion, with increasing refinement of citizen thinking. It runs from

Inarticulate assumptions to

Articulate assumptions (which are debated, often with heat), to

General hypotheses (upon which most can agree for operation) to

Some agreed-upon events which can be anticipated, to

Evaluation (discussion to see whether the hypotheses have been upheld) to

Modification of hypotheses (as a result of evaluation) to

New test. And so on.

There is a companion flow for the social scientist co-experimenters who have been authorized to cooperate. Immediately after general hypotheses have been stated, this flow goes as follows:

Specific hypotheses (for disciplined and exact testing) to

Tests (that do not violate the dignity of the persons involved) to

Proof or disproof of the hypotheses (within a limited time period) to

Generalization to

Report back to the citizen group (as well as write-up for a social scientific monograph).

Both of these flows of research are expedited by the process outline of research design. They work best when the group member and the social scientist collaborator are cooperating, with coordinative encouragement from the encourager.

The community development process makes possible a collaborative relationship, a symbiosis, between the developing citizen and the expert. The citizen helps the technical social scientist to become more humanely sensitive, and hopefully, to modify his operational assumptions toward the optimism of realizable human potential. The expert contributes to the maturation and liberation of the citizen, and hopefully, helps him to achieve attitudes that encourage favorable change in neighbors.[5]

... if experts are able to go into communities and so work that deeper comprehension and liberation is achieved with respect to the issues of life they are the means of promoting freedom and independence. Unless research is designed to measure maturity and liberation as well as know-how it may serve to report further blindness and dependence.

Data Collecting Research

Data Collecting Research is given first consideration for two reasons: It is the more familiar variety and will therefore usually receive first consideration by responsible nucleus members (and possibly also by the social scientists). The idea that all relevant data should be assembled and put in perspective prior to important decisions is commonly accepted (although less commonly put into practice). The keeping of such information up to date for guidance in making further decisions causes no difficulty of thinking (although it is easy to file information and forget it). The expectation that external research of processes of change shall itself produce data (usually measurements of some kind) is not new. But skill in feeding the accumulating data back into the process is new. Both citizens and scientists will have to learn this skill.

CITIZEN PARTICIPATION

A beginning for data collecting research that is to be fed back is found in the setting of a *Base Line*. Some beginning date is chosen, and all pertinent measurements and items of information as of that date are assembled. Subsequent data may then be compared at suitable time intervals, to show progress or its lack. All

[5] Wayland J. Hayes, "The Problem of Community Intelligence," *International Review of Community Development*, No. 10 (1962), p. 161.

this sounds elementary enough, but it is surprising how many so-called experiments in social change will fail to prescribe the base-line starting point. "Experimentation" then follows a "let's put this project into gear and drive it" philosophy; no means for discovering whether change has occurred and whether it has moved toward the desired goals is provided.

The problems that are important to the area served determine which data shall be assembled. Delinquency rates among juveniles, information about the amount and location of substandard housing, employment statistics, the amount of play space available, the incidence of disease, pupil-teacher ratios in schools—these and other measurements may all be significant. Such statistics may be broken down into neighborhood areas or related to different sub-groupings of the population. In time, the actual choice of pertinent data will probably change and so provide new base-line beginnings for new problems. Seldom will a nucleus assemble a complete array of information on the first try. But it can assemble enough data to make subsequently collected information meaningful in terms of the changes it seeks.

Citizen amateurs can carry responsibility for most of this type of data collecting, visiting and revisiting local authorities, making needed surveys, filing and revising the accumulating information, and interrelating and interpreting the cold figures and facts. They will usually call for help from the encourager and the social scientist, but they will grow in objectivity and responsibility by carrying the major burden of such factual research. And they will help scientists to relate data to practical decision.

EXPERT RESPONSIBILITIES

A social scientist co-experimenter can give important help in guidance for interpretation of data. What do all the (frequently bewildering) facts mean, in terms of scientific thinking, in terms of an emerging awareness of community, in terms of human need? Some critics will contend that social scientists are ill-prepared to assume this perspective-achieving role. In their technical training, this is true. In their association with the citizens, however, they learn to adapt to such a collaborative function—or they quickly find themselves unwelcome.

But other responsibilities of the researchers draw more upon their technical training. Some researchers have begun to evolve devices to describe participation in small group processes.[6] These descriptions can be helpful to a basic nucleus—to improve the participation of members. They are more illuminating for interrelationships within the group, however, than for relationships of the group to its emerging community.

A few studies of representative bodies, such as a larger nucleus, have begun to explore relationships to community responsibility.[7] But enough has not been done with a group when it continues over the years and when it authorizes research that modifies on-going process.

There are many kinds of research that can be presented to an authorizing nucleus for approval: records kept of attendance at and participation in meetings and other activities, tape recordings of discussions to make possible the analysis of roles and changes, motion pictures of important events that show action, interviews of participants and nonparticipants (especially depth interviews). These and many other kinds of external research gradually become acceptable to an authorizing nucleus, when explained, when some place is left for participant initiative and choosing, when citizen members are involved in the gathering of information and in the interpretation of the results.

No one knows what the limits are for cooperation of technically-trained co-experimenters, or what new possibilities they may dream up. Who can predict what the creative ingenuity of social scientists may produce for citizen approval once they have become sensitive to development processes, once they have accepted with enthusiasm their role as collaborators?

Several self-disciplines, however, are called for among scientific experimenters. They must avoid the use of procedures that tend to reduce people to the status of guinea pigs or mere objects or that threaten their emerging dignity. They must seek and use experiments that increase the citizen's self-esteem and expedite the on-going process. The experimenters need to display a genuine

---

[6] A. Paul Hare, *Small Group Research* (New York: Free Press of Glencoe, 1962), App. I.

[7] See the publications of the National Training Laboratories, especially Leland P. Bradford, Jack R. Gibb, and Kenneth D. Benne, *T-Group Theory and Laboratory Method* (New York: Wiley, 1963), Chap. 15.

compassion and concern for the people; they need to believe in the people and in their inherent value—as they are, as they may be. Central to the experimenter's motivation must be a concern for the people, their dignity and welfare. Much more is called for than commitment to the niceties of methodological rigor.

All this requires a delicate balance on the part of a social scientist. This can seldom be achieved short of his becoming committed to some of the goals sought by the deciding nucleus, while maintaining a role of separateness to see the process in theoretical significance.[8]

Process Research

... It is an important step forward that the hostility to theorizing which dominated a number of social sciences ten years ago has all but vanished. It has been replaced by a relatively widespread recognition of the necessity for developing better concepts and higher levels of theory. The theoretical development will have to proceed rather rapidly if social science is to reach that level of practical usefulness which society needs for winning the race against the destructive capacities set free by man's use of the natural sciences. . . .[9]

Here is a unique social scientific opportunity for community development, to develop theory from the small-scale laboratory human experience of practical growth. Although the process is used to guide local decision and to increase the compassionate objectivity of participants, out of it also can come basic findings about the nature of human beings when they take part in consciously sought development.

ENABLING ATTITUDE

Since most community developers are hopeful, the process research they encourage tends to open the doors to favorable change, in the manner of a self-fulfilling prophecy. But the doors are not opened wide unless the developers, as experimenters, are optimistic enough about people to convince them to make an effort to

[8] Florence R. Kluckhohn, "The Participant-Observer Technique in Small Communities," *American Journal of Sociology,* Vol. XLVI, No. 3 (November 1940), pp. 331 *ff.*
[9] Lewin, *op. cit.,* pp. 188–189.

improve. That is, belief in the possibility of a favorable outcome for the research is a precondition for the research.

Such optimism is necessary on the part of the community development encourager, but also on the part of the social scientist experimenter. The citizen co-experimenter need not start with any such enabling attitude. He need only hope that something can be done to alleviate the problems that oppress him. He may not become clearly conscious of the development process (despite the adoption of preliminary action and research designs) until he has experienced enough of the process to examine and comment upon the results.

When he can look back upon the base line from which "we" started, when he can see what "we" have done, when he can conclude that "we" have moved even a little toward the values "we" seek, he develops a determination to accomplish more. Then his convictions of guarded optimism begin to grow. Thus the optimistic enabling attitudes of developers and researchers make possible the experiences that can change citizen apathy and discouragement to enthusiasm and hope.

RECORD KEEPING

On first consideration, the task of writing even a brief account of the events pertinent to a process of development seems burdensome. Actual experience with such record keeping indicates that the burdensomeness diminishes fairly soon, when the writing is made routine and when forms to be filled out are available. Most recorders, once they have made the practice habitual, report that the obligation tends to become a clarifying experience, by which events are seen in a more objective perspective.

As part of the routinizing, it is well to write the record of an event within twenty-four hours of its occurrence. If the delay is much longer, the details tend to fade into an indistinct haze of memory. Or even worse, certain details are transposed and attached to incorrect times, places, and persons. When the events are accurately recorded, it is often found that a significance, unrealized at the time, is discovered in later occurrences. At the time of writing the recorder may have had no inkling of the important subsequent events to which an innocuous beginning might lead.

Systematic recording usually begins with the community devel-

oper. His first notes on process can be quite informal, as he records his encounters with people:

Date (most important for a chronological sequence)

Time of Day (relationship to fatigue, discipline of work hours,
and so on)

Nature of Encounter (a conversation—face to face or over the
phone, formal or informal, a meeting of several people, casual
or by invitation, an argument, an agreement, a display of
anger, some shared activity)

Duration (how many minutes or hours)

Nature of Termination (friendly, antagonistic, looking toward
further encounters, or not)

Any Ideas or Problems (that were suggested—or even implicit
—offered by people who took part in the personal exchange)

Already there begins to emerge an answer to the oft-expressed
complaint of the new recorder: "What do I write down? I can't
record everything." The details to be recorded are determined by
the recorder's sensitivity to the process, as he understands it. There
is no final and agreed-upon listing, but with time, certain items of
behavior begin to emerge as significant indicators.

As rapidly as conversations lead on to organized meetings, a
more formal type of recording can begin to supplement the chronological narration of encounters. Numerous forms for recording a
meeting are available or can be evolved. One that we have used
embodies several of the points found in the above informal recording of encounters. The filling out and accumulation of such
forms makes possible an analysis of groups and how they work.

Some forms include items for recording judgments about the
emotional tone of the participants (cooperative, antagonistic,
apathetic, and so on). Others may include analyses of the roles
taken by the participants (and changes in roles). Others may include ratings of efficiency, clarity of discussion, and the like.[10]

There is nothing sacred about any of these forms. They represent a convenience to help people routinize their recording. Such

---

[10] For a discussion of this and related techniques, see Marie Jahoda, Morton Deutsch, and Stuart W. Cook, *Research Methods in Social Relations*
(New York: Holt, Rinehart and Winston, 1951), Pt. II, Chap. 15.

RECORDING A MEETING

Date of Recording ⸺⸺⸺ Date of Meeting ⸺⸺⸺

Name of Group ⸺⸺⸺ Person Reporting ⸺⸺⸺

Occasion ⸺⸺⸺ Place ⸺⸺⸺
   (Regular or Special Meeting,   (Location)
   Work Project, and so on)

Time of Beginning ⸺⸺⸺ Time of Ending ⸺⸺⸺

Citizens Present:

    Name   Occupation   Representing Special Interest?

Helpers Present
    Encourager
    Resource Discussants
    Other Visitors
Matters under Discussion
Decisions Reached
Matters Deferred
Next Meeting (Date, Time, Place)
Significant Side Conversations (before, after, and during Meeting)

forms should be revised from time to time as a result of use. They are frequently used first by the community developer, who then introduces the citizen members to them as rapidly as they will accept some responsibility for recording. (A simplified edition of such forms may be used for less articulate nucleus members.) They are also recommended to social scientists who are learning the self-discipline of participation. From several recorders, a total file of events in chronological order is built up. This file starts with informal narratives of the first encounters and then includes the accounts of meetings from different points of view and also summaries of significant data and descriptions of any actions taken (in cooperative work together, in surveys made, in petitions circulated and carried to authorities, and so on).

This total file is made available to nucleus members. It supplies information for a periodic evaluation of the group's progress. The nucleus members, growing in objectivity as a result, are in position to cooperate with the social scientists and with other formulators of theory and to participate in judgment.

It is important that the writer of the record stress events and avoid judgments as much as is possible. Attention is concentrated, not upon the approval or the disapproval of individual behavior, or upon joy at contribution to group purposes, but upon whatever happened. The touchstone for determining whether to include an item in the record is its contribution to process. And evaluation is left to the group, when it utilizes the records.

A note of realism must be mentioned here. The achievement of such objectivity is difficult—for all people, including social scientists and community encouragers. Some comments upon other people will probably creep into records. The encourager of the process himself may find people making criticisms of his sins and alleged sins of commission and omission. He, of course, can armor himself in advance by training himself to be cheerful in the face of criticism, but the group member who becomes an unhappy victim of an unfavorable judgment, cannot be expected to react so philosophically. The discussion that follows an examination of the record file is the place to assuage hurt feelings and, possibly, also to give personal reassurances to the victim. To be able to bring criticisms into the open, to contend with these judgments and reduce personal defensiveness to a minimum, to keep attention upon the tasks and progress of the group, these are parts of the learning of compassionate but effective objectivity.

We have experimented with forms that call upon the recorder to identify and interpret the roles carried by the members of the group. We conclude that such forms tend to encourage the already existing tendency to pass unfavorable judgment upon any person who irritates the recorder. We do not, therefore, recommend them for citizen recording. Moreover, we have concluded that critical comments about persons may arise in group discussions anyway. And these are better handled there, where spoken words can be explained and apologies can be offered and accepted. Once judgments about persons are written on paper, they tend to become irretrievable.

In all the learning that comes as a result of democraticized research, the skill of the encourager is most important. His explaining, his assuaging of hurt feelings, his mending of the broken bonds of friendship, his appeals for understanding and for toleration of personal idiosyncrasies—these are essential to process, and they are made explicit through record keeping. But the encourager's ability to introduce such responsibility at the proper time and to ask for the acceptance of the accumulating record both call for a sensitivity to the pace of people's growth in objectivity. He has ample opportunity to make mistakes. Fortunately he also has the opportunity to correct them.

A final form, with which we have experimented, enables the members of a nucleus (usually a larger one) to move beyond attention to details and to concentrate more upon the process. This is the *Process Analysis Form*. The mass of reports in the accumulating process file can become cumbersome. It is well if the essence can be put into a brief summary form for quick reading and over-all summation of the process to date (page 143).

The flow of process is indicated by an unending series of brief dated entries. These entries constitute a summary from the beginning up to the latest item. The entries should be clear enough to make possible a determination of the progress that has occurred, or failed to occur.

Two kinds of entries are made: *Events and Decisions*. These are entered chronologically, each preceded by an "E" (for events) or a "D" (for decisions). Each is entered soon after it has taken place, under the date, so that it is possible to gain a concept of the flow of process.

1. *Events* (*E*). These are encounters, meetings, and reports selected out of the accumulating file for significant contribution to process. Each entry includes a statement of what happened and the numbers and kinds of people involved, all in a single paragraph.

2. *Decisions* (*D*). These are proposals, agreements reached in meetings, and stated approvals or disapprovals reached by the nucleus or by some person authorized by the nucleus. These are interspersed, by date, with the events, to indicate whether evaluations that result in conclusions affect the flow of events. The entry names the persons, or group of persons, who have made the decision, describes the conflict prior to the agreement, gives an exact statement of the decision, and provides evidence of the evaluative

PROCESS ANALYSIS
(Page 1)

Face Sheet

Name of (Larger) Nucleus _____

Area of Service (Geographic address, boundaries of area, name of

neighborhood—if any) _____

Date of Beginning (for Nucleus) _____

Date of Last Entry (to be changed each time) _____

First Statement of Purpose (with date) : _____

_____

Later Statement of Purpose (with date) : _____

_____

Continuing Revisions of Purpose (with dates) : _____

_____

. . .

PROCESS ANALYSIS
(Pages 2, 3, and so on)

. . .

CONTINUING RECORD

. . .

discussion. All this can be reduced to a single paragraph for each
entry.

Such a summary can be kept as an accumulating record of progress up to the date of the last entry. It can be kept regularly by
someone with the authorization of the nucleus. It (like the file of
process) is available to the nucleus, but is not for general circulation. Its main purpose is to help participant members achieve a
sense of the onward flow of process. It draws attention to the rocky
road over which the group has come, the triumphs in the face of
difficulty, the unsolved controversies, and the unrealized hopes for
the future.

The final culmination of process research is the production of an *Eventual Narrative* of the process, a case study of people in the process of local development. This will include statistics and other findings from the data research. Not every community development project will produce such a narrative for publication, but the whole new field would benefit immensely if more were published. If the narrative grows out of the kind of process recording that we have described, it will be a product of a co-experimentation that involves the community developer, the citizen and the social scientist. The actual writing of the narrative, however, should usually be placed in the hands of a single individual who has the authorization of the nucleus.

POSSIBILITIES AND LIMITATIONS

Action research that serves community development makes a greater contribution to general than to specific hypotheses. The outcomes of developmental studies like these yield, not so much measurable and final "proofs," as indications of the directions in which human beings may be expected to move—under given circumstances. From an accumulation of many studies of local development there should come presumptive evidence for general conclusions about man's potential for self-improvement. Such evidence is already accumulating in the literature of the field.[11]

There will be social scientists who look upon such research as lacking in the rigor that their particular disciplines have been achieving, often painfully. Their accusations are correct; the methodological rigor is, as yet, low. But citizens and encouragers, working with flexible social scientists, will gradually move the research up a scale of increasing discipline. Narrative reporting has already begun to produce descriptions of process. These should soon result in classifications of the kinds of process that may be seen in relationship to classifications of social situations. Such taxonomies might be expected to yield to both qualitative and quantitative treatment of describable items of experience in the flow of process. These should finally lead to conclusions about man-in-development, which then become new general hypotheses for further testing.

---

[11] See App. II, "Bibliography," Sec. B, Community Development in the U.S.A. and around the World.

Research Attitude

Such cooperative co-experimentation tends to produce an additional maturation in participants. This maturation is seen in a growing tendency to reject formulalike "correct" answers to problems and to place more reliance upon the experimental search for improvements. Thus a gradually growing research attitude toward many of the problems of life tends to replace rigidity of thinking. Both the social scientist and the citizen become convinced that progress will be made, not by their becoming adherents to some messianic doctrine, but by their working intelligently, cooperatively, and ethically, first upon the immediate problems, then upon the more distant and difficult ones. A hope that experimentation can produce favorable results, which is precondition for action research, tends thus to be strengthened.

Dare we assume that most community encouragers possess enough optimism to help other participants gain this reliance upon experimentation?

chapter 9

Microprocesses in the Midst of Macroprograms

A basic nucleus represents a microprocess in the midst of a society that admires gigantism. A larger nucleus provides a means by which several of these microprocesses may be able to relate themselves to huge, attention-getting events and large-scale planning. The comprehensive solution to problems, well-financed, affecting the lives of great numbers of people, and administered from the top, represents a macroprogram. One of the bars to the progress of community development is the widespread belief that only in macroprograms is there hope. According to this viewpoint, microprocesses are foredoomed to frustration.

Macroprograms are characteristically inaugurated by government; the bigger (and therefore more significant?) are federal—for only big government can command the huge sums necessary. But big foundations, big businesses, big churches, big labor unions, these and other great concentrations of decision-making power can also be expected to originate and finance such programs.

A few of the problems that assail modern man are solvable on the simpler local scene. But the bulk of the difficulties, especially the more worrisome ones, must find more comprehensive solutions. Does this mean, as many believe, that reliance must be placed upon the macrosolution in which there is little or no place for the microprocesses of local initiative?

Can the small-scale and local processes of development we have been describing have influence upon the monumental forces of our time? Can they have any appreciable effect upon the thinking of the great decision makers, upon the policy-determining events, the large-scale planning, and the much publicized social movements of a mass-communicated age? There are no easy answers to such questions of democratic vitality. There never have been.

By studying the past it is possible to discover that important movements and headline-claiming events often have had humble beginnings. More important for the future, however, is this: No one can know what the possibilities may be for ordinary citizen contribution to the flow of history until there is more research into the encouragement of human self-development, much of which must begin in local experience.

A development of people to accompany the development of economic systems and facilities is being called for by the more democratic policy makers and sensitive planners. They are questioning whether their programs can succeed without corresponding changes in the human beings who are affected. The more humane these decision makers are, the more they ask for favorable development in persons through participation in the processes of self-chosen change. But most of them do not know how to expedite human growth in the midst of the grand-scale planning. Community development processes provide one approach for experimentation—a local participative democracy by which people may learn to become contributors to the great decisions of our time.

An Era of Large-scale Decision Making

Perhaps the ordinary citizen has always lived with the sense of being overwhelmed by the decisions of the great and powerful. If so, the problem has become more acute in the modern era, when policies are determined, plans are made, and administration is centered in distant capitals of government and of financial control. The freedom left even to members of local power structures, let alone to ordinary citizens, is steadily reduced.

More and more, the great decisions from distant offices of central power call upon individuals to acquiesce. More and more, the instruments of mass persuasion increase the tendency to make a virtue of conformity. More and more, the necessities of interdependence on expanding scale make mockery of claims to individual and local independence. Nationally determined behaviors and standards tend to replace those determined at the community level. And these distantly determined pressures call for some change in people's loyalties and habits. Even the advocates of conservatism call for a change, even if the change is only a return to some (presumed) earlier way of life.

Many of the pressures toward community and individual conformity are governmental, but there are other pressures as powerful and as insistent. Acquiescence in centralized decisions, is demanded by huge employers (corporations with nation-wide operations or with the ability to control the policies of local businesses) and employee associations (labor unions with national or international authority). Various national churches tend to exercise centralized controls, partly because they are in a position to allocate funds. National welfare programs insist (as they should) upon minimum standards. Health organizations seek conformity to better sanitation, diet, and immunization practices. Educational extension enterprises seek the spread of better agricultural practices, better traffic control, cleaner cities. And the list of recommended conformities is endless.

Those who would cultivate citizen initiative cannot avoid urging the people to accept conformity. The problem becomes especially acute when the controllers ask the people to acquiesce in some belief or behavior that is manifestly good—according to the controller. It is easy to urge independence of decision making when obviously bad habits are to be resisted. But what of the changes that distant decision makers "know" to be beneficial? All digit telephone dialing and ZIP codes for mail delivery are "convenient" and "efficient." All such centrally determined changes are forced upon the citizens, who are asked to acquiesce. The only opportunity for independence is found in resistance. And this is often condemned as stubbornness.

Perhaps the benefit in efficiency is demonstrable from these and other changes distantly decided, in an age of centralized mechanization. But how do ordinary persons who benefit from acquiescence also develop as a result of responsible decision making of their own? And can their own initiative be fitted into these and other changes planned from above?

One aspect of life in a mass-persuaded age offers some prospect of hope for a modicum of individual autonomy. This is the existence of multiple persuasions in a free society. Competing advertising is the most obvious, though very limited, example. Rival political and religious propagandas represent another invitation to freedom of choice. Mutiplicity of persuasions, however, grant only the opportunity to choose. It does not provide the experience of intelligent responsibility, upon which autonomy must rest.

Too often, traditional discussions of freedom have been limited to choosing by isolated individuals, as though a single person could hope to resist the organized pressures of a massive social system. Is the only admired free man then the unusual individual resister who can stand out against social pressure and even of historical trends? If so, then freedom is denied to ordinary persons, and responsible freedom (that grows out of participation in change) is denied even to the resister.

Dealing with Distant and Impersonal Authority

A community development nucleus, especially a larger one, provides a means by which an increasing number of ordinary citizens may develop a local voice to influence the great decisions of our time. This is a possibility even though the active members will constitute a small minority of a population at any one time. This is true as long as the door is held constantly open for all to participate if and when they see fit. Experience indicates that when this invitation to participation is kept open, even those who remain inactive develop a proprietary conviction that their point of view has been represented. A community nucleus gives a voice to those who will, to contribute to the large-scale, centralized deciding of our time.

As centralized controls increase, ordinary citizens can hope for independence mainly in a reactivation of localism. But that local initiative can no longer be effective if it relates itself only to processes locally controlled. It must address itself also to the great problems, the macroprograms, the distant decision makers. Community nuclei can provide this renewal of localism, but only as their members acquire the skill needed to deal constructively with bureaucrats, experts, and programs that seek to regiment individuals and "educate" the public.

DIGNITY TO COPE WITH THE POWERFUL

Self-confidence to converse with the powerful on a man-to-man basis is notably lacking in the contemporary ordinary citizen. It is not easy to restore, or create anew, such dignity or confidence in one's self. The assurance that "I" have opinions important enough to gain the attention of influential people is not acquired by mere reassurance. Such conviction grows out of discussion of important matters that helps the discusser to discriminate between important and unimportant opinions.

Nucleus experience provides help in achieving this discrimination. And self-confidence grows when citizens have studied and discussed enough to know that they know what they are talking about. Additional skill in discrimination may be acquired by using the nucleus as a place for examining, criticizing, and verbally resisting the multitudinous persuasions that push everyone toward conformity. This resistance is strongest and most effective when it is not a blanket negativism, but recognizes that all of us must conform at many points, but by our own intelligent choosing. And we learn to resist in the same way.

A task which most nuclei undertake, if they last long enough, is the learning of how to live with omnipresent persuasions, persuaders and wielders of power. Membership in the nucleus provides a sense of group support for conclusions reached or negotiations undertaken. No longer is the single person a lone resister. He is a spokesman for a thoughtful and emotionally supportive group. As such, he can afford to be discriminative, accepting some ideas but opposing others, supporting his conclusions with the reasons for decision.

One of the most interesting and gratifying experiences occurs when a nucleus invites in an awesome person for consultation, or when it sends a delegation to a distant office or to an organization not easily approached. The quizzing, conversation, or petitioning tends to be dignified, with assurance on the part of the member that he is within his rights and can deal with powerful persons as an equal in human dignity. Or he concludes that seemingly impersonal institutions are made up of, or conducted by, human beings who have weaknesses and strengths similar to his own.

LIVING WITH EXPERTS

The representatives of the massive controlling institutions that dominate the lives of ordinary people often appear as experts. These persons, all wise in a limited field, are on the increase as life becomes more complex, as all of us become more dependent upon specialized knowledge, which an ordinary person cannot possess. More and more, the people of specialized wisdom are employed by the institutions (churches, universities, governments, local and federal, and so on) or are licensed by authorities (medical doctors, radio and TV repairmen, qualified auto mechanics, and many others).

Learning to live with these indispensable experts, while at the same time retaining or strengthening a sense of autonomy is, for the ordinary citizen, a problem. It will continue to be a problem, and of increasing difficulty. When a citizen nucleus is used as a local instrument for seeking solutions, it becomes apparent that many different relationships to experts must be tried out, evaluated and modified, adapted and readapted over the changing years. Living with experts in such a manner as to build autonomy and local dignity will prove difficult, but it is necessary.

When the experts respond to invitations from the nuclei or give time to delegations from them, the members become aware of the old cliché definition: An expert is a man who knows all the answers, but does not understand the questions. They discover that he is likely to examine their problem, not within the context of its reality, but within the categories of his field of specialization. He is inclined to offer help as an illustrative case for his isolated wisdom. His approach is likely to be learnedly doctrinaire, not helpfully addressed to the worries and frustrations of people.

In learning to live with experts, therefore, the task of the larger nucleus is to help these specialists learn how to apply their wisdom to problems as these arise, to people as they are. Much patience is required of the members as they confer time and again with the specially-trained. Such patience has its reward, for the interaction of the nucleus with the experts may cause changes in the specialists themselves for which they become grateful—after they have learned how much more useful their skills can be, in the perspective of practical living. But the patience that enables the experts to learn this is an outgrowth of the dignity that the citizen has attained, a dignity that is not threatened by the unrelated self-assurance so often characteristic of the specialist.

The specialists' resistance to the learning of practicality is likely to arise when they discover that their own cherished field of competence needs to be coordinated with the specialties of other experts. They are frequently reluctant to admit that their expertness does not provide all the answers or that real-life problems are seldom classifiable within the prescribed boundaries of any one specialty. Helping the experts to cooperate in order to be more useful may prove even more difficult than achieving a belief in one's own dignity.

BUREAUCRATS ARE HUMAN

Most of the contacts of nucleus members with big decisions, and the institutions that make them, are with the lesser figures, the employed staff who are frequently described as bureaucrats (and who often prove more inflexible than the top-level decision makers). A bureaucrat does not necessarily pose as an expert. He is rather the enforcer and defender of the decisions that his superiors have made. Nucleus members can best deal with such functionaries when they realize that bureaucrats are also human. When these lesser lights are most impersonal and inflexible, they are but responding to a difficult assignment that leaves them little room for making decisions of their own.

A first step toward effective relations with the bureaucracy is taken when the citizens bring themselves to understand the position of the bureaucrat, rather than to blame him for the policy others have adopted. A second step is taken when the citizens come to accept the policy, for the present, even though they realize that it is inadequate. For though the enforcer of the rule may sometimes be persuaded to admit the inadequacy of the policy—if he is not pressed to allow a special exception—changes in the rule are to be sought at a higher level. Nucleus members can often influence this higher policy-making level.

Acceptance of the conclusion that bureaucrats are unfeeling marionettes, indifferent to "our" needs, leads easily to that sweeping condemnation by category to which all of us are liable. The discovery that they are human, even as you and I, opens the way for enlisting a few in the interests and enterprises of a nucleus that serves the common good. A basic principle is involved: When a massive bureaucracy becomes too inflexible to meet human problems, a few individual bureaucrats may be won over, if they are appealed to on a dignified human level. A few may be persuaded to suggest to higher-level decision makers ways to attain greater flexibility. These recommendations can supplement the appeals from the citizens.

LOCAL IMPLEMENTATION OF LARGE-SCALE DECISION

Many national policies and programs depend for their success upon cooperation from local initiative. This is true of federal legislation, of supreme court decisions, and of the programs that derive from both; it is also true of planning agencies, national, state, and regional. The administrators of these programs, frequently finding themselves at a loss because the arousing of local participative responsibility is so difficult, react by developing an attitude of discouraged helplessness, which might be referred to as the "Frustration of the Bureaucrat." There are myriad examples of large-scale programs that have failed or have had only a qualified success, because they have lacked vigorous local participation.

Most federal programs that spend money upon the local scene require the participation of committees representative of community interests in the proposing and approving of activities. In setting up such programs, the Congress intentionally decentralizes responsibility. The good intention has been difficult to implement, however; in thousands of communities that have been served by the federal programs, no vigorous nucleus of concerned citizens has existed, nor has it been possible to create such a nucleus to meet the requirements of specific legislation. Committees, it is true, have been set up, but they are often nominal associations poorly representative of citizen interest, if not wholly inactive. And the frustration of the bureaucrat has increased.

When the Supreme Court laid down the dictum that public

schools must integrate the races with "all due deliberate speed," the actual pattern and pace of integration was left to the decision of local authorities. The implementation of the Court's order and the working out of a response to a growing national consensus that the justice of the Negroes' suit could not be denied, both of these had to be consummated by locally decided changes. A nucleus group that speaks with the conscience of good will then becomes an instrument for influencing school board, merchants' associations, churches, or any other influential decision-making body. After the tumult and the shouting (of the demonstrations for civil rights) have died, there remains the task of experimentally working out the programs that will recognize and satisfy the demands and aspirations of Negro citizens. This task is an opportunity for the local nucleus of good will. The actual patterns of integration must be discovered at the local level, where the members of the two races meet in daily living.

The controversies that receive national attention, but must find some solution on the local scene, will increase in the years to come. The admission of Negroes to first-class citizenship, is but a beginning. Federal legislation, court decisions, changes in the national conscience, all will bring new pressures for local initiative to work out community aspects of national change. The problem is not so much how to relate the small-scale deciders on the community scene to the large-scale problem and program, as how to persuade local citizens to form the association for local initiative—a larger nucleus of good will—that can take its part in the totality of consciously chosen development.

The Democratization of Planning

Even as the controversies over change must be expected to increase, so must the amount of planning increase. Change will need guidance. But is planning an activity limited to a particular breed of experts? Or is it one in which the ordinary citizen of initiative and good will may participate?

Two tacit assumptions underlie much planning: first, that it is a single-shot beginning for improvement, resulting in a "master plan" evolved by experts and subject to only minor modification in the implementing; second, that democratic participation has been achieved when the citizens (vaguely referred to as "the public"), or their spokesmen, have acquiesced in the "master plan" at "public hearings."

Two contrary assumptions need to be made explicit for democratic realism: first, that planning is a never-ending obligation, to be carried on continuously in an age of change; second, that some means for giving voice to the inarticulate, needs to be worked out in order to achieve bona fide citizen participation.[1]

> ... It is encouraging to note that experts in this field are beginning to speak of dynamic planning; that is, planning that is flexible in design and responsive to change. As [Maxwell] Fry put it at a meeting of architects, 'We would be better employed in searching for the rules that govern nature and nature's creature, man; for if this city is to be built it will be built not by one man but many, and not by architects only.' ... The idea is growing that planning can succeed only if it becomes increasingly a shared activity; the different organized groups in the community must have a part in it. This is an idea that was emphasized in a widely read book by [Barbara] Wootten who argued that such control is safest in the hands of the man and woman on the street. ... Progress would be slow, but the results would be more lasting. ...

The processes of community development provide a promising means for the democratization of planning. But two points of sensitivity, at least, need to be kept in mind by the encouragers and the citizen participants: First, it is exceedingly difficult to get ordinary people to voice authentic feelings and opinions, for many average citizens do not know how to express their positive desires; indeed, until they have acquired the dignity conferred by self-confidence, they often do not know that they have positive desires. Second, the contribution from ordinary citizens, once achieved, must be continued indefinitely, so that planners may learn to accept and to live with authentic spokesmen for the citizen interest— so that ordinary citizens may increase their effectiveness as a result of their participation in the making of important decisions.

The processes that offer promise move from basic nuclei to a larger nucleus. The latter becomes effective as it relates itself to many agencies, government offices, institutions, powerful indi-

---

[1] Nels Anderson, *The Urban Community: A World Perspective* (New York: Holt, Rinehart and Winston, 1959), p. 476.

viduals, and the planners, through whom these decision makers operate.[2]

A responsible larger nucleus can be helpful to planners at many points. It can endorse the idea of and necessity for planning and use its influence to assure financial support. It can bring problems to the planners' attention. It can help in the collecting of data. It can join in the discussion of the objectives for a community and of the priorities for progress. The actual technical details of blueprints and specifications remain the responsibility of the trained experts. The administering of the plans and of the supporting laws remain the responsibility of trained experts. The enactment of supporting legislation remains the responsibility of government. But when nucleus members have contributed their thinking to the process by which the plans were evolved and supported, their interest can help planners keep the emerging common good in mind.

When the members of the larger nucleus become involved in planning processes, they frequently discover new necessities for self-discipline. They curb their tendencies to become partisan for particular segments of the population. They also become aware of some of the human tragedy involved in any program of improvement. When the way is cleared for new highways or bridges or housing developments, some people must be ousted from their homes or their land. When zoning ordinances are passed and enforced, when sanitation regulations are adopted, even when children are compelled to go to school, the individual's freedom of choice is curtailed. It is seldom that any important improvement can be brought about without hurting someone. The members of the larger nucleus, aware of the possibilities for tragedy, can urge the adoption of measures that will minimize the hurt. And they can often help to assuage the injury, by insisting that decent homes be found for those who have been ousted and by explaining to the people the necessity for sanitation and education and other self-disciplines in the complexities of modern life.

By preserving a concern for the common good, independent of government or of other authority, a larger nucleus can help to

---

[2] For an example of how this process may operate, see Julia Abrahamson, *A Neighborhood Finds Itself* (New York: Harper and Row, 1959), and Herbert A. Thelen and Bettie Belk Sarchet, *Neighbors in Action* (Chicago: University of Chicago Press, 1954).

make planning humane. And the planners and administrators can be helped to develop confidence in the good sense that ordinary people can learn to exhibit.

From Alienation to Dignity

The fact that ordinary persons resist planning, or stay away from public hearings, or attend only to attack and criticize, is a sign of their alienation from life and from one another, a malaise that is characteristic of our time. There are numerous other signs: a sense of hopelessness, a widespread conviction that "we" can do nothing to improve bad situations, an apathetic refusal to stir out of the accepted routines of life, a fear of making choices, even when it is evident that the traditional ways of life can no longer serve.

Experienced encouragers of community development are aware of local climates of alienation that can infect an entire population. Indeed, they are wise to assume that the citizens' first response to any proposals for action (and even the later responses) may indicate apathy and reflect a hopeless disbelief in "our" ability to do anything positive. The community development process becomes one means for moving from a prevailing alienation to a dignity of belief in "ourselves"—for individuals—for all the people in an area of growing initiative.

Nucleus members who have had the experience of standing up to persons in authority develop a belief in their own significance. They discover that the reputedly powerful often are also hemmed in by circumstance, that they also may be frustrated and impatient, that some who appear to be unapproachable actually welcome contacts. The ability to dominate another person is not necessary to the overcoming of alienation. The opportunity to be heard, to be taken seriously, to make a contribution to important decisions, these are necessary. Necessary also is the growing sense of an effective "we-ness." This awareness of collective influence comes to replace, in part, some loss of the significance of "I," overwhelmed by authoritarian decision and by the sweep of uncontrolled events. Many "I's" begin to gain significance out of association with an effective "we."

It should be noted that the community development process is only one of many that may help persons to mature in dignity. Other processes may be more effectively used in some cases, as for those maladjusted persons who can afford individual professional attention.[3] But for the great number of ordinary people, many adequately conceived and administered community development processes seem to promise the most practical means for stimulating growth in citizen dignity.

A basic nucleus can bring to a few the dignity that comes with participation in an important decision. A larger nucleus can increase the number and can create a social atmosphere conducive to personal dignity for many in a local area. But the totality of people benefited is microscopic as compared with the massed need in our metropolitan-dominated society. Can the microprocesses be multiplied in sufficient quantity to lift a considerable proportion of the population?

This question poses a challenge to the great institutions that make the large-scale decisions which set up macroprograms. Might some or several of these institutions establish a well-financed and properly staffed program directed toward stimulating thousands of nuclei that become effective through larger nuclei? And if they did, would they be wise enough to diminish their long-standing desire to seek citizen conformity? Could they come to admire a large-scale effort that seeks an increase of local and personal variety in initiative? Tentatively, we give a "yes" answer to this query, taking into consideration the frailties exhibited by every human being and posing against this the genuine democratic aspiration to be found in many institutions that operate within an atmosphere of freedom.

But a more fundamental question is: Can these institutions expect to succeed in their macroprograms if there is not built into them some corresponding effort directed toward stimulating the growth of local citizens? Our tentative answer is "no." To make available to people a program of growth in democratic competence is as necessary as are the macroefforts of improvement. Persons achieve competence most surely when they learn to contribute to and help guide the macroprograms set up to improve their conditions.

---

[3] For individual psychotherapy, see Carl R. Rogers, *Client-centered Therapy* (Boston: Houghton Mifflin, 1951). For small groups, see the works of the National Training Laboratories and others working in the field of Group Dynamics listed in App. II.

A Creative Tension

The tension between large-scale programs and small-scale community processes will always exist. The first grows out of legislative and administrative decisions that apply to a whole region or nation. The second grows out of citizen decisions, locally made in face-to-face experience. When the voice of local initiative is strengthened through larger nuclei, the tension can be made creative.

No panacea for the multiplying problems of accelerating change is to be found in community development. Nor are sure solutions to be found in grandiose planning. Both ordinary people and planners, legislators and administrators, must be prepared to seek solutions by experimentation. Community development processes may be used to supplement the thinking of the great deciders by making available to them the creative ideas of citizens who are closest to the problems. The best progress will be made, not by a macroprogram alone, or by a microprocess alone, but by a greater process that establishes a vital interrelationship between the two.

In the processes of community development, the citizens tend to mature; they are no longer content merely to complain. And because they are contributing to the planning process, they become less dependent upon winning and less upset by losing.

The members of larger nuclei can remain close to the people and to the human suffering that is caused by unsolved problems. They are in a position both to expedite and to be creatively critical of experimental tryout of programs. They can give support to programs while criticizing them.

chapter 10

The Rural Scene

When conscientious citizens or professional community development workers survey the contemporary human scene and its unsolved problems, they are often appalled by the variety of the needs and by the poverty of the means available to meet those needs, even in making a beginning. In this chapter and the next we attempt to offer some suggestions for steps to be taken amid some disconcerting realities of our time. This chapter looks at rural life, the next at life in the city.

To divide problems into rural and urban categories is risky; for to do so may seem to be an attempt to dichotomize life into distinct and contrasted areas of experience. Furthermore, the changing circumstances of living necessarily call for constant reinterpretations of reality and for modifications of one's approach to human problems. Our recommendations, we realize, may soon be out of date. Even if this were not so, every community-to-be is unique, as is every personality-to-be-achieved. We do not wish to prescribe formulas of procedure for any typology of communities—even if we were wise enough to work out such a classification.

We feel justified in taking some risk, however, for several reasons. First, community development, as a movement, had its origin in rural settings. The early literature dealt with (and much still does) the small town, the village, and the open country. Certain workers-with-people in cities (but a diminishing number) look upon community development as a rural phenomenon, placing the reliance of their thinking for cities upon community organization.[1] We wish to dispel this historic rural identification.

Second, the community development programs that have been adopted for use in conjunction with foreign aid programs tend to deal with rural problems. The reason is that most of the developing nations that receive such aid depend largely upon agriculture—a fate that they regret and attempt to overcome—as their efforts to industrialize indicate. Although a few studies of urban community development based on the experiences of foreign lands are beginning to appear, the main identification remains rural.

Finally, because of the origin of community development in rural areas and because of its continuing identification, a "Rural Mystique" tends to infect the thinking of certain community developers. This adoration of country life and the small town (it often has a religious flavor) represents an attempted return to the alleged joys of a by-gone era. The Rural Mystique often results in sweeping condemnations of the city as the embodiment of all evil. And it has produced "intentional communities," colonies of people who are to live ideal lives in ideal surroundings usually located in farming regions. The fate of these colonies has frequently been unhappy; the exceptions have been those where the colonists have accepted the discipline of a religious faith that all hold in common.

Decline of the Rural Pattern

The fact of the matter is that the prevailing pattern of modern "advanced" societies (such as that found in this country) is industrial and urban. Not only is a clear majority of United States citizens to be found in cities, but also metropolitan points of view, ways of life, and values have become the standards for imitation and admiration.

METROPOLITAN VALUES

The size of the local population is a less important consideration than the values to which the people aspire. (Demographic experts make arbitrary distinctions as to numbers. According to the U.S.

---

[1] See Chap. 13, "Relation to Social Welfare Work."

Census Bureau, any town over 2,500 is a city; over 50,000, a metropolitan area. In India, a "village" may have as many as 50,000 to 60,000 inhabitants.) The real measure of the quality of life is found in the standards by which people judge material things, behavior, culture, beauty, and belief. And these standards are now determined in cities. They no longer reflect the bucolic values of country life.

The farmer and small-town dweller wants his car, his radio and television (which bring metropolitan values daily into his living room), his inside plumbing and central heating, and an additional income to supplement farming. The citizen of underprivileged areas and nations wants all these also. None seeks the negative aspects of industrialization—polluted streams and air, youthful delinquency and overcrowded dwellings, and many other urban pathologies. But they desire the (to them) positive aspects enough to risk the negative.

Historically, rural experience presented the patterns for thinking about social organization. Now, in developed countries and in those that yearn for development, metropolitan values represent the norm of aspiration, but they provide little pattern for concepts of community. Such structural concepts as town and town meeting, trade area, and even neighborhood (when geographically inflexible) suggest a nostalgic backward look at rural formulations. The newer concepts (which are only beginning to come clear) derive from metropolitan experience, but they rest upon a functional seeking for community in the midst of amorphous confusion.

CHANGING CONCEPTS OF COMMUNITY

A belief that the town meeting represented the ideal manifestation of community life has resulted in too great a reliance upon mass meetings, or upon designation of neighborhoods where such mass gatherings could be held, or upon public hearings. The implied assumption has often been that the will of "the community" was expressed by a public meeting held within an area that resembled the town of old.

As Jane Jacobs has pointed out,[2] much city planning reflects the

---

[2] *The Death and Life of Great American Cities* (New York: Random House, 1961). See especially the Introduction. Available in paperback, Vintage Books, 1963.

planners' admiration of rural life, in garden city developments and green belts around crowded areas. Much planning of shopping centers is based upon trade center concepts, with a surrounding trade area to be brought into being, partly by the construction of the center.

Among the most noteworthy of rural-based attitudes, however, and to be overcome by community developers, is the spirit of local "boosterism." The injunction, "boost, don't knock," harks back to the founding in new territories of settlements that, according to their promoters, were destined to become great cities. The hamlet with ambitions to become a metropolis (often it was hopefully dubbed _____ City) gave way to the town which demanded that important roads pass through its main street or which has wooed industry. Expansion of prosperity and population were believed to be unalloyed ideals to be sought.

"Boosterism" is not all bad. Its spirit of hopefulness, its conviction that "we" can do something to improve our town (or block, or neighborhood, or region) can be used as an initial impulse for a community development process. Difficulty arises when such (usually economic) improvement becomes the only motivation. And when the spirit of town boosting is applied to large cities, it often becomes a burden. In an era of burgeoning metropolitan populations and burgeoning urban problems, the booster's desire to expand, and his refusal to discuss negative aspects of urban life, can hamper social and individual improvement.

These nostalgic concepts of community have proved less and less appropriate to modern experience, either rural or urban. Because they lack usefulness for a development process, we have presented our functional definition in terms of seeking. This is a definition that grows out of experience with metropolitan confusion.

Rural Life in Perspective

Rural life, in contemporary America, represents the starting point of one of the great flows of humanity, which is characteristic of our time. Not only does the rural surplus of children flow into the city, but parents and whole families migrate away from the land. One of the characteristic facts of town and country life in America is a diminishing population. The exceptions to this trend are found in those smaller centers that take on such citylike activities as factories and construction projects or that serve as "bedroom" communities to larger centers of population.

DIMINISHING POPULATION

The trend toward a diminishing population is found in both poverty-stricken and wealthy rural areas. People usually leave the first because of low levels of living. They may leave the second because the mechanization of agriculture makes jobs scarcer, even though prosperity may be high. Any realistic programs for rural America will take this characteristic decline in population into consideration.

That Americans have become a people on wheels needs little documentation. There is travel for pleasure, for business, for transfer of job, and for job seeking. In addition, major population displacements are occurring. One displacement flow starts on the farms or in small towns, moves to city slums, then moves to "better" neighborhoods in the city, then to the suburbs, and eventually, to the exurbs (unincorporated settlements adjacent to cities). For a great number, the flow represents a seeking for better economic circumstances. As the families move from the city slum to the more affluent neighborhood, their number diminishes; those who reach the exurbs (which combine rural advantages with proximity to the city "bright lights") may be but a trickle of the original flow. The end of this flow from the land returns a few to the land in pseudorural living at the edges of metropolitan complexes.

There are other flows of population, involving smaller numbers of people, but all adding up to restless mobility. Some people return from suburb and exurb to city apartment living. Others move about from neighborhood to neighborhood (both urban and rural) and from farmstead to town or from town to town. Then there are the migrants, who travel from one farming area to another each year to work on seasonal crops. The total effect of such flows, counterflows, and cross flows of people is to contribute a geographic rootlessness to the alienation to be found in our age.

Faced with the facts of diminishing populations and inadequate standards of living, people in many small centers have believed that the importation of some nonfarming enterprise is *the* answer.

Though the most frequently sought enterprise is an industry, included also should be the construction of dams, canals, and roads; the exploitation of oil, uranium ore, or other mineral resources; the maintenance of defense or research installations; and the building up of tourist facilities—hotels, shops and restaurants. These activities may bring new income to an area, but they bring also problems—smoke or noxious fumes, industrial waste on land and in streams, jerry-built homes and cheap tourist attractions, and crowds of newcomers. If these new folk are temporary visitors, they are to be exploited and sped upon their way. (This applies both to low-status migrant workers and to cash-paying tourists.) If these new folk are permanent new residents, they are often looked upon with disapproval by the old-timers. The new people sought are often unwelcome when they arrive.

THE HOME OF TRADITION?

Tradition has it that rural life is the home of tradition. This conclusion can scarcely be maintained any longer. Certain old social customs and hallowed political and religious affiliations may be preserved in rural regions, but there is now an avid acceptance of nontraditional conveniences. These creature comforts, mechanical and electronic contrivances, are the beginning of more fundamental change. Machines on the land replace manure-producing animals; there is increase in use of factory-produced chemical fertilizers; there is decrease of rural self-sufficiency. Family life is fragmented by the cars that carry parents and deliver children in multiple directions over improved roads. Because of these and other changes, the image of rural life as devoted to tradition is as outmoded as the vaudeville caricature of the "hayseed."

Often, however, the rural dwellers left behind will fight rearguard battles to preserve some "old order" against impersonal change or against the influence of unwanted newcomers. Their campaigns of preservation are frequently supported by some variant of the Rural Mystique. Examples are found in rural domination of legislatures, in the holding on to local churches and schools when these have obviously lost their utility, in defending "The Southern Way of Life." But such defensive campaigns are not peculiarly rural. They express the people's insecurity in the face of change, which is also part of the alienation of our time. They represent futile reactions, attempts to cling to power privileges when the kind of life for which these were appropriate has passed, or, is passing.

Sometimes a tradition-preserving organization arises to attack an enemy, such as the White Citizens' Councils of the embattled South. As long as their purposes lead to an excluding definition of the common good, they cannot be used as a basis for the community development process. If ever they become all-inclusive in aspiration, they might help to create white nuclei that could combine with Negro nuclei, or with nuclei from other minority groups, to form larger nuclei devoted to the common welfare.

The acceptance of mechanization, of industry, and of factory-made luxuries will destroy rural tradition, by inadvertence. The acceptance of the necessity for change of tradition will allow for conscious reformulation of a rural life that preserves some traditional values but is realistic for modern times.

VARIETIES

According to the Rural Mystique, there is a pattern of farm or small-town living that represents the ideal for all human striving. Actually, rural life encompasses a vast variety of patterns, many of which are harsh and forbidding. The family farm, beloved by romantic novelists, playwrights, and producers of television programs, is rapidly disappearing. The small-town life of nostalgic memory provides fewer innocent childhood memories for the adults of tomorrow.

Economically, life in rural areas ranges from great prosperity to the direst poverty of bare subsistence living. At the prosperous end of the scale are the areas where huge corporation farming is practiced and where cooperative agricultural and marketing enterprises are found. There are towns and small cities with an industry or a tourist trade. Then there is open country acquiring wealth from purchase and subdivision of farm land for city expansion.

Somewhere further down the scale are the boom-or-bust areas, where bumper crops and a favorable market will make farmers rich in a single season or two or where, alternatively, bad conditions may wipe many out. Then there are the areas of smaller operations in such specialties as eggs, broilers, and truck crops, where corporation or cooperative financing, good transportation, and proximity to markets still make possible a type of family farming. Under unfavorable circumstances, these latter turn into areas of deterioration where not even bucolic memory can compensate for continued low standards of living.

At the unfavorable end of the economic scale are the pockets of persistent (rural) poverty, such as the mountain areas where the deterioration of the soil and the loss of natural resources—the destruction of the forests or the depletion of the mines—have caused most families to turn to welfare agencies for subsistence. (And the rising levels of economic expectation make the subsistence living of the past less tolerable.) Then there are the areas where erosion has ruined the land, but where a few people still live. Agricultural migrants should be included also, those whose living depends upon the minute income from following the crops, even though they have a winter residence in some down-at-the-heels shanty town. Rural slums are found on the edge of cities and even in glens or valleys and woods, frequently beyond the limits of police or fire protection and beyond sanitary supervision. What of the low-income rural areas that fringe the expanding metropolitan areas, where overcrowded shacks and the lack of community identification increase social pathologies of every kind? Are these sections, usually outside municipal boundaries, to be regarded as rural or urban? And what of the trailer settlements of more or less permanent transients? Are these rural?

Dwellers in pockets of poverty find that they have little in common with the privileged rural dwellers. Even when rich and poor are found in close proximity, sympathetic communciation is difficult. Take, for example, the privileged and underprivileged sections of the same town (the division may be ethnic as well as economic) or the labor of migrants which is welcomed while the migrants themselves are rejected. Classification as a part of rural life presents little in the way of a common pattern or a common aspiration. And those patterns that seem ideal are more and more found among the privileged who do not readily find community with the disadvantaged. The privileged may indeed maintain their advantages by exploiting their poorer neighbors.

The variety of patterns again illustrates that modern rural life is but a part of the totality of a social order in (often painful) transition. Rural life cannot be treated as a distinct phenomenon or as the correct goal of striving. It offers certain values by which intelligent choices for the future can be selected. But so also does metropolitan life.

Search for Community

An awareness of the great and changing variety of patterns of rural life makes any generalization difficult. The recommendations given here are offered as points for discussion by those who wish to move forward with community development on the rural scene.

PROSPEROUS AREAS

Wealth is a relative matter. Especially is this true of rural towns or regions. One area is affluent in contrast with another; not all residents share in the economic well-being; economic level is determined by averages that draw attention away from extremes, both favorable and unfavorable.

In the more prosperous rural regions, community development enterprises are likely to reflect a class-determined exclusiveness. Specifically, community improvement nuclei tend to be composed of the more comfortably fixed and more permanent citizens. They frequently exclude the poorer, less socially acceptable, more recently arrived, or transient elements in the population. Community development nuclei that grow among the excluded tend to reflect a comparable narrow interest. And the all-inclusive search for community is separated into noncommunicating efforts.

Community development activity among the prosperous is conducted by the old-line farm organizations or by agricultural extension service to the successful farmers. A structure of county-wide community improvement may be set up, which rests upon the initiative of established local leaders. Or community interest may be stimulated by the establishment of cooperatives.

Cooperatives may have been started to serve an economically distressed population. But when they achieve success, the members become conscious of being part of a "proper" social classification. Moreover, rural cooperatives tend to emphasize the interests of the producers more than the consumers. They, therefore, tend to limit participation to people of substance. Consumer's cooperatives are potentially more inclusive, because all human beings are consumers. But only a limited number of people may qualify as important producers. So community activity through rural cooperatives is likely to exclude the folk of lesser economic influence.

When prosperity rests also upon industrial or commercial activities, service clubs and chambers of commerce may be the vehicles for community development. (These organizations will be found also in smaller cities and in some municipal fragments of metropolitan areas.) These organizations also tend to exclude representation from the economically disadvantaged and the socially unacceptable.

As long as rural aspiration derives from a vision of an ideal past, it is easy for the community development process to serve the privileged. But as rural life is understood within the context of the total modern life of change, responsibility for serving the disadvantaged is more readily seen to be important. Should these unfortunates be served by inclusion in the nuclei of the privileged? Or should they be encouraged to form their own? This is one of the questions that calls for experimentation. In any case, the nuclei of the privileged will be more realistic when they give attention also to the problems of their disadvantaged neighbors.

RURAL RESIDENTS

On the modern rural scene, there is a steady increase of people and families whose major occupation is other than farming. They live on the land or in town, but they are, at best, part-time farmers.

Since these rural residents cover the full gamut from great wealth to great poverty, the problem of achieving community is as great for them as it is for those who make a living from the land. Perhaps the difficulty is even greater, for these people give loyalty to a great diversity of income sources and of social identifications.

At one end of the economic scale are the gentlemen farmers with estates managed by employees. Less prosperous, but often well-fixed are the "sun-down" farmers, those who hold paying positions in factories, offices, or schools, but cultivate their acres in spare time. Lower on the scale are the householders, with smaller acreages, fewer farm machines, but capable of producing a few eggs or broilers or small quantities of fruit and vegetables. Many of these householders live in the country by choice. Lower still are those who live in rural shacks, because they are forced into such misery.

Or they may have migrated into a haphazard, unincorporated area in hopes of finding (usually) nonfarm employment. These more or less impermanent residents will produce little or nothing for home consumption or sale. Their homes compose the rural slums or headquarters for migrants or depressed fringes to cities, without adequate governmental or social services.

The problems of the common good that catch the attention of those high on the economic and social scales are quite different from those that interest the disadvantaged. And even among the disadvantaged, varieties in social outlook will be found. All this suggests that adequate rural community development calls for several nuclei in the beginning, especially in areas of population movement. Out of such beginnings in variety may come the larger nuclei that serve the common good.

DISTRESSED AREAS

One particular kind of rural life needs special mention, the distressed area. This is a section of the country with poor or exhausted natural resources where people continue to live in persistent poverty. There is usually a residue population, left behind, after many have fled to greater hopes elsewhere. Such areas may be small and isolated and spotted around in the back country, as in several New England states, or in sections of the Rocky Mountains. They may include whole regions, such as the Appalachian Mountain area that extends over parts of eleven states.[3]

The people who inhabit such pockets of poverty are likely to be suffering from long years of hopelessness and frustration. They will believe that they have been by-passed by an advancing civilization, and may be very defensive as a result of neglect, or pauperized by ill-advised charity. Often ethnic differences make the problem even more acute, as in Indian reservations, in Negro hamlets in areas of the South that no longer need hand labor, and in Spanish-speaking settlements in the Southwest.

The distress of people in these areas is compounded by the "Revolution of Rising Expectations." They are no longer willing to remain outside the mainstream of material advance. Even if the subsistence living of their ancestors were still possible, they would

---

[3] Our case study in Chap. 3 deals with the people in this distressed area.

not be content to accept it. But they find themselves caught between migration to the city slum (or the rural slum on the fringe) and continuing in poverty at home. Neither choice promises much material advance.

Effective solutions to the problems of distressed areas call for macroprograms. Only the large-scale organizations (such as government, state and federal, national churches, huge foundations, universities, or some combination of these) are capable of undertaking such programs. Difficulties arise, however, when the huge organization provides for a statistical survey of the needs of the area, for economic steps of improvement, and for the large-scale expenditure of funds without giving attention to the need for microprocesses. For the crux of development for such people lies in strengthening their initiative to contribute to the solutions of the small and the great problems.

Perhaps the responsibility for encouraging many small nuclei, that grow from the grass roots, could be written into and financed by the macroprograms. Or alternatively, public schools, universities, or churches scattered throughout the distressed area might accept the assignment, in coordination with the grand program. Whoever takes the initiative to stir local people out of defensive· ness and despair will encourage nucleus building by the disadvantaged themselves, in response to their perception of need.

Rural Problems—Opportunities

Certain characteristics of the current American rural scene are to be found frequently enough to provide the basis for valid generalizations. Depending upon the encourager's point of view, he may regard these characteristics as problems or as opportunities for local development.

AVAILABILITY OF ORGANIZATION

Farm organizations are frequently to be found. Or if they are not, there are services that may be used to form them—the Agricultural Extension Service, the organizers from the Farmers Union, or the Cooperative League or the Farm Bureau or the Grange.

Churches are everywhere in country and town, though most may be indifferent to their responsibility to the community. Fraternal societies are frequently encountered although they also need encouragement to move beyond their middle-class loyalties and exclusiveness.

Towns and small cities are filled with social organizations. In fact, local residents will tell you that "our town is overorganized." Churches, fraternal societies, and service clubs make up only part of the accumulation. Beyond these clubs, associations, and "circles" are legion. So much is this true that proposals to form a nucleus may be rejected as "just another one." Wise relating to organizations that can be inspired to have a civic interest, can provide a basis for nuclei among the privileged. And once started, their point of view can be broadened to include their disadvantaged neighbors.

CONFLICTS

If the bucolic dream of rural harmony has been shattered by conflicts with migrants, with newcomers, with persons of a different race or religion or political persuasion, there is an opportunity for the rural inhabitants to discover how friendship can work. The challenge to nuclei that seek the common good does not consist in a return to a Rural Mystique, but in a discovery of how neighborliness and brotherhood can be inculcated in spite of the barriers of human differences. Rural people are capable of exploring such possibilities—if they are encouraged to do so.

LACK OF SOCIAL SERVICES

Most rural areas and towns have a shortage of those social services that may normally be found in cities. Thus many acts of kindness can be direct and personal. The hungry may be fed, and the sick cared for, without the intervention of professionals. There is an advantage to the person expressing brotherhood, if he can avoid becoming pious or self-righteous. Nonetheless, as time goes on, and as the rural experience approximates the city experience, it is desirable that social services be set up to care for the unfortunate. Once such organized services become an aspect of the emerging community, they should be administered professionally.

An opportunity is available to rural nuclei, therefore, to work for the establishment of social service agencies, both those publicly and those privately supported. Perhaps such nuclei might even evolve new patterns of support for and cooperation with the agencies they help create.

MUSCULAR ACTIVITY

In rural areas, it is easier to find cooperative action projects that stretch the muscles and bring perspiration to the brow. There are definite advantages to such physical work together; one of the best solvents of misunderstanding in conflict is the experience of working and sweating together, to accomplish some agreed upon purpose.

In city environments, opportunities for physical labor together are harder to find. More often the interest of urban nuclei will turn to "social action" (that is, the passing of resolutions, the circulating of petitions, the bringing of influence to bear upon public officials, and picketing or public demonstrations). There is a place for social action in rural settings, but such pressure tactics are less acceptable there than in the city. If undertaken early in the community development process, they may have a divisive effect. Because it is easier to find cooperative activity that clearly serves the common good, it is often easier to start an all-inclusive nucleus in town and country, than in the city.

SPECIAL SERVICES TO YOUTH AND AGE

Beyond the early phases in work projects, there are many opportunities of a planning and less muscular nature. Among these are two services worthy of special mention; services to youth and services to the aging.

Throughout American history young people have left the farm and village to seek their fortunes in the city. (One of the chief products of rural life has been children.) When the members of this exodus have been well educated in high school or in college, they have usually done well in cities. But when poorly educated youths have made the transfer, they have swelled the ranks of the urban unemployed and maladjusted. Responsible rural people, therefore, have an obligation to prepare their young folks for the life they may encounter when they depart. Community nuclei might undertake vocational education and discussion of adjustment to urban living, as serious obligations.

In a time when the number of retired people is increasing, some thought must be given to providing places in which they can live. Institutional "homes" and retirement villages are being constructed. Too often, however, the planning of such facilities originates in cities, though the buildings may be located in the country. Rural nuclei are missing an opportunity if they do not assist in the planning of such construction, and in the operating of the facilities, so that the elderly benefit by the friendship that welcomes them.

AMBITIOUS PLANNING

Any mention of the providing of services to the youth and the aged suggests that it is possible for rural people to participate in ambitious planning, once they have moved beyond their preoccupation with the limited community concepts of the past. Already the existence of good roads and the ownership of automobiles has made the village of yesteryear obsolete. Such institutions as schools and churches are already being abandoned or consolidated. Shopping centers are beginning to serve larger areas. Cultural centers—for religion, education, entertainment—may be planned for the larger areas made possible by transportation facilities and necessitated by diminishing populations.

The search for a meaningful community good may start with numerous small nuclei composed of different groups on the rural scene. But it is incomplete if it stops there. It can press on through the larger nucleus process toward ambitious planning for a larger area, even a region. The search looks for the common good in the context of a whole society in transition.

Realistic Attitudes

Rural people need to overcome twin but opposite errors of attitude. The first is that "we" are superior and the pacesetters for the good. The second is that "we" are inferior because "we" lack urban amenities and cultural advantages.

When they become members of active nuclei that are expanding the horizons of responsibility they tend to discover that "we" are an important part of the fabric of modern life. If the color of that fabric is largely determined by metropolitan values, these values can be somewhat shaped by themselves. Rural people can contribute importantly to the weaving of the fabric.

chapter 11

The Metropolitan Scene

If the urban case study in Chapter 2 does not present as clear a picture as the rural, this lack of clarity is characteristic of the predicament of modern metropolitan man. Urban community development does not, as yet, show an established methodology, nor does it claim as many triumphant outcomes. However, methods are being worked out, often painfully, amidst the enormous complexities of city life. We can report, not a generally accepted procedure, but rather some ways in which numerous experimenters are feeling their way into an endless reshaping of metropolitan life.

When we talk about metropolitan life, it is important to realize that more is contemplated than mere residence in a city. Cities and city-dwellers have been known in human experience for thousands of years. But we have encountered a new experience more recently, in the metropolitan complex, in ways of thinking and behaving imposed by sprawling urbanization. Some observers are so impressed by the newness that they refer to an Urban Revolution. Others are seeking to arrive at an "Urban Mystique," the counterpart to the "Rural Mystique."

The "Urban Mystique" [1] grows partly as an exaggerated correc-

---

[1] For some examples, see Editors of *Fortune, The Exploding Metropolis* (New York: Doubleday, 1958), or United Presbyterian Board of National Missions, *The City, God's Gift to the Church* (New York, 1963), or Lawrence H. Janssen, *These Cities Glorious* (New York: Friendship Press, 1963).

tion for the age-old contention that the city represents a concentration of all that is evil. But when a majority of the population lives in urban areas and their standards become a determinant for all of life, then there seems to be some justification for prettifying the ugly place of yesteryear. The difficulty is that the Urban Mystique is unrealistic and diversionary. Our task is to discuss as realistically as possible social problems and prospects for human development in the metropolis, not to sing its praises.

Almost all students of urbanism, but especially the supporters of the Mystique, look to citizen participation as *the* way to a better metropolitan life. We agree. But the question is: How, in the midst of the confusion, the masses of human beings, the problems of monumental complexity, and the general sense of helplessness, is this participation to be achieved?

Spreading Metropolitan Areas

For most of recorded history, the city has been an exceptional pinpoint upon a map. Now urbanization sprawls across the landscape, undeterred by county and state boundaries. Cities merge into each other, and with satellite villages, suburbs, and unincorporated settlements, to form more or less uninterrupted inhabited areas. Such great conglomerations of people, which like Topsy "just growed," provide the metropolitan environment for modern man, in the United States and in certain other industrially advanced nations.

The confusion for urban man is illustrated by the difficulty of giving a name to the supercity. First, there is the city itself with its municipal boundaries. Then there is the "greater" city, usually including the commuting suburbs. Then there is the metropolitan complex, or "Metroplex," which includes towns, villages, smaller cities, and even some sparsely settled territories, all of which are economically dependent upon some central core. Finally, there is the continuous area of urban living, sometimes referred to as the Metropolity. The term "Metropolitan Area" may refer to any one of several central cores with satellite settlements, or to the continuous urbanization that encompasses several central cores and the less densely settled territories that connect them.

Cities of old had several reasons for being. Sometimes they grew at transfer points for transportation, for example, from water to land travel. Sometimes they served as trade centers for the hinterland. Others grew up around factories or other industrial activities. Their location was often determined by roads, railroads, and other shipping lines.

Modern metropolitan areas are no longer bound to such fixed places as ports, distribution centers, or factories that must be located on railroads or canals. Power for industry or homes now comes over wires or through pipe lines, not by the bulk transportation of freight car. Materials for factories or consumers may arrive by truck over the paved highways that spread over the land. Therefore metropolitan areas can spread out from any center to any adjacent territory where an exploding population chooses, or is forced, to live. The facilities of streets, shopping centers, schools, and churches are located to serve the accumulating people, rather than the reverse. Speculators, land "developers," or planners may anticipate, or even seek to guide, metropolitan expansion by laying out or plotting these facilities on vacant land.

As a matter of actuality, the spreading metropolis is less planned than it could be. Characteristically, in the United States, new territory is added to the metroplex by profit seekers who hope to benefit by the expansion. These promoters are not likely to seek the common good, except as they decide that the allocating of space for conventional service facilities is good for their business.

INCREASE OF POPULATION

If the demographic determinant for rural life is a diminishing population, the opposite is true for urban life. The fact of increasing population may be obscured when attention is given only to the statistics from the central city. It becomes alarmingly apparent when the accumulations for an entire metropolitan area are considered. Then, urbanization, usually ill-planned, is seen to be encroaching more and more upon land formerly used for agricultural purposes. Indeed, in some sections of the country that have been highly productive of food and fiber, such as California, the turning over of productive acres to pavements and buildings has aroused opposition. The increasing number of people must be housed somewhere. But food to feed them must also be produced. Thus planning for an increasing population must give heed to homes *and* to the productive areas that feed the people who live in them.

Socially responsible planning for metropolitan living usually comes belatedly and at excessive cost. It is normally delayed until an area has been built up. Then the space for throughways, bridges, schools, cultural centers, parks, and so on can be made available only by pre-empting scarce land from other uses. The pre-empting is expensive and always inconveniences the people who are removed from homes, shops, recreation facilities, or other accustomed places.

An additional difficulty of planning is found in the confusion of responsibility in great metropolitan areas. Consider the complexity of planning for through roads or adequate drinking water in the continuous urban settlement that extends from north of Boston to Norfolk, Virginia. Or consider police protection, zoning for factories and homes, and sewage disposal in the continuous settled area from southwestern Michigan, through northern Indiana, through Chicago and its surburbs, to Milwaukee, Wisconsin. In all such areas, there are fragmented municipal and state jurisdictions, with little in the way of over-all authority. Even within a particular larger city or metroplex, functions may be split between several local governments, several school districts, port authorities, and community chests, each with its own peculiar area of responsibility.[2]

At one end of the problem, the macroplanning and programing have not caught up with the metropolitan sprawl. At the other end, the individual citizen has been paralyzed in his efforts to understand or influence the course of events, even for the limited planning that does exist.[3]

DEMOLITION AND CONSTRUCTION

A second characteristic of the metropolis is the cycle of demolition and construction. This is one spectacularly visible evidence of the turbulence of metropolitan life. The restlessness is to be ob-

---

[2] The exploding metropolis of Los Angeles is especially noteworthy. See Winston W. Crouch and Beatrice Dinerman, *Southern California Metropolis: A Study in Development of Government for a Metropolitan Area* (Los Angeles: University of California Press, 1963).

[3] Francis C. Rosecrance, "The Community Then and Now," *You and Your Community,* Discussion Series of New York University, 1954.

served also in personal lives and in unstable social customs. The changing sky line is symptomatic of changing aesthetic and ethical standards.

With constant demolition and construction, one wonders if change is not sometimes admired for change's sake. There are New Yorkers who claim with pride that the song of their city is the compressed-air jackhammer, tearing up pavements, destroying old buildings, digging out foundations.

Much destruction and reconstruction is the result of belated planning. It comes about because there has been a lack of foresight. Other episodes come because of new demands that no one was wise enough to anticipate. When streets were first laid out, who could have predicted that subways or limited-access six- and eight-lane highways would one day be needed? Even when a city is planned, as Washington, D.C. was, it is designed for the kind of traffic and kind of living known to the planner. L'Enfant laid out a gracious city for an age of horse-drawn vehicles and for a population that did not live in slums.

Construction arising from belated planning is often ill-conceived; the planning frequently is for a limited future period only. Or it fails to take into consideration the side effects of change. The most notable of these little-considered side effects is the impact upon human beings. To overlook the human factor is easy when there are so many people and always more coming, so that concern for persons is lost in the planning for the masses.

PEOPLE OR AUTOMOBILES?

The automobile, and motor transport in general, have made the great sprawling metropolis possible. Yet the areas of congested population are in danger of being choked by their own means of transportation. The question has fairly been raised, Are the cities for people or for automobiles?

The whole character of urban living is being modified by the motor age, and many modifications of construction and living are beyond present predicting. The whole character of streets is changing. Once they were meant to be connecting links for social intercourse. Now they have become arteries for traffic flow, and are hazardous to people of all ages.

The electric transit rails that once were located on or off these streets, and which connected urban centers in the metropolity, have all but disappeared. (Some experts predict they will have to be rebuilt one day, at great expense.) Trackless buses grow in number, adding to the traffic and to the air pollution.

Throughways, a triumph of the demolition-construction cycle, speed some of the heaviest traffic through the congested areas; they are seldom built rapidly enough to keep pace with the increase in motor vehicles. Ordinary streets, therefore, remain as hazardous as ever, while the throughways become choked with commuters twice every working day and at the beginning and end of each holiday period.

Someone has estimated that one half of the available territory of metropolitan Los Angeles is utilized for the care and nurture of transportation. Included in this estimate would be such uses as streets, freeways, service stations, salesrooms for automobiles, parking areas, and repair garages; but also to be included are railroad rights-of-way, yards, and stations, airports and docking and shipping facilities. It would be difficult to prove or disprove the estimate; do you include, for example, home garages and driveways, junkyards filled mainly with wrecked automobiles, hotels and motels, and storage areas for supplies and for many kinds of vehicles? In any case, it should be clear that a great proportion of such metropolitan space is devoted to the business of moving about rather than to living in areas with which the residents can identify.

The problem of air pollution has no easy solution. Carburetors can breathe the smog-laden air, but can human beings do so without jeopardizing their health? Experts are not in agreement as to whether factories or motor vehicles are the chief contributors to pollution. But both are important to the total accumulation of foul air.

Yet the inhabitants of cities are dependent upon transportation to bring supplies in and to take refuse out of the congested area. Water and sewage are handled through pipes, but all other supplies and disposal must be hauled by truck or railway and distributed or collected by delivery vehicles. So great is the metropolitan dependence upon haulage that some economists refer to "technological tenuousness" and make dire predictions of short periods of life for city dwellers if a strike or natural disaster should disrupt supply lines. Quite as much are people dependent upon mobility within the metropolity, from home to work, to recreation, to cultural experiences, and back again.

Thomas Jefferson predicted that Americans, having become urbanized, would lose in self-sufficiency, would become more dependent. He was right. He was wrong, however, in believing that the trend toward city living would be resisted. Independence has been replaced by interdependence. Has this change been registered in inferior attitudes, behaviors, and ethical sensitivities of people? Jefferson feared that it would be.

New ways of metropolitan living are being worked out in the crucible of paradox and confusion. We need not despair, as a literal reading of Jefferson or of latter-day prophets of gloom might suggest. But we cannot yet discern the pattern of life or the kind of human beings that may emerge.

The Mainspring of Alienation

We have already mentioned tendencies toward alienation upon the rural scene. These same tendencies reach their high point on the metropolitan scene, not because city life is evil, but because it represents the most advanced stage of whatever it is we are advancing toward.

It would be a mistake to ascribe all alienation to urban living. There are many other pressures that break down traditional habits and standards and make life frightening for many. It is rather that, in metropolitan living, these pressures reach their nth degree. It is here that the revolution of fundamental changes speeds up most.

The impact of rapid change upon individuals becomes more explicit when we make clear what we mean by alienation. Sociologists, social psychologists, psychotherapists and psychiatrists have given their interpretations. We present ours, which is couched in terms of an analysis of the metropolitan experience.[4]

HELPLESSNESS

Individuals feel they are helpless to contend with impersonal forces or powerful organizations, all of which are felt to be beyond

---

[4] See Russell Middleton, "Alienation, Race and Education," *American Sociological Review,* Vol. 28, No. 6 (December 1963), for a summary of much thinking in this field.

their ability to influence. This despairing helplessness is easily reached in the midst of huge populations, where the separate person is just another among the faceless millions. Policies are made, laws passed and enforced, styles set, and opinions crystallized and expressed by an isolated few, who are often vaguely referred to as "the power structure." The whole of life is complicated and remotely controlled. And all the helpless individuals can do is to take out their frustrations in complaint or in an occasional riotous demonstration.

Much of the frustration is voiced as protests against symbols of authority. Accusations of police brutality represent one example of such alienated reaction. There may be actual episodes of such brutality that need correction. But the accusation too easily outdistances the provable event, because the police are the local symbols of rejected and overwhelming authority.

DETERIORATION OF VALUES

Traditional standards of right and wrong are slipping away. The deterioration of that which has been right in the past is found in metropolitan living, all the way from the member of a delinquent gang, or of a teen-age peer group, to the man in the gray flannel suit, to the acceptor of "payola." Traditional virtues, such as honesty, integrity, and compassion, are unacceptable to much city sophistication. They are even "corny."

As a consequence, individuals often find themselves doing things they suspect are wrong. A sense of guilt grows, but the individuals feel powerless either to return to the value system of yesteryear or to create a new scheme of values for contemporary times. There are few, if any, means at hand for seeking for reinterpreted values in new patterns of city life.

LOSS OF DIGNITY OF JOB

At the privileged end of the economic continuum, paid work is no longer an integral part of the individual's way of life. The job is divorced from the rest of life, both in function and in location. To many persons the job becomes a means for obtaining money to purchase the things that are more and more necessary. Therefore work is less satisfying in itself. There is less pride in a job well done. There is a greater scramble for higher pay and for a better title or prestige or other status symbol.

Toward the underprivileged end of the scale, poor pay, insecurity of employment, or unemployment, reduce the citizen's self-esteem. In a society that has measured a man's personal worth by the size of his income, vast hordes of city dwellers are cast upon a psychological junk heap. Especially is this true of those who live out their lives on various kinds of relief.

One of the great values of Western civilization has been found in the dignity and importance of paid work. The number of those now denied this recognition increases in cities. The fact that minority races are overrepresented in this alienation does not limit its impact to those ethnic groups only.

LACK OF NEIGHBORLINESS

Individual loneliness is a phenomenon of metropolitan living. Many individuals feel lost and forgotten in the mass. Geographic neighbors may meet each other daily and look through each other.

Many persons overcome the loss of neighborliness by associating either with others who are perceived to be part of a micropopulation in the city or with peer group members in opposition to others. Thus the loneliness of metropolitan anonymity is relieved by an association in conflict. The concept and experience of neighborliness, which follows Judaeo-Christian values, is difficult to recreate. The person who is "different" is looked upon as an enemy, even though he may live nearby.

Mention of loss of the experience of neighborliness is another way of referring to loss of sense of community. In the metropolity, community is to be rediscovered in some smaller area usually referred to as a neighborhood. This is a small enough area to allow for friendship with those who live nearby, whether these be like "myself" or different.

LOSS OF PERSONAL IDENTITY

The loss of personal identity is a maladjustment of our times [5] that is related to all the above—the loss of dignity, the lack of

---

[5] Erich Fromm, *The Sane Society* (New York: Holt, Rinehart and Winston, 1955).

neighborliness, the sense of helplessness, and the deterioration of values. It is found in exaggerated form in cities. Since much of life is beyond the control of the city dweller or is meaningless to him, he finds his own significance reduced. He begins to wonder who he is and what the purpose and meaning of his life is.

Much of the loss is, for many, a by-product of the anonymity of city living, but also of the fact that "I" have no importance in the eyes of others or even of "myself." There is a lack of the warmth of human understanding or of concern for "my" ideas or ability to think for "myself"; "I" am afforded little or no opportunity to contribute "my" decisions to the guidance of change.

Note that in discussing the varieties of alienation, we have stressed those that weigh upon the ordinary citizen. An urban-dominated society is filled with people who feel lost and over-whelmed, for whom traditional standards of value have become meaningless. We are thinking of the majority whose sense of personal dignity and confidence to contribute is undermined by urban living. We are concerned also with the better standards they may be able to create in the midst of urban living.

Our discussion does not call for a condemnation of metropolitan living. Nor does it call for a flight to an Urban Mystique. Rather it recommends that the metropolity be accepted as the growing edge of change. It is to be redesigned continuously by the coura-geously intelligent. Part of the problem for community development is to find a sizable number of these courageously intelligent among the ordinary citizens who are now frustrated into apathy.

Many programs have been proposed for curing our urban ills. Most of these programs stress things to be done to or for the people—more relief, the cleanup of slums, job training and re-training, the introduction of new industries, and so on. All these aims are good, but they lack the essential personal development experience. Community development processes are addressed to this essential need.

These processes provide, not the answers, but the means by which citizens shall seek the answers. They may be able to over-come the individual's sense of alienation by drawing him into par-ticipation in community development. In a basic nucleus, the citi-zen may find the warmth of recognition that allows the helpless to become constructively articulate, to achieve new values, to live with his neighbors. A larger nucleus provides a deciding entity for helping to plan the specific programs of improvement.[6]

To achieve an effective program of continuous community improvement requires the resources and involvement of all types of groups working on many facets of community problems. *Informal groups are the foundation upon which any sound program must be built.* [italics were added] A program involving informal groups must be realistic and directed toward the achievement of purposes which are within the experiences of the members of the groups. Without the establishment of functional relations with these basic groups, no community endeavors can hope to be successful on a continuous self-maintaining basis.

Urban Varieties

There is an enormous variety of life in a metropolis. Even though the total impact of the city contributes to the citizen's alienation, his rescue from this condition will be found in experiences characteristic of some specific variety of urban life.

The sociologist Morris Janowitz has criticized his fellow sociologists for finding urban society impersonal, self-centered, and barren, because they believed the importance of local community had declined into disorganization and a mass society. According to Janowitz, these sociologists have failed to take into consideration that "impressive degrees and patterns of local community life exist within . . . metropolitan limits." [7] Such patterns of community life are often visible only to those who are especially discerning and compassionate. And when patterns of community have been discovered, the problem is to find ways for utilizing them to expedite development.

We will have to look at several varieties of urban life (realizing that we will not mention every kind) to inquire how ordinary citizens might begin a process of development. In a great metropolitan area, the problem is to make the operative social units small enough to reach the individual (basic nuclei), yet large enough to achieve persuasive influence (larger nuclei).

---

[6] Hurley H. Doddy, *Informal Groups and the Community,* A Research Study of the Institute of Adult Education, Teachers College, Columbia University (New York: Teachers College Bureau of Publications, 1952).

[7] Morris Janowitz, *The Community Press in an Urban Setting* (New York: Free Press of Glencoe, 1952), p. 19.

NEIGHBORHOOD ORGANIZATION

Numerous cities are now experimenting with neighborhood improvement programs, some of which are moving from an emphasis upon demolition and construction, or upon political propaganda, toward the development of more competent citizens. It would not be possible to mention all of these programs nor to keep up to date on the changes in each. But to give some impression of the scope of movement toward community development processes, several may be mentioned.

In scores of cities will be found urban renewal projects. These include both privately financed apartments for the comfortable and wealthy, and federally subsidized low-income housing. A need for development processes, especially among residents in the low-income housing projects, has become clear. Federal officials and local authorities have called for the development of community programs. These are usually assigned to social welfare agencies. These programs contribute to development of persons to the extent that they utilize basic-nucleus-to-larger-nucleus processes.

Because urban renewal has often destroyed traditional neighborhood communities and produced an alienation that is difficult to overcome, emphasis has been placed more recently upon neighborhood rehabilitation. In Philadelphia, to choose one example, block nuclei are being encouraged, to make the local decisions of self-help.

In New York City, an elaborate structure of neighborhoods was worked out by municipal officials, and neighborhood councils were created by appointment. In theory, such councils might constitute larger nuclei. But it has been difficult to move from the appointive top of the neighborhood level to the level of inarticulate citizen initiative. Like many another neighborhood organization, the democratic contribution to citizen development has been curtailed by a failure to develop basic nuclei.

The Chicago Neighborhood Conservation Program makes community development processes more articulate, at least in printed form. Published booklets [8] call for the formation of Neighborhood

---

[8] City of Chicago, Housing and Redevelopment Coordinator, *Neighborhood Conservation* (April 1956).

Committees and Citizen's Action Projects. In handbooks on how to start a program in a neighborhood, the word "nucleus" is used, though the term more often refers to two or three initiators than to the long-lasting primary group we have described. As a consequence, more emphasis is placed upon organizational structure than upon the process by which the participants develop beyond alienation.

A closer approach to the community development process that we have outlined is found in Boston,[9] where neighborhood nuclei have been created around specific problems of local interest. The writers who have described the Boston program use the terms "community organization" and "community development" interchangeably, but the processes are similar to those we have been describing.

INNER CITY—SLUMS

Some proponents of an Urban Mystique and worriers about urban problems, talk much of the inner city. By this they mean the down-at-the-heels (and deteriorating) sections frequently described as slums. They say or imply that here the accumulating problems of the city reach a crescendo that must awaken the consciences of people of good will.

Actually, those who know slum dwellers intimately can often find evidences of community loyalty that may be used to stimulate the growth of nuclei. There is often a warmth in the fellowship of a shared fate, even an unhappy one. Furthermore, it would be unwise to find all the problems or even the most serious ones in the slums. There are many other parts of the metropolitan area that need compassion, though the need elsewhere may not be as spectacular.

Characteristically, the slums house the poor who have arrived more recently on the urban scene, those who can be expected to move on up the economic scale. These people may come from other nations or from other underprivileged sections of our own country. But in the slums, there will also be found those who have

---

[9] William C. Loring, Jr., Frank L. Sweetser, and Charles F. Ernst, *Community Organization for Citizen Participation in Urban Renewal* (Boston: *Housing Association of Metropolitan Boston,* 1957).

remained and have no expectation that they will move somewhere else. These latter will include the people who have given up the struggle or who have found some warmth in poverty. Some of the inhabitants of slums are handicapped by racial or linguistic differences. Others are the down-and-outers of "skid row." The most unpleasant of vices may be well represented (the genteel vices will be scattered elsewhere throughout the metropolitan area).

Conflicting ethnic groups are often present; frequently one self-conscious group will take over a block or a neighborhood; and misunderstanding and suspicion between these ethnic or racial ghettos will provide the frictions that lead to gang warfare.

Often the slums, characterized by decaying structures, vermin, and ethnic groups in conflict, will be found located close to the luxury of the central core of the city. But not always; slums can develop wherever neglect or disadvantaged human beings make deterioration more likely.

How to meet the needs of people in such areas has worried social and religious workers, educational authorities, police, and others for a long time. Various approaches have been tried—neighborhood houses, block organizations, recreation for young people, institutional churches, store-front churches, vocational education —the list is long and often disheartening. It is probable that no one method, or combination of methods, can provide a satisfactory answer. A determination is needed to try out many approaches, to study and keep studying the situation, to adapt and readapt methods to change.

In one of our projects, the inner-city area in which we were interested was inhabited by a confusing ethnic mixture of Negroes, Italians, Greeks, Mexicans, white migrants from the rural south, and a considerable trailer population (of many origins). Some families were "squatters" living in "do-it-yourself" tarpaper and tin-can shacks on land that often flooded, whereas other families were middle-class owners of modest homes. The one interest that these diverse people held in common (we discovered) was a concern for their young people, who were dropping out of school, being injured by factory traffic, suffering from poor police protection and saloons, and straying into delinquency.

We tried to interest public school authorities, church pastors, and social welfare workers in inaugurating a development program

—with no success. At length, we started a basic nucleus process with the factory workers and the housewives. The nucleus received the interested but nonparticipative blessing of schools, churches, and social welfare agencies. Each of these institutions, however, later gave help, providing meeting places, financial support, and, ultimately, members of the nucleus.

The process began with the three members who started the nucleus. But as it continued over a period of years, the number of participants rose to some three hundred, and the group became a larger nucleus with numerous subcommittees that constituted the smaller nuclei. The major beginning activity was the conducting, equipping, and supervising of a vacant lot playground. From this the process moved into volunteer home repairs, a job-opportunities program (for minorities), a city-wide human relations council, and efforts for the introduction of such programs as urban renewal and racial integration.

Of particular interest was the fact that though many residents of the slum were transients (and might be assumed to have little loyalty to either neighborhood or larger community), responsibility to serve the common good did grow.

We offer this brief account, not as an example to be followed, but as evidence that the process may be expected to produce results when used with imaginative experimentation—even in unfavorable circumstances.

MORE PROSPEROUS NEIGHBORHOODS

The term "neighborhood" is as ambiguous in people's experience as is the word "community." Whether there are distinct neighborhoods with boundaries and a character of their own is highly debatable. Even when such neighborhoods do exist, their boundaries and characteristics shift with the restless movements of humanity and with deteriorations and improvements. The best we can say is that the consciousness of belonging to a neighborhood is something to be sought as a part of the metropolitan experience of community.

The neighborhoods which are more favored economically may also be lacking in neighborliness. Though often a casual inspection will lead the observer to the conclusion that though people appear to live in satisfied comfort, closer observation will show that many of the residents are "upwardly mobile." That is, they are expecting to get a better job or an advancement that will allow them to move to what they regard as a "better" neighborhood. Therefore they do not wish to become involved in any effort at local improvement.

A more prosperous neighborhood will also often include a definitely disadvantaged area or group of families. It may be possible to draw the boundaries of the area in such a way that the low income people are excluded, but such an exclusion does violence to most contemporary city life and makes striving for the common good a less meaningful and even hollow aspiration.

One such neighborhood of all-inclusive economic levels is found in an action research project now in process in a large city. The development began with a larger nucleus made up of mildly prosperous people, two or three representatives of the disadvantaged, and with a goodly number of social welfare and public school personnel. In fact, the trained members from the helping professions were so numerous that, for a time, it was difficult to find enough ordinary citizens willing to do the contact encouragement work to form smaller nuclei. As a result of conscientious recruitment, however, enough nonprofessionals were brought in to make positive work possible.

Several smaller nuclei have developed and continue to be active. Two of these nuclei serve ethnic minorities, Negroes and Mexicans. One serves an economically disadvantaged micropopulation, the dwellers in a limited income urban renewal project. Then there are two nuclei serving school dropouts. (Two were necessary, and perhaps more will be formed, because small numbers seemed to be necessary to provide the warmth of primary group experience, so important for these alienated teen-agers.) Another basic nucleus has been formed among the blind and those threatened with blindness. (This particular interest was evolved by a member of the larger nucleus who himself is blind. In addition to acting as an encourager in a basic nucleus, he operates the tape recorder for the discussions of the larger nucleus that are a part of its ongoing research.) One of the particularly noteworthy activities introduced by the basic nucleus of the blind is the production of recorded readings by seeing citizens who will give time to help their handicapped neighbors.

The larger nucleus has several triumphs to its credit. In a government-subsidized housing project, the management was persuaded to make an apartment available, rent free, for the developmental activities of the residents. Teachers, recreation leaders, and counselors were provided for the different groups that utilize this apartment. Funds to help the school dropouts were provided by a local Optimists Club, which takes great pride in "their" service activity. The local Lions Club provides financial help for the blind and near-blind. The local Junior Chamber of Commerce insists that it be allowed to make some contribution commensurate with those made by the Optimists and the Lions. The local school authorities have begun to re-examine their programs to see first, whether they can reduce the number of students who are dropping out of school, and second, whether they can develop educational activities that will serve those who have already been lost.

The activities of this action research project are not limited to these local interests, however. Discussion within the larger nucleus has covered such matters as pending state legislation regarding racial integration in housing. The larger nucleus has taken a position in favor of the legislation and has transmitted its recommendations to the proper authorities.

Many other kinds of action programs can carry the larger nucleus process into its developmental task. The specific activities of the basic nuclei of this project represent the expressions of service to the common good discovered, so far, by larger nucleus members. The larger nucleus can be expected to become involved in additional activities, as will other larger nuclei elsewhere. The members still worry about recruiting enough people to do the jobs they have undertaken. They still worry about finding adequate financial support. But even the worry contributes to the development process.

AREAS OF URBAN REHABILITATION AND RENEWAL

Sometimes urban renewal projects can be included as part of general neighborhood areas of development, as in the instance just cited. More characteristically, however, each large housing project or high-rise apartment building can be treated as its own neighborhood. This is often true also of the areas chosen for the rehabilitation of old structures.

When the decision has been made (usually at some governmental headquarters) to preserve the structures and social life of an area, the recommendations just made about neighborhoods apply. The larger nucleus that takes responsibility for planning, however, may want to give serious thought to encouraging basic nuclei in each of the city blocks. This will often mean that the smaller nuclei will be organized on a monoracial basis. It will then be the responsibility of the larger group to encourage the members of the basic nuclei to establish relationships and to assume responsibilities beyond the confines of a single ethnic classification.

When the decision has been made (again by governmental authority) to construct new buildings, the human problems become much more complicated. First, there is the question of what happens to the people driven out of their homes by the destruction of the slums. No research studies of adequate compassion have been made of the fate of the dispossessed. It is generally assumed that these people will go somewhere, that their lot there will be no worse than it would have been in the conditions from which they were driven, that the neighborhood will be better for the improved housing. It is probable, however, that few of the displaced families will be found among the tenants of the new housing when it is completed. Do those who are not accommodated in the new buildings become new slum dwellers?

Such unhappy results follow from "planning from the top" that fails to enlist the participation of the citizen. Might the residents of a neighborhood that is about to be demolished and rebuilt be drawn into the process before the bulldozers move in? It is difficult to involve people only to work in a rehousing program that has already been adopted by a distant authority. The need can be met by enlisting the interest of a larger nucleus for the area, assuming such a body exists and has been active.

The usual course of events, however, is that the housing authority tears out the old structures, builds the new (sometimes high-rise apartments, sometimes smaller buildings with garden apartments, but apartments nonetheless), leases to tenants (who must qualify according to income range), and *then* begins to worry about a program to deal with the problems of human development. Such belated concern makes the task most difficult, but not hopeless.

Again, there is an opportunity for public schools, social agencies, churches, and even for the housing authority itself to act. Any of these institutions can start by placing friendly encouragers in the new housing development. Such encouragers should avoid professional manners and compulsions; their chief asset is simple friendliness and neighborliness with people who cannot be expected to have deep and vital roots in the new housing facility. Through his friendly and sympathetic attempts to discover the people's needs, an encourager can hope to see the development of nuclei that will begin to lift the people out of their alienation.

A few social science studies of alienation, conflict, and problems in housing projects have been made. Few, however, are based upon a utilization of nucleus processes. Here is an opportunity for community developers to make important research contributions to a problem of our time, one that will increase in complexity in the years to come.

SUBURBS

Then there are the suburbs, which are, for the most part, locations of the privileged.[10] These areas for the well-to-do are usually incorporated municipalities that lie outside the central city. They tend to be "bedrooms" to the big city, supplying the commuters whose work and some of whose loyalty is centered away from the suburb.

Because the suburbs are separated governmentally from the central city, they tend to insulate themselves from "unwanted" ethnic populations (except as these are admitted as servants), from high taxes, and from low standards of living. Yet, despite the insulation and the withdrawal of taxes and responsibility, the suburban dwellers are an integral part of the metroplex.

It is not too difficult to discover some sense of community loyalty in most suburbs. These municipalities are frequently small enough to allow for formation of one basic nucleus, and the first may give birth to others. There is often enough identification with the name of a town to instill a bit of pride to be used as a basis for improvement. The difficulty arises when the community development process deals only with suburban problems. The process is incomplete until the suburbanites accept responsibility for the entire metroplex.

The suburban community development process is cut short

---

[10] The underprivileged urban fringe we mentioned in the preceding chapter.

unless these nuclei of the privileged relate themselves to other nuclei —first, of their own less affluent neighbors, perhaps in the same suburb—then, of people in the nearby city neighborhoods. This is an assignment for encouraging agencies.

"SLURBS"

A particular new kind of local environment, a product of the metropolitan population explosion, presents another challenge to community development. This is the growth of "slurbs." This term, combining the words "slum" and "suburb," is probably a shortened form of another term, "Sluburbia." It refers to the mass-produced housing projects, built upon open land, usually outside of any municipal boundaries. Homes by the hundreds or thousands are erected for sale to middle income buyers, mostly commuters. The chief planner for the entire enterprise is the real estate "developer," whose major motivation is usually a quick profit. Planning for municipal services, schools, recreation facilities, churches, libraries, or even for beauty or variety is likely to be neglected. Sometimes county planning offices or state law may set some limitations upon the "developer," but these restrictions usually prove inadequate to the creation of a physical environment for the development of the semiaffluent families that move in.

How to encourage the people of a slurb to create the experience of a community is a problem for much action research experimentation. Some of the more conscientious builders have begun to design a physical layout of homes, recreational areas, educational and religious and shopping facilities that, it is hoped, will tend to help the inhabitants find a sense of community. But the growth of people toward neighborliness demands, in addition to facilities, developmental processes.

In one such housing development (incorporated as a suburban municipality after the homes had been built) we have seen an encourager strive to find some common problem or interest, that would provide a basis for a nucleus process. He discovered that a great many of the homeowners were unresponsive because, they told him, they expected to sell their homes soon at a profit and move on to the next new construction. Thus the expectation of a quick profit had infected the new owners as well as the builder. The only leads for service to the common good, he has wondered about using, are concerns about teen-age problems and about the early deterioration of quickly built homes. Can these worries become a basis for nucleus growth?

Another area is about to become a slurb. The open farm land has all been purchased by the wholesale builder, and his bulldozers are scheduled to move in within a matter of months. An encourager on the scene is attempting to create a larger nucleus of present, older residents to welcome the newcomers as rapidly as they buy into the surrounding city-to-be. So far the encourager's progress has been slow, for he must work against the residents' desire to keep things as they are and against their resentment at the probable newcomers (even before they appear) and at the builder who is bringing the newcomers.

The slurb, the slum, the urban renewal or neighborhood conservation project, all these and many other metropolitan environments call for experimentation that stresses human development. Many adaptations of basic-nucleus and larger-nucleus processes are called for as means for involving the developing city dwellers in the planning for their emerging way of life.

POLITICAL INFLUENCES

It is in the midst of the frustrating complexities of metropolitan life that the effective influence of basic and larger nuclei will be tested. For the most part, the test will come in the pressures, counterpressures, and dialogue of politics. But the kinds of political influence that are most compatible with the processes of community development are something other than partisan campaigns, election victories, and negotiating for personal and group advantage.

Just how citizen groups that seek for the common good are to operate in the controversial field of politics will be determined by action research studies of effectiveness. We can give one example that is suggestive of possibilities for such experimentation.

The scene is an industrial municipality, part of a huge metropolitan complex. The original impulse for a larger nucleus grew out of a conviction that the local government needed improvement. When the group was finally formed, however, the members decided to work upon lesser specific problems rather than directly upon political reform. These problems were the replacement of public buses that were decrepit and dangerous, the improvement of the public library, the upgrading of the schools, the improvement of slum housing, and the development of better recreational facilities. The choice of these problems was a deliberate limitation imposed early in the process by the members themselves. Through work on such questions, it was hoped to influence government to become more democratic and efficient.

After about a year and a half of the larger nucleus process, a municipal election was scheduled. The members of the nucleus conceived the idea of formulating a series of questions on the problems with which they were concerned to be addressed to all candidates for office, including the incumbents. These questions were published in the local newspaper as an open letter from a group that sought the over-all good of all neighbors.

Soon the secretary of the group received a telephone call from the incumbent mayor, a candidate for re-election, asking for an opportunity to meet with the nucleus to answer these questions, and any others, in a direct conversation. Each of the rival candidates for mayor or city councilman made the same request. The members of the larger nucleus, with invited guests, carried through a series of conversations with these aspiring politicians and received statements from each about how he would act if elected.

The incumbent mayor was re-elected. And he proved as good as his promises. He asked the members of the group to obtain data on unsafe buses to be used in enforcing the laws on safety. And soon thereafter, many decrepit buses were discarded, and a new and more responsible company took over the bus franchise.

Then the members of the group were asked to report details on the violation of laws in slum housing, so that the safety and sanitary ordinances could be enforced or changed. The nucleus members took photographs of uncollected garbage and obtained affidavits on unheated or rat-infested apartments. Some progress in clearing up the abuses was made, although the results were not as dramatic as in the case of the buses. The clearing away of slum dwellings is a most difficult long-time obligation.

Emboldened by the mayor's recognition, the members brought pressure to bear to improve library services for children and to upgrade the schools. The latter proved difficult because the board of education (an appointive body) was not responsive to the political influences that were effectively exerted upon the mayor and the city council. The attendance of nucleus members at board meetings (wholly legal) alarmed the school authorities, who could not believe that any group could genuinely serve the common interest. Nonetheless, progress is discernible in the building of new facilities and in changes in the schools' programs.

The larger nucleus later suffered a setback when its chairman used his position to support a candidate for governor. The candidate lost, and the group broke into conflicting factions. Recovering from this reverse, it has gone on to interest itself in the original problems, but it has taken a new interest in such questions as the pay of policemen and the administration of social welfare funds. It has re-established its reputation as a group devoted to the common good, despite the bad judgment of its chairman (who resigned after his mistake). It seems to be gaining influence as a nonselfseeking voice for the community good and as a group that is open to all who will give time, study, and thought to general improvement. The members are convincing themselves and their neighbors that they can overcome the alienation of helplessness.

Problems—Opportunities

As larger nuclei feel their way into new responsibilities, certain basic principles emerge for the guidance of their further effort. And there are some suggestions, growing out of experience to date, that implement these principles.

FLEXIBILITY

The members of larger nuclei must expect to adapt and readapt procedures endlessly. Sometimes experimentation is justified on the ground that "We are learning. Once we learn, then we will be wise enough to use the correct method." This is a vain expectation, whose popularity in the past has often made good programs ineffective. Even when a specific program (such as one to combat delinquency or to raise money for hospitals) has worked well for a time, it needs to be modified as people change, as they perceive their needs differently, as new problems arise.

Even more, the expectation that methodologies are transferable needs to be examined with skepticism. Because a particular organizational structure works well in St. Louis does not mean that it will yield the same results in San Francisco. Even the transferability of specific methods from one section of the metropoly to another is doubtful. While following basic processes and principles, there must be an endless willingness to let the participants work out those procedures that are meaningful to them.

BASIC PROCESS

The larger nucleus process presents a generalized approach and principles that can be adapted to many varieties of metropolitan life. The details of the operation will vary enormously, depending upon the institution whose encourager initiates the process. The process may start with a church, a public school, a social agency, a chamber of commerce, a housing authority, or some other special agency, but the initiating organization will inevitably add some flavor of its own purpose and mode of working to the process. Thus the initiating organization should seek a coalition with other organizations as rapidly as possible and should direct its efforts toward creating a larger nucleus with unique characteristics.

USE OF AMATEURS

So enormous are the needs for human development in the metropoly that there are never enough trained professionals to go around. Fortunately, so much does the process rest upon the warmth of genuine friendship, volunteer encouragers can be used effectively. These amateurs require training, however, and they should operate in collaboration with professionals. The actual relationship between the volunteers and the paid staff, the amount of time to be given, the kinds of jobs to be undertaken, all these require working together on an experimental basis.

Fortunately, there are many people of conscience in the teeming population of every city who will themselves grow in neighborly responsibility by becoming involved in community development. One challenge to the initiating agencies is to recruit volunteers, train them, and maintain contact with them as they participate in the process, so that they, and other citizens, will benefit.

STUDY—PLANNING—PETITIONING

Muscle-stretching cooperation is much less possible in the city, as has already been noted. But in the city there are more agencies, governmental authorities, and official red tape through which citizens must proceed as they solve their problems. The process therefore must rely more upon study, discussion and planning and upon arguing, petitioning, and persuading in order to get jobs done.

Such less physically vigorous activity is satisfactory for the educated. What about the disadvantaged who are less accustomed to intellectualized procedures? Experience indicates that the poorly educated and even the illiterate can take part in their own concept of study, can discuss serious matters responsibly to develop worthwhile ideas, and can meet with the great and powerful with genuine dignity. Their confidence to confer with and request help from authoritative decision makers, grows out of an assurance that they know what they are talking about.

CONTROVERSY

Urban community developers should not be afraid of controversy, for controversy often provides the impetus to nucleus building. Their problem and opportunity is to help people learn how to handle conflict in a rational and constructive spirit.

In the work of any larger nucleus, it should be assumed that there will be conflicts between microneighborhoods. These internal controversies are to be recognized openly. They require of participants the skill to resolve disputes sufficiently to allow positive efforts to go forward. There will also be external conflicts when the nucleus seeks to influence the authorities and other powerful decision makers. The problem here is to avoid seeking the satisfaction that comes with a great volume of complaint and, instead, to discover those methods that are most effective in influencing decisions. Though pressure may be brought to bear through publicity, demonstration, public debate, or legal action, the ultimate purpose is that reconciliation which ultimately benefits everyone.

One of the broad experiments open to larger nuclei is the tryout of good will in action. How far is it possible to go with the hope that an opposition faction in conflict wants to be rational, wants to do the right thing? Pressure tactics that will force the opposition to cooperate can be held in abeyance until, or unless, this hope has been proved fallacious. Then the experimentation with different kinds of pressure may be undertaken.

The experimental attitude goes further. After pressure has been applied, there is the follow-up that seeks positive steps to resolve the conflict. After an adversary has given some response (hopefully yielding a bit), there comes the period of thoughtful planning with him.

In short, controversy is a part of the totality of development. It should be handled in such way as to increase community-serving responsibility on the part of all parties to the conflict.

PATIENCE

Community developers should not be discouraged by their slowness in achieving positive results, by the poverty of the people's response, by the complications of the problems, or by the unpredictable changes that are beyond their control. They must realize that the experience of community development is new to metropolitan citizens. They must guide their thinking by the realization that all of us are in the midst of revolutionary changes to new ways of life that no one can, as yet, predict.

Starting Points

Although metropolitan citizens contribute eventually to the fundamental repatterning of life that is now going on, they must have some starting points for the process that develops them. Their competence to contribute grows as a result of a process that has humble beginnings.

Their alienation, expressed as helplessness and as a lack of confidence in their own abilities, can be relieved as they discover that they can do something to better immediate conditions. Among these simple beginnings are the following:

Block or Small District Improvements. In some cities, small nuclei of neighbors have worked together to clean up backyards, repair steps, paint exteriors and interiors, and install window boxes. They have undertaken sanitation efforts, an antirat campaign, the putting of lids on garbage cans, and the replacing of the old ones.

In other cities, they have begun with petitioning for better police protection, for better rubbish collection, for better schools, for the introduction of training for dropouts in schools or elsewhere. In cooperative endeavors of these kinds, in which all work together for the common good, the members of the small nuclei have often found that ethnic animosities and other conflicts tend to resolve themselves.

Cultural, Recreational, and Youth Improvement. Some city neighborhoods are working on a musical group, or a little theater, or a gallery for local artists. In others, public parks become a target of attention, seeking better play equipment, lights for night recreation, and employed supervisors for either public or private facilities. In addition to school and recreation improvements, there are counseling and job clinics for youth. Recruitment for service in work camps and Peace Corps, either foreign or domestic, can interest a nucleus. Teams of young people that can work on some of the block improvements above, can be part of the challenge. Another most difficult, but most necessary, activity is the setting up of treatment facilities for drug addicts; however, the setting up of such a program usually requires trained professionals.

Quiet Influence. There are numerous agencies, both publicly and privately supported, that will welcome intelligent and informed help from local nuclei. In fact, some agencies all but beg for cooperation. In some cities, overworked social welfare agencies discover that nucleus interest will put them in contact with needy individuals, thereby making their work more efficient. Housing officials, when they find responsible nuclei, may be willing to invite their participation, beginning with surveys of need, moving to decisions of plans, to caring for the ousted, and to plans for personal development of new tenants. There are many places where friendly influence can be exerted—planning commissions, church councils, boards of education, police offices, and so on.

Publicity-Seeking Influence. Sometimes a nucleus (more often a larger nucleus, and better later than earlier in the process) seeks to gain influence by publicly supporting or opposing such matters as the issuance of bonds to finance public construction, the raising of teachers' salaries, the employment of minority group members on the police force. When such matters are at issue, it is important that the decision of the nucleus, whether to support or to oppose, be made not in a spirit of partisan benefit, but in a spirit of service to the common good. The nucleus, but especially the larger nucleus, needs to maintain its identity as an association devoted to the all-inclusive good of everyone.

Influence that is sought through publicity is a poor objective for the formation of a larger nucleus. Those who start the process would be wise to postpone such attention-getting activities until the group has achieved some loyalty to the over-all good. The desire for headlines leads to the recruitment of publicity seekers; it does not provide a solid base of service and tends to give a partisan character to a larger nucleus.

These, then, are some points at which to begin—but not at which to stop. The constant effort is to give a voice to the inarticulate, the fearful, to those paralyzed by the alienation of metropolitan living. There is no one best way to do this. There are starting points of immediate need that can grow into important influences, if attention to them inaugurates a process. The process will have many varieties. But the community development processes we have presented can serve as guides.

Community development processes do not provide formulas for metropolitan improvement. They do provide a means of experimentation for seeking answers. By using them, citizens can grow into ethical responsibility that reduces alienation—as they contribute to the repatterning of metropolitan life.

chapter 12

Scientific Relatedness

Most community developers have come into the work from backgrounds other than scientific. Indeed, some recruiters for this new field regard traditional training in research as a handicap. As one administrator for overseas community development remarked, "We do not seek people with advanced degrees in sociology, social psychology, or anthropology. They do not come to the job prepared to meet people's needs. They come hoping to collect data for a monograph which they can write to enhance their reputations."

That is, a social scientist is looked upon as a specialist with little or no commitment to people, but with great commitment to some technical methodology, the use of which will excite the admiration of fellow scientists. The practical encourager of community process is likely to have little patience for such a theoretically oriented person, and vice versa.

Community developers would be less isolated from social scientists if they could select the theories and methods in these disciplines that are compatible with local human development and if they could also gain some self-confidence in realizing that they can contribute importantly to scientific research.

Before going too deeply into this matter, it would be well to realize that all scientific disciplines (including those called social and behavioral) are in the midst of great ferment. There are rival

schools of thought, each often defended with the fervor of embattled political ideologies. There are discernible trends of change,
some of which we will mention, but very briefly. To summarize
scientific controversy is not our present purpose. Instead, we propose primarily to examine the relatedness of various disciplines to
local human development.

Interdisciplinary Background

Community development depends upon or borrows from several
social scientific disciplines. These appear, not in their separated
neatness or purity, but in the slovenly interrelationship dictated by
the actual problems that people encounter. The chief social scientific fields are the behavioral sciences already mentioned—sociology, anthropology, and social psychology.

SOCIOLOGY

Sociologists lay much claim to community development, because
"the community" has long been a major responsibility for this discipline. When "the community" has been analyzed as a social structure that exists (or is supposed to exist), the influence has often
been stultifying, for it has featured verbose descriptions of rigid
social structures, class subdivisions, and hierarchies of power. Actually, the reality of these concepts is in flux, in sociological thinking, as in the reality of living.

When some of the more realistic sociologists have stressed the
development of the community more than its structure, they have
been more helpful.[1] They have begun to correct the remoteness
of sociologists from urban society, quoted from Morris Janowitz
in the preceding chapter. They begin to provide a theoretical basis
to support the search for community.

An awareness of, and sense of, responsibility for development
reintroduce moral values into sociological thinking. For long the
discipline fled into an essentially amoral objectivity, by way of
overcoming its reformist and "do-gooder" origins. But more recently certain sociologists have come into line with the growing

---

[1] Irwin Sanders is one example, especially in his *Making Good Communities Better* (Lexington: University of Kentucky Press, 1950).

sense of scientific responsibility to be found even among atomic physicists. They are beginning to take ethical thinking into consideration. All social scientists are especially involved because they deal with people. Sociology must therefore respond to moral judgments.[2]

Moreover, the most fundamental methodological dogma of modern social science—most firmly held in sociology and in the so-called "behavorial sciences"—is an insistence on the absolute distinction between facts (including theories explaining them) and values. Behavioral scientists dread being caught out making "value judgments" or using "value-loaded" terminology—dread it to a degree that is easily satirized by less inhibited and more old-fashioned scholars. . . .

What is required is more sensitive awareness of the inevitable interaction between factual knowledge and values. Insistence on their *logical disjunction* need not prevent recognition of their *psychological connection* and of the modes of reasoning from fact to value and vice-versa to which this connection gives rise. The social scientist too often clings to an early and narrow "logical positivist" view of the fact-value dualism and ignores more recent trends in philosophy which, while not denying the basic distinction, nevertheless recognize a rational dimension in moral and political discourse. . . .

ANTHROPOLOGY

At one time, anthropology gave most attention to ancient, far-away, and bizarre people. Anthropological studies laid stress upon how quaint and odd these other people were—from the point of view of an observer habituated to western civilization. More recently, this social science has been applied to contemporary societies, even to our own. When allied with purely descriptive sociology, it has exhibited both the static quality and the amoral objectivity. But as it has become concerned with people like "ourselves," it has increasingly used a dynamic description of change, in which the scientist could not avoid responsibility for outcomes.

First was the movement away from the outside, uninvolved observer to the "participant observer." There was a realization that the outsider never could understand what was going on, why people

---

[2] Dennis Wrong, "Political Bias and the Social Sciences," reprinted from the *Columbia University Forum*, Vol. II, No. 4 (Fall 1959), pp. 29, 31, by permission of the publisher, Columbia University, Copyright © 1959.

did what they did, and how they felt about it.[3] If an anthropologist
was to get the facts about a process or to interpret it, he had to
be a part of it, while yet maintaining his objectivity to describe.

Then there was the even more significant development known
as "action anthropology," [4] in which the anthropologist not only
observes people in the process of change, but takes steps to encourage certain kinds of changes that have been chosen as valuable
according to ethical norms. Then he tries to record how successful
or unsuccessful he has been. More is involved than the participant-
observer technique, for the anthropologist may intervene in or influence the process. He becomes a part of the process, even as he
observes, and commits himself to securing a favorable outcome.
He is observing himself as well as others, himself in interaction
with others.

SOCIAL PSYCHOLOGY

The most fruitful identification for community development,
however, is with social psychology.[5] If the tendency of sociology
is toward social structure, and that of anthropology toward process,
then the tendency of social psychology is to give attention to people.

Again, contending schools of thought need to be distinguished.
Although we speak of social psychology generally, there are many
other kinds of psychology that presume to speak for social phenomena. And every psychologist tends to reflect the viewpoint of
his own specialty. These specialties are ranged over a vast spectrum, from studies of animal behavior, to studies of human beings
in the mass, to studies of individual persons and the treatment of
individual maladjustments. The psychologists may be ranged in another way, from those who seek to control, to those who would
teach and persuade, to those who place reliance upon inducing

---

[3] For a classic description of the participant-observer technique, see Florence Kluckhohn, "The Participant-Observer Technique in Small Communities," *American Journal of Sociology,* Vol. XLVI, No. 3 (November 1940),
pp. 331 *ff*. For one that comes closer to community development, see Severyn
T. Bruyn, "The Methodology of Participant Observation," *Human Organization,* Vol. 22, No. 3 (Fall 1963).

[4] See Sol Tax (Department of Anthropology, University of Chicago) in
an address given at the University of Michigan, March 20, 1958, entitled
"Action Anthropology."

[5] Here a bias of the writers becomes obvious.

processes of development. Then other contrasts between psychologists may be noted, between those who find ultimate reality in atomistic concepts (such as habits, traits, conditioned reflexes) and those who seek to deal with the whole human being. The wholeness may consist of the person as a total organism, or it may refer to the organism plus the total environment in which he lives. The term "social psychology" does not, therefore, designate any agreed-upon point of view.

Psychology has long been dynamic. It has dealt with learning and forgetting; with growth, maturation, and the decay of intelligence; and with patterns of behavior and attitudes. Only recently, however, have a few psychologists begun to study the processes of planned development in which the personality involved (the self) became a contributor to the process. Psychology has long been atomistic. Only recently have some psychologists returned to an earlier concern for the total person. A minority seeks to make psychology holistic in the midst of purposeful development.

Other influences toward new emphases have come from clinical psychology, which has studied development of whole individuals within the context of a psychotherapist's office.[6] In something of the same spirit, the group dynamics people have experimented with the changes that persons can bring about in themselves through small group experience. Perhaps the best-known of these experiments are carried on by the National Training Laboratories,[7] which use the "T" (training) group. Genuine holistic development has taken place in participants, but these groups have been too much inward-turning in their attention. They have not utilized enough obligation to serve people outside of the experimental group. More recently, these laboratories have turned toward community obligation in forming "T" groups that resemble community nuclei— except that they are of short duration and do not go into action to serve a common good external to themselves.

Certain other group dynamics people have explored the concept of a group's serving a common good.[8] But experimentation with

---

[6] See the work of Carl R. Rogers, especially *On Becoming a Person* (Boston: Houghton Mifflin, 1961).

[7] See the publications of the National Training Laboratories.

[8] See Ronald Lippitt, Jeanne Watson, and Bruce Westley, *The Dynamics of Planned Change* (New York: Harcourt, 1958).

a long-lived, intimate group of people that creates its own wholeness in an emerging community has not as yet engaged the attention of psychologists. May it when community development presents
the opportunity?

The clearest expression of the new emphases in psychology that
are meaningful to community development is found in "Humanistic
Psychology," which draws together several emphases already mentioned, along with various other emphases devoted to human potentiality for development.[9] We will follow this emphasis more fully,
later, after mentioning some other scientific disciplines. In many
ways, humanistic psychology summarizes trends in various related
sciences as well as in social psychology.

As a pulling together of the three behavioral sciences, consider
Paul Goodman's conclusion that community development represents a "pragmatic social science." [10] According to Goodman, community development allows a scientist to enter a real-life situation
and irradiate it with whatever knowledge (and sensitivity) his
disciplines have given him. The social scientist then goes on to
search for both theoretical and practical answers to questions. In
this endeavor, community development provides one opportunity
for a creative interrelating of these three important scientific disciplines.

OTHER DISCIPLINES

Because community development deals with real people who are
contending with real problems in the context of real living, it may
call upon any scientific knowlege for help. All the other social
sciences are potentially involved. Economics may be consulted,
especially that branch which studies local consumption and production in relation to the statistics of macroprocesses and planning.
Political science is often important, not so much for the study or
teaching of the machinery of national or international or even

---

[9] See Nevitt Sanford, "Social Science and Reform," an address given at
the annual meeting of the American Psychological Association, Washington,
D.C. (August 28, 1958). For a specific statement, see J. F. T. Bugental,
"Humanistic Psychology: A New Break-through," *American Psychologist,*
Vol. 18, No. 9 (September 1963), pp. 563–567.

[10] See Paul Goodman, *Utopian Essays and Practical Proposals* (New
York: Random House, 1962), pp. 18–19.

state governments as for its yielding to the people an understanding of the process by which they may learn to govern themselves.

Demography cannot be overlooked. How many people are there? How rapidly is their number increasing or decreasing? What are their movements into or out of the local scene? What kinds of people are there? What are their hopes, their fears, their prejudices? The securing of these items of information calls for the application of human geography, human ecology, topography, climatology, and so on to human problems and capacity for growth.

A sense of history is important—not so much that entombed in books, but more the kind which is lived. The individual's experience of development can be discussed as part of the history that is recorded in books. And even the small processes of change in a nucleus or neighborhood can take on significance as part of great flows of events into the future.

Failure to mention a specific discipline does not imply that we think it unimportant. Any scientific inquiry that affects human beings may be called upon in community development. Many non-social sciences are, of course, utilized, especially the applied sciences. The various kinds of studies that are indispensable to agricultural pursuits draw upon the biological disciplines. Medicine, sanitation, and nutrition are important. From the physical and chemical sciences, engineering and planning are contributors. The list could go on and on, for no significant contributions to the understanding and improvement of man may be excluded when great problems are being considered.

Various professions that lean upon scientific disciplines are to be noted also. Some of these, the "helping" professions, will be mentioned in subsequent chapters.

THE HUMANISTIC EMPHASIS

The contemporary concentration of science upon mass data and technology has resulted in a social science of computers. The admired evidence of scientific respectability has become the use of technological gadgetry, by which experimental results can be collated statistically. To many scientists, the findings of research are not acceptable unless they have been produced by the most complex of machines, a mechanical "brain." Human beings are observed, as it were, through the punch holes of an IBM card.

The humanistic revolt against such mechanization does not necessarily call for a repudiation of such research, for in fact, many
processes and findings from impersonal mass studies must be used.
What is required is rather a supplementation of the impersonal
mechanisms and techniques. If we are to learn about man, we need
information about him in the mass, but also as a unique person.
This supplementary point of view, attention to which might keep
research in balance, may be epitomized from the writing of J. F. T.
Bugental.[11] He presents eight modes of psychological thought that
are being questioned, especially as a result of the social scientist's
dealing with human beings in clinical situations. We adapt these.

First, there is the atomistic emphasis, the tendency to think
about a man as a composite of parts. Psychologists and other
social scientists, in keeping with the analytic urge, have examined
human beings as assemblages of abstract fragments. Human beings
need to be treated as whole organisms, whole persons.

Second, there is the model of science taken over from physics.
Bugental should be referring here to preatomic physics. The newer
physics, which made atomic fission and fusion possible, presents
concepts much more in keeping with the humanistic emphasis.

Third, there is the model of the medical practitioner. This pattern is changing. Both the doctor who looks only at the patient's
symptoms and the specialist who concentrates upon a small portion of the patient's anatomy are sharing attention with teams of
health workers who examine the person in the context of his physical and social environment.

Fourth, there is the pattern of the departmentalized university
faculty by which psychologists are trained. The subdivision of the
faculty into compartmentalized and often noncommunicating specialties is compatible with the atomization of the individual that
is produced by analyzing him into separate intellectualized fragments.

Fifth, there is the reliance upon the statistical treatment of masses
of data to establish truth. Nonstatistical information is also scientifically respectable. Furthermore, research allows for variation in
the results caused by the uniqueness of individuals and of social

---

11 Bugental, *op. cit.*

situations. These unique variations are glossed over in data that are gathered and collated mechanically.

Sixth, there is the idea that research must precede practice, that the researcher develops knowledge and the practitioner applies it. Basic contributions can be made by the practitioner also.

Seventh, there is the idea that a research team must consist of, or be dominated by, professionals. Laymen can also make an important contribution to research.

Eighth, there is the belief that a cordial relationship with the persons who are to be helped is more important than a thorough diagnostic knowledge about them. Research about people may require objective information, but before the researcher can assist in the progress of persons, the essential humanity and individuality of people must be accepted. And it is precisely this progress that community development seeks to investigate by research.

Although Bugental presents these points as new, the fact is that the humanistic emphasis is a return to certain forgotten themes in scientific thinking. Jane Loevinger [12] points to a long-standing conflict between "holist" and "dissectionist" approaches to nature. The process-oriented view is ancient, and so is the concern for the person. Indeed, the humanistic revolt is symptomatic of that ferment in scientific thinking which is found in the physical sciences and which has been infiltrating the social and behavioral disciplines, and even philosophy and theology. There is, as yet, no organized and systematic philosophy of science to replace that which is being challenged. The search for wholeness, the respect for moral values and for the people who hold them, these at least are essential to the new (but old) scientific world view.

Community development, in scientific relatedness, belongs within the scope of the newly vitalized search for more humane and realistic patterns of thought. The search for wholeness in the person (who is valued) is expedited by the search for wholeness in community experience (which is based upon the ethical good of all neighbors). When there is some success in finding comm-*unity* in town, city block, neighborhood, or area of service, this success

---

[12] "Conflict of Commitment in Clinical Research," *American Psychologist,* Vol. 18, No. 5 (May 1963), pp. 241–251.

contributes to the internal unity of those who are doing the searching.

Is there also a possibility also of a search for unity among the separated and often jealously conflicting scientific disciplines, through community development experience and research? Might the attention given to the problems that arise in a "pragmatic social science" help scientists to submerge their rivalries in a cooperative search for the answers to real problems, as real people perceive them?

Research Contributions

Further achievements for the social sciences may be hampered by the progress made to date. Success in research tends to enshrine accepted methodology as something sacred. New concepts may seem to break away from established practices even when they actually build upon the earlier work. The pioneers of social science will be honored, however, not by continuing to cover the same ground they explored, but by pressing on into new territory. . . .[13]

Community development practitioners have come to look upon themselves as the users of scientific wisdom developed by others. They have a sense of inferiority produced, in part, by their admiration for a theoretical wisdom that may or may not be directly useful. The encourager on the community scene may feel that he is the adapter of the purer knowledge developed by more renowned researchers in university laboratories, libraries, and swivel chairs.

"PURE" VERSUS "APPLIED" RESEARCH

Part of the sense of inferiority of community developers (and many other practical people) lies in the commonly accepted description of research as "pure" or "applied." As long as something "pure" will be contrasted with something "impure" or "adulterated," the "applied" is clearly seen to be inferior.

Actually, the distinction (often tacitly accepted) is unreal. Some of the most basic theories have developed out of practical research.

[13] William W. Biddle, "A Major Breakthrough for the Social Sciences," University of Wisconsin (June 1958). Unpublished paper. See also William W. Biddle, "The Challenge of Major Research," *Adult Leadership,* Vol. 7, No. 5 (November 1958), pp. 123 *ff.*

The germ theory of disease grew out of Pasteur's experiments to discover means for keeping wine from turning sour. Other theories developed out of quite impractical scientific curiosity. Basic research can be carried out in many contexts, not only in carefully controlled laboratories, but also in practical settings. It all depends upon the skill and the imagination of those who do the work.

When it comes to research in human development, the social context becomes most important. Are the conclusions reached in the classroom, learning laboratory, or psychotherapeutic clinic applicable to the problems of delinquency in complicated city life? Is it possible to learn what potentialities for leadership and ethical sensitivity people may have until they have been encouraged to develop these characteristics in the context of their daily living? In other words, it is probable that basic conclusions concerning the development of people will require research *in situ* (to borrow a medical term).

Such a necessity gives a new dignity and importance to the community developer. Instead of being a mere applier of someone else's wisdom, he may also become a producer of findings that grow peculiarly out of the process he encourages. He will undoubtedly need help in this endeavor. But, without his efforts, the findings might never be made.

A FRESH LOOK

Community development affords an opportunity to the scientifically minded to take a fresh look at the phenomenon of man in the process of choosing to become better. A scientist who responds to the opportunity must attempt to free his thinking of previous judgments and theoretical constructs. He must plan to learn from the phenomenon he is observing. He must agree to concentrate more upon people than upon any approved research technique. His every intervention in the course of events should expedite a process that people come, more and more, to control. For the becoming he hopes to observe is one of increased autonomy for people.

When human beings are thus approached *in situ,* it is probable that new findings and new theories will emerge. A scientist who is learning from the people's development retains still the insights and sensitivities of his training and his respect for disciplined thinking, even as he avoids categorizing events in a predetermined way. He will begin to formulate new categories, which, hopefully, will be closely related to the realities people face.

Important scientific advances have been made before by men of originality who took a fresh and unstructured look at reality. Galileo observing the motions of the lamp in church, Darwin traveling over the world to describe animal species—both were taking a fresh look through eyes unclouded by previous intellectual formulations. And both, in consequence, were condemned by those who were threatened by their unorthodox conclusions. Perhaps community developers, trying to learn from man as he develops, can expect similar condemnation. But is it possible that they might evolve enlightening new interpretations that would open new vistas of scientific thinking?

The realization of such possibilities will require the research team we have already discussed.[14] The community development encourager on the team is likely to be the pacesetter for the social scientist. But he, in turn, will take his pace from the developing citizens. He should welcome trained social scientists, on condition that they agree to certain stipulations:

Any research that is undertaken must not impede the process of development.

No research that will hurt people or impair their dignity will be permitted.

The social scientist researchers must be willing to enter into a warmth of relationship with the people whom they are observing, and they must include themselves among the observed.

Social scientists cannot always guarantee that their research efforts will meet these criteria, any more than the community encouragers can. But they must make an honest effort, and keep on making it.

COMPASSIONATE EXPERIMENTATION

When social scientists, especially behavioral scientists, accept their relatedness to community development, they must accept also an ethical responsibility for the outcomes of the processes. They

---

[14] Chap. 8, "Research Design."

cannot guarantee the outcomes, but they are obligated to throw their influence on the side of humane and democratic normative values.

Such an obligation is consistent with the methodology of action research, but it is also in keeping with the scientific thinking of the atomic era.[15]

> As psychological knowledge grows, the possibility of more effective control over human behavior increases, with profound consequences for ethics. The very process of enquiry that promises to improve decision making also adds to the gravity of the decisions made.
>
> Increasingly man will be able to employ the results of psychological science to manipulate his fellow man, often without his victim knowing that he is being controlled.
>
> Developing psychological knowledge presents the same conjunction of good and evil that we have all felt so keenly in the development of atomic energy. Atomic energy can ease man of drudgery and disease, and it can also annihilate him. Psychological knowledge can bring man increased certitude, dignity, and joy, and it can also enslave him. These antinomies are among the most exciting and demanding developments of our time. They have within them the seeds of ultimate tragedy or triumph. The stakes seem to be getting even higher, and the rules of the game, embodied in ethics, ever more important.

The humane emphasis also calls upon the scientist who takes part in compassionate experimentation to respect the prosocial potentialities of the people in the process of development. Such respect is mentioned by psychotherapist Carl R. Rogers, who terms it "Basic Trustworthiness of Human Nature." [16]

> It will be evident that another implication of the view I have been presenting is that the basic nature of the human being, when functioning freely, is constructive and trustworthy. For me this is an inescapable conclusion from a quarter-century of experience in psychotherapy. When we are able to free the individual from defensiveness, so that he is open to the wide range of his own needs, as well as the wide range of environmental and social demands, his reactions may be trusted to be positive, forward-moving, constructive. . . .

---

[15] Nicholas Hobbs, "Science and Ethical Behavior," in *Personality Dynamics and Effective Behavior,* James C. Coleman, ed. (Chicago: Scott, Foresman, 1960), p. 533.

[16] Rogers, *op. cit.,* p. 194.

The compassionate experimentation of community development processes makes more probable the participation of ordinary citizens in research. A productive democratization of social science becomes possible.[17]

Fourth, I have suggested that one value of the scientist is that certain values of the scientific community concerning the use of scientific method should become common values of the total community as the basic approach to the continuous assessment of action and reconstruction of values. It seems to me this is probably the meeting point of the scientist's value system and the general ideology of democracy. . . .

Certain fundamental changes in the whole orientation of scientific progress are noteworthy. Unique social science contributions are made possible for community development by scientific thinking that moves beyond the rigidities of logical positivism. It was some such revision of the modes of thought in physics and mathematics that made the atomic age possible. This whole shift of models for disciplined thought is much too complicated to be covered here. Certain aspects of what Ruth Nanda Anshen calls "World Perspectives" [18] can be mentioned, however, by way of clarifying the possibilities for research.

Among the revised emphases that open up research opportunities to community development are the following:

A tendency toward holistic thinking by way of corrective for the overreliance upon analysis into fragments. That is, the meaning of organisms and even of events is not to be reduced to the characteristics of their fragments. It is to be found more importantly in the wholes, in the total realities, in whole persons.

A realization that for objectivity the observer must be considered as part of the total situation. An observer (either a person or an instrument) affects the phenomenon being studied, and therefore

---

[17] Ronald Lippitt, "Value-Judgment Problems of the Social Scientist in Action-Research," in *The Planning of Change,* Warren G. Bennis, Kenneth D. Benne, and Robert Chin, eds. (New York: Holt, Rinehart and Winston, 1961), p. 694.

[18] This is the title of a series of books by scientists, philosophers, and others, edited by Ruth Nanda Anshen and published by Harper and Row.

the observer is also observing himself and his own impact upon whatever is "out there."

A realization that a scientist has ethical obligations in his research and even greater obligations for whatever use is made of his skills and products. His objectivity cannot be used as a justification for his employment by antisocial forces or for his engaging in an activity that is antihumane.

A willingness to accept qualitative as well as quantitative differences. Although measurements that can be treated statistically are much to be depended upon, there are other differences that are discontinuous (in quanta and in human beings) and thus understandable only as unique phenomena or organisms. Especially is this important for the integrity of distinct persons.

Finally, a realization that causality, as an explanation for events, needs supplementation by some concept of purpose. Certainly, as far as human beings are concerned, the purposes that guide the decisions of ordinary people, of the powerful, and of the social science experimenter become part of the explanation of the events that occur.[19]

A Beginning

As an example of beginning relatedness to the social sciences, we present a book review of an important contribution to community development. This review was written by two psychologists, husband and wife. It refers to an overseas program rather than to one in the United States. And it was administered by an engineer rather than a professional community developer. With all these interesting variations, it does present an excellent example of the way in which the community development process makes available basic findings about man in development.

This volume [20] is at the junction of two main highways of modern social-science research. One of these roads marks the develop-

---

[19] For a brief summary of newer emphases in scientific thinking, see Peter Drucker, *Landmarks of Tomorrow* (New York: Harper and Row, 1957), especially the Introduction and Chapter 1.

[20] Albert Mayer and Associates, *Pilot Project India* (Berkeley: University of California Press, 1959).

ment of the experimental study of the community. . . . all of this work represents the best tradition in the action research of Kurt Lewin. The task to be done dictates the working concepts, the methods, the types of reports drawn up, the type of conclusions and applications formulated. The other road represents a more general movement in social science toward the clarification of concepts as to what goes on in a scrambled and bewildering social situation, in which experimental intervention is possible only on a very limited scale, yet in which there is an achievement of some sort of broad, human generalizations that go beyond the local and particular needs to be met. We think Lewin . . . might be distressed at our implication that action research as such could not ordinarily achieve broad clarification and order but must limit itself to the attempt to derive local and particular working conclusions to be plowed back into more local and particular research efforts. There seems, however, to be coming into existence a type of social research in which wide human generalizations can be experimentally tested. This book by Albert Mayer exemplifies the trend.

When we talked to Mayer in Bombay in 1950, we felt that his tough realistic approach as an architect and city planner, and his sensitive, subtle perception of the enormous capacity of modern India to use generous, imaginative methods of self-education and self-development, could give a very rich orchestration of new ideas. India was proving to be the natural habitat for a down-to-earth practical planner, not only because of the desperateness of its need, the seething demand of the hungry and bewildered population, but also because of the availability of a trained "village-level leadership." There was likewise a general readiness to accept lower-level and middle-level types of activity that had long been underplayed in the British regime. And, finally, there was a sensitization everywhere to the critical importance of acting because of the fierce light that beats upon a really new situation in which a country suddenly finds itself (as it may once in a thousand years) ready to do something fundamentally, heroically new.

The present volume tells how Mayer and the top-level, middle-level, and lower-level leaders with whom he worked found a dynamic way in which to increase enormously the agricultural yield of a large region in northern India, while they were, at the same time, providing vast increments of education, applied science, and sheer self-respect to the millions of simple people who were ready for—they did not know quite what until they saw it taking all these forms, themselves giving more than they knew they were capable of giving. For example, we saw there a new road that had been made at night on village initiative after the villagers had spent the day on tasks agreed upon with the planner.

This volume explains how it all began in 1946, when Mayer, after war service, had the chance to talk to Premier Pant of the United Provinces in north central India, and then with Pandit Nehru himself (who, though he had no time from dawn to midnight, could still talk for a few minutes with Mayer every night as he got ready to go to sleep). Such talks convinced Nehru that the originally contemplated "model village" would be of no use, and that the thing to do was to work through with village people themselves the pressing problems of ways of increasing agricultural yield, improving sanitation, and so on. Soon it became clear that everything had to be done at once.

Mayer and his American collaborators here fit together their memoranda, interim reports and retrospective reflections, to give vivid pictures of the project from 1946 to the present. All the time they were immersed in many concrete and grubby realities. Better seed, better food for the animals and better veterinary care, better wells, better communications between villages, better schools, better adult-education programs, all had to be thought through in a staggered or even a simultaneous co-working program with well-trained, multi-purpose "village-level workers" brought in and helped to understand local village problems. Along with the Mayer staff itself, they were ready to get dirty and exhausted in bucking the most formidable of the problems, without waiting for the administrator to tell the villagers what to do. The records, kept constantly, made it possible to say afterwards just what targets had actually been achieved and at what dates. The records showed that the objective gains could be used to reduce the tax burden which had been willingly assumed by the local and more general public, so that more and more tax support could be made available for more and more ambitious expanding projects.

Does it sound easy? One must remember that the Indian villager had always been told what he ought to do. Over and over again, the narrative reminds one how wells had been built and abandoned, how tools and tractors had been imported and fallen into rust and disuse. In the new approach each step had to validate itself, and that could be done by vigilance, by careful watching for signs of faith and despair, not only by the local elected leaders ... but also by the cultivators themselves.

Now what "generalizations" does this volume yield? The most extraordinary thing in this extraordinary book is the sensitive essay it writes on "ego-involvement" and "group-involvement" without ever using these words, and the way in which these principles are thrown into relief as general psychological principles, with an even greater clarity than has been achieved in the experimental "small group research" of the West. People had to be shown that the problems were theirs and that they were soluble. The traditional teachings methods had been failing right and left, but now a practical democracy, instead of being preached, was being ocularly exhibited, day by day, as fully capable of getting the necessary jobs done.[21]

Basic Contribution

Community development helps people to solve local problems. But it can have significance far beyond the local scene. An accumulation of many community development processes might affect the progress of a nation and even redirect some of the course of history.

But community development viewed as research opportunity will also make a basic contribution to scientific thinking. New possibilities become available for social scientists and for those who would catch their spirit when they will open-mindedly learn from local dynamic processes. By pursuing this opportunity, it may be that new concepts of man as an endlessly developing organism and personality may be achieved.

The more dynamic social scientific point of view which supports community development experimentation has been summarized by psychologist Theodore M. Newcomb.[22]

> ... The late Professor Kurt Lewin used to express the experimentalist's credo by saying that if you want to improve your understanding of something you will observe it as it changes, and preferably as it changes under conditions that you yourself have created. He might have added (and perhaps he did) that there are special advantages in observing it in *statu nascendi*—that is, in watching the emergence of variables that initially were not there. Basically, even if not in the restricted, laboratory-like sense, any procedure is an experimental one if it systematically observes the emergence of phenomena under conditions that have been designed to make them emerge.

[21] Gardner Murphy and Lois Murphy, "The Ego at Work in India," *Contemporary Psychology,* No. 4 (September 1959), pp. 267–268.
[22] Theodore M. Newcomb, *The Acquaintance Process* (New York: Holt, Rinehart and Winston, 1961).

chapter 13

Relation to Social Welfare Work

Perhaps social work at its best represents the prototype of all "helping professions." Social welfare workers are the professionals whose business it is to aid people in trouble. They do this without demanding a payment in return. Neither money nor adherence to a political or religious loyalty is expected. And there is minimal demand that the beneficiaries conform to any prescribed behavior. Help is given because it is needed.

Then why is not community development the same thing as social work? Why has community development come to attention as a separate entity? Should it be a subdivision of social work (as some claim)? Why should it be regarded as a field in its own right? Is it less useful when claiming separate identity?

Because community development seeks to bring about growth in competence more than alleviation of misery, it needs to maintain its own identity as a discipline. It serves many people not reached by social workers. It uses processes and skills not ordinarily taught in schools of social work. It involves many practitioners in addition to welfare workers, encouragers who do a commendable job without benefit of social service training.

Social work can benefit, and is benefiting, from community development. But such benefits can accrue only when community development has an identity of recognition. This is true even when it operates from a base in a social agency.

Professional Recognition

For two generations or so, social work has been working hard to gain recognition as a legitimate profession. Its leaders have insisted that the practitioners in the field have postgraduate training, certified by a master's degree at least. They have been seeking to overcome several historical handicaps, such as the idea that any good-hearted amateur can render adequate service; or the widely held notion that they are the agents of the rich serving the deserving poor; or a reformist zeal to change political or economic arrangements; or a tendency to identify their work with sectarian religious evangelism; or an impersonal objectivity of social science, to which the field turned for theory. They have been working to establish the idea that their field of work is analogous to the medical profession.

The endeavor to gain recognition and upgrade standards is to be admired. It has been successful in considerable part, more so in large cities, less so in rural areas and suburbs. Generalization is difficult, however. Some of the above handicaps may be overcome in one locality, and in others not. And even in a given geographic area, professional standards vary from agency to agency.

Will community development, after becoming defined and organized, go through similar struggles? That there are dangers in the outlining of method and process, even when this is necessary, may be illustrated by the experience of social work. There is the hardening of once flexible skills into approved, labeled, and outlined procedures. There is an institutionalization of practices and services, according to the rule book. Will such hardening of the procedural and institutional arteries occur as community development also becomes an identified field? The possibility is always present.

Once any field of work, especially one that serves human beings, is conceptualized, organized, and reduced to approved procedures (we are recommending some such systematization in this book) it runs the risk of becoming inflexible and even sterile. A strait jacket of organization always imperils the practitioner's freedom of creativity. Could community development, however, minimize the probability of strait-jacketing by learning from the experience of social work?

Community Organization and Community Development

Before going too deeply into how an emerging humane speciality can minimize the dangers of institutional rigidity, we need to clarify a point about which there is some confusion. This is the distinction between community organization and community development. Community organization is one of the three major classifications of systematized social welfare work.[1] (The other two are casework and group work.) Community development belongs outside the classifications of social work. It is a process that encourages the citizen in his personal development. The encourager may be, but he does not have to be, a social worker.

Community organization is structural. It relies upon a concept of community as an already existing social system, with institutions to be coordinated. Some of the institutions to be organized are governmental or governmentally controlled—city councils, police and fire departments, schools and school boards, and numerous commissions and public offices. Others are private organizations—churches, service clubs, social clubs, and so on. But most typically, community organization deals with social welfare agencies, both public and private. The purpose of community organization is to interrelate the functioning of these institutional structures in a manner that will give the best of service to the people who need it. Attention is given to the possible overlapping of services as well as to gaps in services.

The thinking of workers in community organization is often influenced by the necessities of raising funds to support their work. In the United States most attention has traditionally been given to some united fund-collecting program, such as a Community Chest, or to working out an agreement among the campaigns whereby they will not interfere with each other. The tax-supported welfare services that have become important since the days of the New Deal also give their character to community organization. The impetus to coordination is more likely to be found in financial necessity than in sensitivity to people's needs.

---

[1] See Ernest Harper and Arthur Dunham, *Community Organization in Action* (New York: Association Press, 1959).

By contrast, community development is functional. It initiates a people-directed process that is based upon their own perception of their needs. It recognizes the necessity for the discovering or creating of a community, in a process that will utilize the existing social structures, but that will help to create new organizations and institutions when needed.

The social agencies that provide services are indispensable in a complex urban and industrial society. The organizational thinking that keeps these institutions in balance and efficient is important. But the necessity for community organization should not bar the exploitation of the possibilities for the community development process.

But the contrast made so far is with one of the conventional subdivisions of social work. Community development is related more closely to the entire social welfare profession, with which it shares a number of objectives. Both fields are devoted to people and interested in their welfare, their progress, and their ability to cope with a difficult world. Both seek to discipline efforts by the use of social scientific thinking. Both work through the concepts of community and neighborhood.

As social work hardened into prescribed subdivisions and techniques, it tended to profess the humane objectives at a verbal level and to concentrate more upon the correctness of methodology. Community development may avoid this hazard if it keeps paramount its objective, the urging of the initiative of the people and the processes by which this initiative may be strengthened. The disciplined skills in which encouragers are to be trained are those of sharing a process with, rather than bringing help to.

Contrasts

Social work early came to believe that it must function through an agency. This idea took form in either of two ways—as a neighborhood center, or as a headquarters for services. This excessive attachment to the agency has resulted in an inflexibility in adapting practices to changing times. The people served by the agency have tended to develop a special loyalty (or resistance) to it. The identification of the social services rendered with a particular building has often created the suspicion that there is greater enthusiasm to serve the institution than the people.

So all-pervasive has the "agency approach" become that community development efforts often tend to be interpreted as propaganda to build a "community center." During the exploratory phase of the community development process, especially in cities where the agency approach is familiar, an encourager must often spend much time and energy convincing the people that he is not asking them to create a "house of neighborly service" or a "community center."

The people's reaction in such cases poses a real dilemma for any helping profession, for the work must be institutionalized if the profession is to provide enough help to be effective, if it is to provide continuity in giving help. The need to serve people more than an institution makes development processes necessary. These depend upon a participant-created nucleus that scrupulously avoids ever becoming an operating agency. The dilemma is not eliminated, however, for unless some institution (or several) assume the responsibility for community development, this new field will remain a sporadic phenomenon, less than effective to deal with the great problems of our day.

The practice of social work has seldom displayed an adequate understanding of the concept of process. The emphasis, instead, has been upon the specific service to be rendered with rising standards of professional discipline. Because process has been insufficiently utilized, the responsibility of people for their development in ways that they have chosen has remained at low ebb. Social work has given attention to people, but as clients to be benefited and not as collaborators who will take the initiative in their own improvement. The benefits have gone from the trained workers to clients in a one-way flow. A relationship of cooperative search for the answers to problems might threaten the self-perceived importance of the social worker.

The community organization approach to social problems has had unfortunate publicity results. The means used to attract donations (whether from voluntary contributors, as to a community chest, or from legislative appropriating bodies) has tended to limit the kind of programs undertaken. For campaigns among voluntary givers, there has been the heart-rending appeal to help the unfortunate. For obtaining tax moneys, there has been the insistence upon defeating a rival political ideology. In gaining "public" support, it has been thought that the need for citizen participation was met by putting a few "big name" people, or good money-raisers on the advisory boards of the agencies.

Community development, when true to its method, avoids publicity that might jeopardize the process. It is, or should be, dissatisfied if it has only the support of prominent persons who can be listed on a letterhead or in promotional brochures. It should even be suspicious of any progress that is made by the use of the "natural leaders" who are recommended for community organizers. It should be much more concerned to create new "emergent leaders" through the use of the community development process.

Finally, by its devotion to health and welfare, social work has limited itself to offering specific skills that may be obtained from trained professionals. "Welfare" has seldom been interpreted so basically that it was understood to include the development of individuals who could then provide for their own welfare. Health and welfare services must be made available to the needy, it is true, but such emphasis tends to concentrate attention upon aiding the casualties of a rapidly changing industrial society. Of more basic importance is the development in these unfortunates of the dignity that accompanies competence, of the knowledge that they have the abilities and skills to do for themselves some of the things that need to be done.

Community development, in contrast to social work, gives attention to all citizens in a totality of the emerging common good. More privileged citizens work with (not for) the disadvantaged. And the disadvantaged are stirred out of the torpor induced by pauperism. This new field is devoted to strengthening in everyone the skills he will utilize to meet his own needs as well as the needs of his neighbors. Community development strives to help all people make use of professional agencies and services, to strengthen self-help.

The importance of social work is not reduced; it is often enhanced by new emphases. Agencies can discover ways to make services available to the needs of self-motivating citizens.

Mutual Helpfulness

Social work and community development have much to offer to each other. The two fields can coexist with much mutual benefit. Certain social workers can become community developers, if they will stress the original humane impulses of their field by searching for new techniques of encouragement. Community developers can utilize social services in ways that will help these services become more efficient.

The contribution of social workers to this mutual helpfulness might be clearer if those social workers who are devoted to community development were so named and designated. Then they would be less condemned by their professional associates for a lack of devotion to the standards of excellence that the profession wishes to attain. There might even grow a realization that another, and equally to be admired, array of skills is required to induce self-help. In other words, social work might become a sponsor of community development work—but not the only one.

Community developers, on the other hand, can contribute in several ways to increasing the effectiveness of social welfare work. Some of these can be made specific.

First, it will be found helpful to invite representatives of the agencies to become members of larger nuclei. These professional welfare people usually participate, not as working members, but as consultants, advisors, and discussants. They may choose not to attend meetings regularly, but they should feel at home and be accepted as participants when they are present. Many social workers welcome the invitation as an opportunity not only to advise, but to sensitize themselves to the problems discussed.

It is possible for the nuclei, and even more for the larger nucleus, to discover individuals who have special needs in a specific area of service and then to bring them to the attention of service agencies. Welfare workers often point out that people in need do not reach them until their difficulties have reached a crucial point. Nucleus members who become sensitive to the problems of their neighbors can urge them to visit clinics, to seek counseling services, or other help long before a crisis has been reached. Furthermore, when these members discover that the particular need of a number of persons has not been filled, they can ask the agencies to provide the needed service, or may even bring into existence a new agency that will satisfy the need.

Such cooperation is often received most gratefully by social workers. Numerous are the areas—rural, in small-town, but also in parts of many a metropolity—where the standard social welfare services are not available. One task for a responsible larger nucleus is to strengthen the social welfare agencies or to help create them when they do not exist.

In an emerging community the members of the nuclei can build up in their neighbors a disposition to ask for and seek professional services, rather than to wait until these services are imposed. The seeking out of services can become a matter of dignity, when the seeker has had a choice. The development of a community atmosphere in which the seeking of professional help is regarded as wise and not an admission of pauperism or helplessness can be accomplished by nucleus members.

But perhaps the greatest contribution of community development to social work will be an urging that social workers reconcentrate their attention upon persons. The people served by the workers can be regarded as more important than the refined techniques of service. Social workers will become more aware of this urging from community development when they turn attention to stimulating initiative in these people.

There is one more point at which cooperation between the two fields becomes very important. This is in the attack upon persistent poverty. In the years to come, it is to be hoped that valiant efforts will be made to bring into the mainstream of economic well-being, those who have been cast aside. Social welfare agencies will be called upon in this endeavor. But they will need the help of community development, for the alienated must overcome their inner handicaps, partially through the cultivation of their own initiative.

The most advanced industrial society has produced a new proletariat, the more or less permanently unemployed and unemployable (some of whom are young and untrained for any income-producing work), the people on relief, the workers displaced by automation and a lowering of the retirement age.

Members of the new proletariat suffer many negative reactions symptomatic of an alienation. Not the least of these is the tendency of these alienated to resist the programs and services that are designed to help them. Sometimes the resistance is justified—when the programs imply charity from superior to inferior; sometimes it hinders the development of that competence which overcomes the negative reactions.

Great skill is required of the encourager as he tries to help these victims of change move beyond their resistance to a realization of their good potential. They will develop through cultivation of their initiative, but not in response to the first or the second, or even the tenth or twelfth invitation to growth. The skill needed to overcome the resistance is embodied in the process of encouragement in community development.

Many social workers become discouraged or even cynical when their services, generously proffered, are rejected—or when those whom they have aided take selfish advantage of the generosity. Community development encouragers, however, have learned to expect negative responses, displays of ingratitude, and temporary defeats. These reactions are all considered a part of the development process, a process that requires patient understanding of how people can grow, even in the worst of unfavorable environments.

Ferment

In keeping with the dissatisfaction and the self-criticism that may be found in many helping professions, social work is also in ferment. Leading spokesmen for the profession have made all the criticisms that we have mentioned—and more. Some of the dissatisfied have looked to community development as a means of rectifying some of the inadequacies of social work, especially those that are products of a failure to enlist citizen responsibility. Others have been contributing mightily to the emerging field of community development.[2]

Those who are not social workers should look upon the achievements of the profession with gratitude. They should be sympathetic

---

[2] See the writings of Arthur Dunham, especially "Community Development," *Social Work Yearbook,* 1960 (New York: National Association of Social Workers, 1960).

to the self-examination being made by sensitive leaders of the field. Community developers especially should welcome cooperation from social workers, even if these should attempt to pre-empt the emerging field for themselves. Other professions will also lay claim to it. Let us have more, not fewer claimants. Social work has much to offer.

chapter 14

Relation to Religion

Community development processes seek to bring about changes in the lives and motivations of people. If the processes work properly, they should help the participants to achieve a more meaningful existence, to become more responsible to an expanding common good, to become more responsive to human needs, and to become more competent to live harmoniously with neighbors. These expectations bring them into relationship with religion.

We approach any discussion of religion apprehensively, not only because we cannot pose as theologians, but also because religion is a potent force and has been for ages. While preaching good will, it has divided men into mutually misunderstanding groups, and has been a historic cause for savage wars. Experts in the field can wholly disagree with each other, each with a strong assurance that his point of view alone is right. So it should not be surprising if we, too, are belabored for our nontheological approach—which may ultimately have theological implications.

In spite of the negative things that can be said about religious thinking, it is so basic to all hopes for human development that it cannot be ignored. It is potent for good as well as for divisiveness. Without the guidance of religion, any planning for the future would lack direction; indeed, without it there may be no future.

In our discussion of the relation of community development to religion, we seek to point toward the commonalities of good will that could unite the adherents of many faiths and denominations. In so doing, we will undoubtedly betray our own affiliations and backgrounds. We ask only that our peculiarities in the matter be treated with the same understanding and respect that we try to show toward others of different affiliations.

The Origin of Values

One of the points to be made clear, especially in American experience, is that "religion" and "church" are not the same. The first is that realm of thought which deals with ultimate values in life. The second is the instrument, notably in Western civilization, that gives expression to these values. Though the late Archbishop Temple was credited with stating that the best expression of Christianity was to be found outside the churches, we would insist that churches are the custodians of basic values. With all their faults and failings, they are the instruments for keeping religious thinking alive.

Values act as guides for living. These values may be openly stated or tacitly held, consistent or inconsistent with each other. They may be posed as absolutes for acceptance and reassurance or as goals for seeking and the discomfort of striving. In either case, these normative values give meaning to life. Their absence may make life meaningless.

Religious thinking, kept alive by churches, has given form to much of Western civilization. The concept of political democracy is an outgrowth of the Judaeo-Christian belief in men and women as the children of God. Art, music, and literature are tinged with religious themes—or, more recently, with the rejection of these themes. The repudiation of religious values found in modern revolts against the Western tradition, known as fascism and communism, develops not so much from the ideals as from the failure of Western nations to live up to the ideals.

The church, as an instrument for the perpetuation and expression of religious values, has had wide influence in western societies, far beyond the numbers enrolled, far beyond the political power available. Often this influence has taken the form of pioneering in response to the demands of a humane conscience. Slavery, war, and racial discrimination have been challenged by religious voices before these practices were legally condemned. Churches have led the way in setting up the helping professions and in providing such facilities as schools, hospitals, clinics, and welfare agencies.[1] Frequently these helping institutions have split away, their support being assumed by various nonchurch interests that still feel the persuasiveness of humane religious teachings.

Now an opportunity presents itself for the churches to pioneer again—the opportunity to give form and impetus to another humane endeavor, community development.

Though the system of values that has led to humane pioneering does derive from religious imperatives, the emphasis upon serving humanity does not represent the whole of religion. The emphasis on serving mankind derives from that part of religion which deals with man's relationship to man. It stems from the second great commandment given by Jesus, "Love thy neighbor as thyself."

Churchmen may bewail their lack of influence in society, or in another mood, when attendance and membership are increasing, they may boast about a "return to religion." But they would be more realistic to be aware of the influence their message carries, and can continue to carry, when it is addressed to the problems of man's living with man. Theirs can no longer be the power to dictate or demand righteousness. Theirs is the influence of an appeal to men's consciences, an appeal expressed in terms of a value system that could continue to guide development into the future.

The community development process is always value seeking. Consciously chosen development must have objectives. This is true even when the process is free-flowing and its encouragers try to avoid domination or instruction. It must have goals in the thinking of both encourager and participant citizens. These several normative directions may be contradictory, and they may often change, but, in general, they will tend to serve the chooser's implementation of the commandment concerning love of neighbor.

However, at least two great difficulties arise. First, most community developers eschew religion, not because they reject the values involved (they assume these tacitly), but because they fear any identification with partisan denominationalism. Their fear is too often justified, for many churches engage in doctrinal disputes

---

[1] See Haskell M. Miller, *Compassion and Community* (New York: Association Press, 1961).

that impede interfaith and interdenominational cooperation, divert idealistic energy into conflict, frighten citizens away, and make unavailable the good will upon which all could agree.

The second difficulty is that many religious workers are reluctant to trust ordinary people to make ethically good choices. Their working belief in the good potential that could develop, falls short of the "Basic Trustworthiness of Human Nature" described by psychotherapist Carl R. Rogers.[2] Thus, in the name of righteousness, they place major reliance upon their own ability to dominate others. They are reluctant to place reliance upon an altruistically motivated process that allows people to make choices, choices that might move them closer and closer to the proclaimed ideals.

This reluctance is produced, in part, by a lack of experience with such community-seeking groups as basic and larger nuclei. Religious workers have yet to discover that such groups tend to make better choices when they have discussed and comprehended a wide range of alternatives, and that the groups tend to develop an ability to hold an antisocial deviant to a prosocial collective decision. Many religious workers have yet to discover that they can have a new role, that of an encourager of process.

Talking About versus Doing

The community development process we have described is threatening to many churchmen, for it tries to put neighborliness into daily conduct instead of merely preaching about it. This effort is disturbing to those whose major satisfaction is found in proclaiming the message.

Talking about religious values has often become an important substitute for living them. The success of the church is too often measured by the size of the audience that comes to services, by the verbal affirmation of belief or commitment (which may or may not be reflected in behavior), by the giving of approval to the correct formulation of creed or doctrine, and by the measurement of the number of people who have heard the message on radio and television.

Word and deed need not be separated. But the church's rejec-

---

[2] In Chap. 12.

tion of the implementation of the word, as in community development, makes it clear that too often they are.

One is reminded of the apocryphal story that was told in the days when Europe was recovering from the shambles left by the Second World War. A team of Quakers was working in Germany to help the people stay alive and rebuild their lives. One of the citizen beneficiaries, impressed by good will in action, finally asked an encourager, "Why don't you people preach what you practice?"

Many churches, perhaps most, impair their own effectiveness by assuming that religion is more a matter of what one believes or professes than a matter of what one does. Yet it was the Apostle Paul who pointed out that faith without works is dead. And great religious teachers have again and again laid down rules by which life is to be lived. Belief gives the motivation, but belief must also be apparent in behavior.

Yet many churchmen take their satisfaction in words, whether delivered from pulpit or in conversation. And they are uneasy in the presence of a process that seeks to implement the ideals they talk about. Their uneasiness is the greater if the sought-after ideals are not stated frequently in orotund phraseology. The process that expedites the ideals seems incomplete to them without the blessing of approved words.

In becoming involved in community development, churches have the opportunity to put word and deed together, at least on the local scene. Their determination to proclaim a message to an audience will not cease, nor should it. But they can supplement the words with discussion, study, decision making, action, and evaluation by small nucleus groups that seek to put the ideals into practice. The participants in the process soon learn that there is great room for honest differences of opinion as to what the sermonizing calls for when carried into everyday life. Is it the fear of this discovery that makes the sermonizers uneasy about authorizing a process that implements?

The churches have tended to neglect community-serving small-group experience and to prefer multitudes in an audience. The listeners have been comforted, of course, and this is good. At other times they have been urged to better conduct, but little opportunity has been offered for experimenting with the exhortation. Frustration has frequently been the result, or indifference, or even cynicism. The utilization of small groups that seek to establish a community might give the members of the congregation an opportunity to experiment with the implementation of their beliefs.

A few churches, of course, are experimenting with small groups, but seldom have these experiments involved community responsibility. Instead, stress has been placed upon an inward-turning examination of the participant's faith or upon the way in which the group might serve the institution better.

Religious workers are no more free from overregard for the institution than are members of other helping professions. That churches are the custodians of the religious ideals does not exempt them from worship of bigness—in numbers, in budget, and in headaches. Indeed, a tendency to succumb to such objectives (and these nonhumane matters must be given consideration) causes the churches to be all the more condemned for the contrast with the ideals that they preach is readily apparent.

A religious worker, when he is trusted by the people because he trusts them, when he addresses his attention to their worries and not to institutional aggrandizement, when he helps them seek an expression of the ideals that will also serve their neighbors, and when he avoids ecclesiastical jargon and piousness, can utilize primary-group experience to carry ideals into the conduct of the people he loves.

Church as Sponsor

In the United States, the churches have a superior opportunity to be sponsors of community development. Not only are they custodians of the tradition that would make life more abundant for "even the least of these," but they are located everywhere. So ubiquitous are they that few community improvement efforts can hope to succeed unless they have church support.

But many churches encounter difficulties when they try to make their teachings relevant to local people and to local problems. In rural areas, the diminishing populations call for larger parishes that are organized around the problems of change. In metropolitan areas, increasing and shifting populations create tensions that challenge idealism to evolve new patterns of operation. In fact, the only churches that can rest secure upon traditional methods are the city cathedrals and those well established in privileged suburbs. And how secure is their comfort? Churches have much to gain from accepting responsibility for community development processes.

Equally important, community development needs to make articulate the religious values it pursues. It is incomplete, and often unconvincing, unless it quietly acknowledges its debt to the great humane themes found in religious thinking.

A NEW BREED

One kind of church acceptance of the challenge would call for finding or training community developers who will accept some nontraditional functions. Such a church community developer must meet certain requirements. He should be a person who gives greater priority to human need than to proselytizing for a particular doctrine, denomination, or congregation. He must give loyalty to the great ethical imperatives of his religion, yet acquire the skill to help all kinds of people criticize and evaluate their own conduct by *their understanding* of those imperatives. He must place greater reliance upon a process in these people's lives than upon any program he asks them to accept. He must utilize the idea that a basic tenet of his religion is a trust in the goodness that people can be encouraged to find in themselves.

All this calls for a new breed of religious worker—not the preacher, not the usual religious educator, not the pastoral counselor, not the traditional religious social worker, not the ecclesiastical organizer, not the defender of denominational orthodoxy. Even when this worker serves the community development function only part of the time, he must take on a role other than these traditional assignments. He is called upon to be a warm friend who believes so deeply in his religious values that he creates an atmosphere in which people may prove these same values in their lives. His quiet belief is a chief element in the creation of that atmosphere.

LOCAL ECUMENICITY

The acceptance by churches of a responsibility for the community development process calls for a united effort to search for the local common good. The churches cannot hope to succeed on a basis of denominational separateness. So great are the problems, so difficult is the task of finding a workable common good, that all the forces of good will need to be mobilized. This calls for and tends to create a local and practical ecumenicity.

There is no need for an erasing of denominational differences. Each church can preserve its own identity and uniqueness. Each must, in order to contribute its point of view to the common search. Usually community development efforts start with one local church, which then invites other churches to work on specific problems within the chosen area of service. In this way a larger nucleus is built up from all the cooperating churches.

In the forming of a larger nucleus, it is often found that some local churches will refuse to join the effort that seeks to be all-inclusive. The more they are convinced of their exclusive claim to righteousness, the more likely they are to become "holdouts." Such churches should not be condemned for their lack of cooperation. Instead, every effort should be made to enlist the interest of individual church members, without trying to pull these persons away from affiliation with the uncooperative congregations.

Though the result may be locally ecumenical, the basic motivation is not church unity, but the desire to serve the developmental needs of human beings. People, their needs and their potentials for growth—both economic and personal—these are central to the development process. Such an emphasis gives a new vitality to religious activities and institutions. And as a result it will often be found that people who have strayed away from churches become interested once more.

Such a multidenominational good will makes the religious heritage available for the human struggle upward. One of the central values of this heritage is diversity. Thus there is ample room for denominational differences; and these differences are welcomed and honored. For out of the discourse between differing interpretations of ideals comes the process by which the whole of civilization moves forward. Ecumenical discourse goes on at high organizational levels, but it may also take place within the community, at the level where the local churches are to be activated.

Another way in which churches can accept community development responsibility is to persuade a nonchurch institution to take the initiative that points toward local working cooperation. One such an institution in American society is the public school. The local schools, when they go beyond their thralldom to instruction and interest themselves in the educational growth of people, might become the institutional focal points for rallying the forces of good will in which the churches could join.

EXPERIMENTATION

Obviously, a community assignment for churches calls for a shift away from the tendency of each to speak with a "thus saith the Lord" finality. If religion is to become the direction-giving influence it could be, in an age that admires scientific thinking, its spokesmen must accept experimentation. That is, the determination to try out many different ways for moving toward ideals becomes another of the values of religious thinking.

The movement away from authoritarian finality is easier when the focus of attention is upon specific immediate problems. The different proposals for solutions and for the steps to be taken toward solutions, which are brought forward by nucleus participants, make an experimental approach necessary. The representatives from the different churches, while adhering to different creeds, can yet respect each other's sincerity and agree to try out one proposal after another. Their agreed-upon purpose is to determine which proposal or combination of proposals works best in service to humane ideals. Their basic agreement is not upon doctrine, but upon the determination to see the people grow toward their expanding concepts of a more generous and abundant life.

In this process, one of the discoveries made by the participants is that there are basic commonalities of good will, frequently unstated, that all may accept. These can ultimately be stated openly as guides for experimentation. There is the rediscovery, through action, of those values of good will that are held in common by members of various faiths. There is likely to be an acceptance of a new value—the experimental search for ways to implement these ideals. This approach offers a method to relieve the paralysis of uncertainty and disbelief in which the people give up trying to find favorable answers to the difficulties that overwhelm them. And a grass-roots experience that supports high level ecumenical discourse is created.

Stumbling Blocks

Some stumbling blocks that hinder the involvement of the church in community development can be pointed out in addition to those already mentioned.

When specific problems are encountered, it is easy for the religious worker to persuade himself that the obstacle is the reincarnation of the devil and to call for the believer to do battle with satanic forces. Such human embodiments of the evil that is being attacked in particular programs of study and action are numerous—landlords who refuse to rent to the members of minority groups or who perpetuate slum conditions, employers who refuse to employ people because of race or creed, upholders of white supremacy, militant Negroes, lazy and timid and corrupt government officials, atheists, communists and their defenders, liquor dealers, vice overlords, dope peddlers, purveyors of pornographic literature, and even sometimes believers in another faith. The list is endless. And many churches have discharged their community obligation by the condemnation of such "villains."

Many such targets of attack may be persons whose behavior is to be condemned. But it becomes easy to forget that the "devilish" individuals are also human beings who have potentials for good. The directing of energy into an attack may result in an insensitivity to the processes by which both the attacked and the attackers may develop in ethical sensitivity.

An overemphasis upon a single proposed solution to a problem can lead to the ignoring of the interrelatedness of all things within the common good. Thus a conclusion that the racial integration of the public schools is the only objective worth fighting for draws attention away from the improvement of education for all children. The single-minded approach to this problem may cause the citizens to ignore more basic proposals for achieving integrated neighborhoods, proposals that would automatically bring about racial balance in the schools. An idealistic program in advocacy of a single proposal is less likely to achieve a balanced idealism than the patient process within a larger nucleus.

Still another difficulty with the church's concern for social issues is the program that calls for a single great effort—the money-raising campaign for a hospital or community center, a dramatic demonstration against chosen enemies, organized pressure to obtain legislation against pornographic literature, and so on. Any of these single-shot campaigns may be justified as serving a good cause, but such dramatic efforts seldom start a process that extends over the years of development.

Often these intensive programs are justified by intellectual or theological explanations, high-level verbalizations that may be essentially meaningless to the ordinary people who are potential participants in the process. The explanations often deny to the participants the developmental experience that is possible when they follow their own logic of approach and analysis. The problem for the religious worker is to share the participants' approach, while preserving the integrity of his own trained thinking.

All this suggests one final fundamental roadblock to the involvement of the church in community development. This is the self-perception of the professional religionist, whether he is a pastor, a priest, a social worker, or an educator, but especially if his duties as any of these includes that of a preacher. Such a religious professional tends to look upon himself as a person with special knowledge (largely theological) and special authority (ecclesiastical). He thinks of himself as the man in front, the one who proclaims from the pulpit, who presides at the meeting, who prepares the agenda and advances the ideas to be adopted, who is the spokesman to be heard and the voice of the church in all local problems (and beyond, if possible). He, or his professional colleagues, he believes, must do all the important jobs, using laymen only for the auxiliary and non-policy-making functions.

His belief in his own importance makes it difficult for him to sit in the rear of the meeting and say little while the people wrestle and worry their way through their perplexities. He often finds it uncomfortable to trust them to have worthwhile ideas, good intentions, initiative, or to develop leadership ability. In short, his perception of his own importance stands in the way of his placing reliance upon the humble, yet noble qualities that may be potential in people and upon the process that might cause these qualities to emerge into usefulness. He often prefers to retain his position as a man of prominence, even in a small circle. He wants to be calleᴅ upon to give the correct formulation of the problem and its solution rather than to accept a role as a friendly collaborator who encourages others to find words as well as deeds.

And he is too prone to seek credit for his own institution, the church, as the only possible initiator of programs that may serve ideals. He easily forgets that the churches have pursued their ideals by inspiring schools, hospitals, social welfare agencies and programs, and even government to serve human needs. He needs to realize that, in community development, the churches may lead once again by urging the initiative upon other institutions, while expecting to cooperate in any joint efforts.

This is to say that preachers, too, are human. But some of them might catch the vision of the greater satisfaction that is possible when their triumphs are sought in the lives of other people and institutions and in processes of development that follow the proclaimed ideals.

The churches in the past have been the carriers of hope, a role that they can continue to perform, in spite of difficulties, in the future. If they face up to the "here and now" problems that lie close at hand, attending to the realities of the local environment and to the process by which persons can develop there, they can help people to lift themselves.

chapter 15

Relation to Education

Community development is an educational process. It is this, first, last and all the time. All else is secondary to it and must take its place as a reflection, not as the end result. Community development is not better roads, better beehives, pure water nor sanitary privies. It is something of the spirit not something material. It must reach into the deep cultural patterns of people, examining them and testing them as principles of faith. It is not a temporary, physical construction. It is a building within the hearts and minds of men, not a recreation center in the middle of a playfield. It is these things because without them it relatively matters little whether the road is paved or not, whether economically you and your community are materially blessed. It is these things because with them all physical solutions follow in their proper order.[1]

The community development process is clearly educational. It is so recognized by men who have worked long in the field. But the process is educational in a fundamental sense that goes beyond formal teaching and disciplined drill. It re-emphasizes the outcomes of learning in terms of people's lives, value systems, and competence.

---

[1] Fred Wale, Director of the Division of Community Education, Department of Education, San Juan, Puerto Rico. Quoted from *Community Development Seminar Proceedings,* Department of Health Education, University of North Carolina, May 1963.

Among the helping professions, education gave early and persistent recognition to community development—especially adult education. The Adult Education Association has a community development section. So does the National University Extension Association. And when community development is sponsored by economic, planning, health, religious, or other noneducational organization, it is accepted for the educational effect it may have upon people.

Education is defined as progressive or desirable changes in a person as a result of teaching, study, and (as some insist also) experience. The changes that come about by reason of chronological maturation or deterioration are not included.

Teaching is defined as the art of assisting another to learn. It includes the providing of information (instruction) and of appropriate situations, conditions, or activities (experiences) designed to facilitate learning.

Learning is defined as changing one's ways of acting, as a result of practice or of other intervening relevant experience. Such change in conduct assumes changes in the responding person.[2]

To the extent that the community development process is concerned with favorable developments in people, as well as with economic, social and governmental improvement, it is an educational process. Its main concern is with adults. But since infants, children, and adolescents are a part of most local accumulations of people, they must be included within the scope of community development. This is true even though these others may be served by other, more formal educational processes and institutions.

In covering educational relatedness, we lay special stress upon adult educational thinking. But we press on to cover the responsibility of the whole university and the public school.

What Do You Mean—Education?

Education is another word to be used with caution. It has a wide variety of meanings ascribed to it. Even among educators them-

---

[2] All three definitions are adapted from Ava C. English and Horace B. English, *A Comprehensive Dictionary of Psychological and Psychoanalytical Terms* (New York: Longmans, 1958).

selves, there is confusion. The word covers such diverse activities as programed instruction by machines and the creation of an atmosphere of freedom in which the learners find their own way or a highly organized system of formal teaching from kindergarten through graduate school, contrasted with casual personal contacts between parents and children in a family. Especially among those who classify themselves as adult educators is there variety in conflicting points of view.

Whenever community developers admit that they are educators, they encounter this confusion of interpretations. They may quickly find ascribed to them intentions and supposedly typical behaviors that, because they are incorrect, tend to hamper their work. The expectation that they wish to assume a schoolmaster's role, for example, can arouse resistance among adults and make the participant-initiated process most unlikely even to begin.

SCHOOLING

When adult educators seek to become community developers, they find themselves handicapped by an interpretation of education that makes schooling the prototype. This concept (held by citizen participants and by many educators as well) arises from years of classroom experience. The schooling experience began in childhood and may have continued into young adulthood. It leads many to conclude that education cannot be meritorious unless there is a teacher (human, mechanical, or electronic) instructing learners who are not so well informed or less mature. These latter look up to the schoolmaster for correction of misinformation or error. Discipline is imposed by the teacher or the institution, whether direct and harsh or gentle and disguised by cordiality. The learners respond in various ways, depending upon the attitudes they have brought to the learning experience, whether a welcoming of the opportunity, a defensive indifference, or an open resistance.

The belief that education means schooling colors many innovations that move beyond or modify the classroom. There is the teaching machine (the teacher uses the contraption to "reinforce" the proper learning that has been programed into it). There is teaching by radio and television (the teacher is electronically projected to the learner, who, whether in a classroom at school or in a living room at home, is called upon to complete prescribed lessons). There are group discussions (the teacher, as discussion leader, devotes himself to covering the prescribed material—"great books" or liberal education—but he remains the chief controller of the process).

All these procedures, and many other methods of teaching, have their places and values. But they should not be confused with the community development process, which has other objectives and methodologies. When the learners wait upon instruction, they are less likely to assume the initiative to guide their own learning. But even more, any expectation on the part of the community developer that he must instruct curtails his ability to create an atmosphere conducive to learner-motivated development.

TELLING

At this point we encounter a major block to effective community development work by educators. This is the teacher's concept of his own role and responsibility. He is likely to believe, or to act as if he believed, "Woe is me if I do not instruct." (We know; we have been teachers for many a year.) The teacher's self-dignity is undermined if he is not afforded an opportunity to tell the people about the things in which he is expert.

Teaching is likely to be defined as telling, whether by words, pictures, pantomime, books, or discussion. The full gamut of teaching, however, covers a number of things auxiliary to telling. These include the repetition of the learning in recitations or examinations, the giving of rewards and punishments according to teacher-determined standards of excellence, the giving of marks for performance, the promoting from grade to grade, and the certifying with diploma and degree upon graduation. Throughout this regimen, the intellectual goals are very likely to be stressed more than the totality of personal development. Excellence is usually defined in terms of accomplishment that can be registered on an examination paper. Sometimes the learning of sympathies for people and habits of working with them are openly disavowed as objectives. Sometimes these goals of personality growth are merely ignored. When they are recognized in formal schooling, they are usually accepted by an individual teacher, beloved but regarded as a bit queer. And his salary and professional advancement are seldom bettered by his concern for the totality of personal development in students.

Once again, let it be clear that, in formal education, we are in favor of the emphasis upon telling. We have indulged in it, and will again. There is a place for such teaching. But the community development process, considered as education, is something else again. It has a different purpose.

SPECIFIC SUBJECT MATTERS

Another interpretation of education that may be ascribed to the community developer by the citizens may even be accepted by him —if he is unwary. This is the idea that he should make instruction in a specific skill or knowledge his central responsibility.

There are many valuable subject matters that may thus be demanded of him. In dealing with disadvantaged people, he may be asked to instruct for literacy, health habits, better farming practices, or vocational skills that increase employability. In dealing with more privileged populations, he may be asked to set up classes in group dynamics, parliamentary procedure, or even in such skills as how to live in a city, how to live happily with people of another race, how to garden in backyards, how to paint and make household repairs, or how to write petitions and be persuasive in influencing the powers that be.

The paradox is that though these learnings are good and even necessary to adequate development, if the community developer allows himself to become the instructor, he tends to lose the relationship of shared friendship. And thus he curtails his usefulness for the encouragement of process.

If a specific subject matter or course needs to be taught, an expert whom nucleus members or the community developer have secured will be best employed to teach it. If no such person can be found, and the educational task devolves upon the encourager as the only person with the requisite knowledge, then the information should be offered casually, as a part of personal conversations or nucleus discussions, in which the participant-friends are free to counter with other ideas, to reject, or to modify. It is highly important that, as far as the citizens' attitude toward the community developer is concerned, the acceptance of ideas or information be on the basis of the material's making sense to the citizen, not on the basis of a teacher's authority.

The community developer, as an educator, must realize that the basic things he has to teach, in terms of attitudes, skills to work with people, competence for living, are learner-acquired more than teacher-instilled. The citizen with whom he associates as a friend, not as an instructor, is likely to accept the values that he has seen in action and in aspiration, because these values have assumed meaning for him. Long before community development was ever heard of, sensitive teachers had learned this fact. But in community development it becomes central to the process.

EDUCATING THE PUBLIC

Another type of educational enterprise into which the unwary community developer may stray is propaganda, or "educating the public." To some people, any community effort is quickly translated into a campaign of public persuasion, one which hopes to gain support for some meritorious proposal. Teachers will often deny that such a campaign belongs within the proper definition of education. But advertisers and public relations people will justify public persuasion as education. And even schoolmen will use propaganda—when they believe deeply enough in the cause they are advocating.

An additional paradox is here evident. Any nucleus may decide that "educating the public" to accept some worthy cause is important. In that case, the community developer advises and helps the nucleus to be successful in its efforts. But he does not himself become the public relations man. He may advise the members of the nucleus to get help from advertisers or other publicity professionals, the experts who know the mass-communications field. His own expertness has to do with the process of development, and within that process the persuasive campaign is but an incident. His obligation is to keep the process active and vital, so that people may learn from it, not to be a successful public persuader.

A UNIQUE KIND OF ADULT EDUCATION

The prototype for community development as education is not a classroom (inherited from childhood experience) nor a publicity campaign (in imitation of high-or low-pressure salesmanship). It is the gathering together of a small group of friends who are devoted to the local good. The community developer is an educator who becomes a friendly consultant to such a committed, thoughtful, yet active group. His role as educator consists not in his instructing, but in his quietly encouraging the process by which the involved adults become more competent to serve an expanding neighborly good.

Action Research Approach

Community developers will be more convincing educators when they are aware that their approach illustrates a pattern of research more than a pattern of instruction. They depend not upon telling and other formal instruction, but upon helping people discover the experiences that may cause them to bring about favorable changes in themselves and in others. They seek for answers, but also for development. The hope for development invites the discipline of action research.

Since in such a search the outcome cannot be predicted with certainty, the community developer is an initiator of a process that he cannot expect to control. He hopes that the outcomes will yield social improvement and simultaneously produce beneficial changes in the lives of the people. Even if he does not set up a disciplined research procedure, he operates in a spirit of research, for he is expediting a process that is seeking, but that is never sure of the outcome.

RESEARCH THAT SERVES INSTRUCTION

Encouragers of community process may, for various reasons, be wary of accepting a research approach. First, they are likely to be so busy keeping the process going that they have little time for keeping records or philosophizing about the methods used. Then, if they investigate the research in adult education that is available, they find it disappointing, for such research serves instructional rather than developmental purposes. It is directed, by and large, to the necessities of institutional instruction in classes and courses.

A recent (1962) symposium on the subject [3] points out that the research has been scarce, although it is increasing in amount.

---

[3] *Objectives and Methods of Research in Adult Education,* report of a conference by leading figures from several universities (St. Louis: Washington University, 1962).

It deals mainly with the recruitment for classes, the outcomes of formal teaching, the characteristics of those who enroll and attend, and the like. An earlier (1959) and more comprehensive study [4] covers learning, motivations, and attitudes in adults, and the methods used to instruct them, within the assumptions of institutional operation. When the authors, true to their material, discuss the community, it is in terms of the institutions involved. And community development is discussed from a community organization point of view. There is little research into the processes by which adults develop, especially the processes that are operative in normal living situations.

Stirrings of dissatisfaction within adult education circles, however, point toward a more fundamental interest in how adults learn and become more adequate persons. In a small but significant pamphlet,[5] a commission of professors of adult education point out that as a discipline the field has not yet become firmly established. Adequate knowledge about adult development, maturation, and learning is far from complete. Research for needed information about adult processes is a matter of secondary interest both to educators and to social scientists. As they point out these lacks, the members of the commission recommend systematic research, but they also recommend variety in new programs, including community development projects.

Such proposals tend to break the shackles of dependence upon instruction. They imply a dawning recognition of the difference between adult learning and teaching addressed to adults. Only if the interpretation of teaching can be broadened to cover the experiences that help people to develop can personality growth become a focus for adult education.

RESEARCH FOR ADULT DEVELOPMENT

It is relatively easy to discover how different kinds of instruction can be used to teach a foreign language or such a skill as typewriting. It is much more difficult to discover how people become more

---

[4] Edmund de S. Brunner and Associates, *An Overview of Adult Education Research* (Washington, D. C.: Adult Education Association of the U.S.A., 1959).

[5] *Adult Education: A New Imperative for Our Times* (Washington, D C.: Adult Education Association, 1961).

ethically sensitive problem solvers. The second kind of learning is of greater consequence. It has to do with the learning of fundamental personality attitudes and habits. Knowledge about the "how" of such changes must be sought through action research, for dynamic processes of growth are involved.

Years ago, research on the school learning of children was supplemented by research on how they developed. Child development came into being as a specialty that looked at the totality of the child's growth as a person. It was holistic, including not only school experiences, but also dietary and health influences, the impact of parental discipline or its lack, play contacts, and so on. Might a similar specialty of adult development arise to carry the research into the years of chronological maturity? Adult development might use data from school studies, but also learnings from experiences in family life, in work situations, in recreation, and especially from conscious efforts to serve neighbors and to grow into responsibility for the common good. That is, the community development process would be central to the totality of adult development. This fact adult educators will discover when they give serious attention to the favorable changes that can occur in people's lives.

Adult education refocused upon action research into development will carry on many educational functions, but in new contexts. It will require also many learnings from experience not provided by traditional educational practices.

It will still be important to convey information to learners, but in service to a process of development, rather than in service to a job or a liberal background or learning for learning's sake. Responsible decision making still must rest upon adequate knowledge. But more important than the evidence of knowledge that can be reflected in recitation or examination is the disposition to seek reliable information, to recognize it when discovered, and to utilize it in decisions for action. The mere acquisition of information is not enough to serve in the development of persons. Adult educators must look to supplementary learning experiences in the making of decisions and in the criticizing of the action that results.

Community development makes available to people the experiences that create the social skills needed to deal with each other, with neighbors, with experts, and with the powers that be. Some of these skills include the ability to discuss without rancor or recrimination a controversial proposal, the ability to cooperate and to take satisfaction in cooperation more than in conflict, and the disposition to accept a problem as a challenge and as an opportunity rather than as a fearful thing to be avoided. These and other pro-social skills can be learned, as a part of participation in process. Some instruction in group dynamics, and the like, can speed the learning. But such instruction should be used with caution, lest the subtle relationship of friendship between encourager and citizen be replaced by one of schoolmaster to pupils. Again, there is a need to experiment to discover which kinds of experience, and in what timing, produce the desired learnings.

A community developer is interested also in seeing shifts in the emotional orientation of the citizen, from despair to hopefulness, from self-centered values to neighbor- and community-serving values, from the timidity that clings to the reassurances of the past to the courage to venture forth into the unpredictable future. To what extent are such changes in the citizen's attitude toward life an educational by-product of his experience with process? An action research approach will help adult educators find out.

NEW VISTAS

Centering adult education upon action research in the context of community development opens new vistas—both for teaching (the kind that includes encouraged experience) and for the discovery of new understanding (about human beings in the process of becoming more competent). By welcoming such an opportunity, adult education could find a new focus in adult development. This new orientation could free adult education from its slavery to present-day demands for instruction in multiple specifics (instructions for truck drivers, courses in parliamentary procedure, and so on).

The action research approach frees the adult educator also from a slavery to a fixed location. No longer must he limit himself to the formal relationships of classes conducted in an institutional building. He is now free to go to the people wherever they are—at home, in church, on a playground, in a factory, or in any environment in which the people feel comfortable as they seek the experience of community.

Training

Most outlines of the community development process make a provision for the training of the various people involved. So do we. Many academic disciplines may be called upon to give instruction. When we indulge in such training, then, are we violating our own recommendations that basic learning come through encouraged experience? Is there an inconsistency in suggesting that those who help people to discover the skills that will enable them to develop themselves need formal instruction? An inconsistency, no, a paradox, yes—but a productive paradox. Because training for community development needs to be set up differently for different types of trainees.

PROFESSIONAL TRAINING

True to their academic limitations, most institutions that train professional community developers give major attention to the courses and the credits that can be added up to produce a certificate or degree. We have sympathy for the institutional insistence upon a proper academic background, as certified by accumulated credits. In fact, we have joined in debates over whether three more points are needed in sociology or in economics or in anthropology, ad infinitum. But these debates are endless, and any decisions are always subject to revision. So we prefer to pay more attention to the skills to be mastered, the functions to be met, and the kind of person necessary to meet them.

A liberal arts undergraduate schooling is recommended for a professional community developer. A graduate degree that stresses the social sciences (as discussed in Chapter 13) is desirable. But more important than these formal learnings are the kind of person the encourager becomes and the attitudes he develops toward people.

In giving attention to the more significant training for the professional encourager as a person, we can benefit by the recommendations of T. R. Batten.[6] He divides the required experiences

---

[6] T. R. Batten, *Training for Community Development* (London: Oxford University Press, 1962).

into two categories: Orientation and On-the-Job Training (more accurately termed, On-the-Job Learning). The first experience gives a background of information but also seeks to change attitudes in an abstract way. The second brings the trainee into contact with the process and with the people who develop through it; the information acquired is tested against reality, and attitudes are subjected to the criticism of contacts with people as they change.

A means for expediting these two learning experiences is available. It is the small and intimate group, which compares learnings, discusses the knowledges and attitudes in relation to events and to basic values, and does all this in the presence of an experienced and (we hope) wise person. This sharing experience is a seminar. During orientation, a seminar integrates the information gained from many sources, and interprets meanings as an aid in forming abstract points of view. The problems likely to be encountered later are used as (verbal) reference points. During on-the-job learning, the seminar interrelates the theory with the actual responsibility for starting and continuing processes among the people. The discussion shares the successes and failures, the new insights, the inevitable modifications of the theoretically stated points of view. In the orientation and in the seminar that examines field experience, constant reference is made to the values by which individual learners make a choice of skills and attitudes. The small group provides an arena in which these values may be critically examined and compared.

A seminar that provides primary group warmth as atmosphere for open expressions of differences of opinion is central to professional training. Such a seminar begins with the orientation training and continues throughout the period chosen for on-the-job training, but it is also useful for the unending learning that is a part of the community development process.

VOLUNTEER WORKERS

The members of a larger nucleus who will accept responsibility for working with basic nucleus groups are volunteer workers. These people often become as important as the paid professionals; indeed, without the cooperation of such amateurs, the professionals will be unable to do the job. The training of responsible and active volunteer participants is one of the chief obligations of professionals.

Again the distinction between orientation training and on-the-job learning is applicable. But in the training of volunteers the amount of time devoted to each type of training is shorter and the level of skill that is to be expected of the worker is lower. Brief periods of orientation, such as weekend programs of intensive lectures and discussion (given at the beginning of the formation of the larger nucleus and repeated from time to time), are useful. But the on-the-job encouraging of, and counselling with, volunteers, in and out of nucleus meetings, provides the opportunity for a professional to make training-in-action meaningful.

ORDINARY CITIZENS

The ultimate educational beneficiaries of all the above training are the ordinary citizens—the members of the smaller nucleus groups, some of whom will one day volunteer to lead community development work with others. But during their training they concentrate most attention upon solving the immediate problems that worry them. Such folk are initially only dimly aware of the changes in themselves that may be brought about by their learning from their experience with process.

The chief educational outcomes for these adults develop out of learnings from actions in which the learners have themselves participated. Whatever instruction these citizens receive is likely to be that offered by the consultants whose wisdom bears upon some problem under discussion. These experts come by invitation to confer with a basic nucleus group, the invitation usually being extended by the professional or volunteer worker. The worker's patient, day-by-day contact with ordinary citizens is the chief educational influence in their experience. The influence may be observed in his quiet comments, in the questions that are raised by him, in his being present and remaining silent upon many occasions. Because the worker is the kind of person he is—friendly, warm, concerned but nonpartisan in conflicts, willing to worry along with the group—his influence helps to bring about the citizen's learning through experience.

NONACTIVE CITIZENS

The dwellers in the community-to-be who are seldom, if ever, involved in nucleus activities are the nonactive citizens. Though they receive no instruction per se, and take part in little or no planned experience, they may exhibit discernible educational changes. It is possible to discover and even measure general attitude improvements in a population. There may be change from a conviction that "this is a poor place in which to live" to a pride in locality, from an attitude of "what's the use" to a conviction that "we can do something," from hateful reactions against minorities to an acceptance of them as good neighbors.

Such learning seems to come about as a result of several influences—word of mouth transmission of the ideas being tried out by a nucleus, the knowledge that the nucleus has carried certain projects to completion, publicity in newspapers or on radio and television. "Educating the public" can result from nucleus activity, but the educational impact upon a local population needs much more research.

CONCEPTS TO AVOID

As adult educators become community developers, they must avoid several concepts, of themselves and of education, that will impair their effectiveness. Some of these concepts have already been mentioned. Some that concern training for the community development process may be summarized here.

First to be avoided is the expectation that "I" can tell other people how to develop. Actually, the learnings of development are acquired almost wholly through experience, with only occasional encouragement and cautions from the encourager. And the learning, if vital, is shared cooperatively; the encourager learns from the experience as well as those he would teach.

There is also the idea that a teacher must "sell" other people, persuade them to become active, or "motivate" them into good works. Actually, the motivation for people's growth comes from within them. A community development encourager can help them to discover the worries that will galvanize them into action, help them articulate these worries, and help them strengthen and discipline their determination to act in service to their understanding of the common good.

The emphasis is upon a process of inward-originated growth. This concept, incidentally, reflects the original meaning of the verb "to educate." It means to lead out (it is assumed that there is something within to be led out). Training for community development, therefore, provides points of view and social atmospheres that, hopefully, will make actual the good potentials that are assumed to be within the learners. The skill required of the teacher then is less the ability to instruct effectively, and more the ability to provide the circumstances that expedite self-chosen learning.

Institutional Responsibility

The many educational challenges and opportunities made available by community development call for some institution to assume leadership. One institution stands out as being pre-eminently fitted for the responsibility—the university—when it will take the role. Various other agencies and institutions look to the university for leadership—government programs, churches, social welfare agencies, foundations, civic organizations of various kinds, and other educational enterprises, such as colleges and public schools.

Already many universities have departments, institutes, or research activities that could be a part of the role of leadership in such education—extension services, adult education, bureaus of applied research, and urban and planning programs. They have as well multitudes of professional schools and academic departments. These university programs might focus part of their attention upon community development by accepting responsibility for selected human laboratories, either in metropolitan areas or in regions that include both industry and agriculture. The focusing becomes meaningful in action research into the problems that worry citizens, a research that calls for an interdepartmental, interdisciplinary approach.

Two benefits to the university accrue from such focusing upon the actual problems of real people. First, there is the opportunity to re-relate the vast proliferation of academic specialties around service to human needs. Second, there is an opportunity, for those professors who are willing, to experience educational processes outside the context of formal classroom instruction, an experience that is almost always enlightening and humanizing.

Certain new attitudes and skills develop in university personnel as a result of their participation in community development. Such new attitudes may be evidenced in a willingness to listen to the people in the hope of understanding them and their problems, in a desire to adapt their learning to the people's needs and levels of understanding, even in a willingness to see the relationships between their own specialties and those of another academic department. Participation in community development makes it easier for the professors to abandon the false doctrine that anybody is ever fully trained or educated—to understand that education is not a status to be achieved, but a process that continues throughout the lifetime of the learner, whether he is an ordinary citizen or a highly trained university graduate.

Continuous training for adults, research adapted to problem solving, service to developing people, a refocusing of academic fragments, all these are opportunities for universities that become involved in community development. But the need of thousands of localities will not be met by university involvement alone; there are too many potential communities to be served. Other institutions should be inspired by university leadership. Notable among these are the public schools.

Inspiration for presently constituted public schools to take on new responsibilities will not be enough, however. The challenge cannot be met by teachers or adult educators who take on extra responsibilities in their spare time, if any. New personnel—full-fledged and adequately recognized encouragers of further adult development—will be required.

chapter 16

The Encourager

Community development is, essentially, human development. In the field of community development, the goal is to create an atmosphere in which men and women can express their inherent right to "life, liberty and the pursuit of happiness," unfettered by the chains of hunger, poverty and ignorance. The attainment of that goal must start with the basic need of the human soul to express, to grow, to build a life that will fulfill its dreams. He needs only the stimulus of understanding; the knowledge that others recognize his individuality and respect it; and the guidance that evokes his latent ability to achieve his goals.[1]

A nucleus-level worker [2] is the central figure in the drama of community development. He is the instigator of process. His responsibility is significant, but difficult, for he has a role of paradoxes. He is called upon to take actions that seem to be contradictory in themselves or to run counter to much conventional wisdom. He is a central figure who seeks prominence for others.

---

[1] Glen Leet, *Partnerships Available in the Community Development Foundation Counselor Corps* (New York: Community Development Foundation, n.d.).

[2] Compare the term "nucleus-level worker" with that used in community development for newly developing people, "village-level worker." We believe that nucleus-level worker is more widely useful for both overseas and domestic operation, and for both rural and metropolitan accumulations of humanity.

Is a nucleus-level encourager an innovator? Most people use the word "innovator" to describe the inventor, the introducer, or the promoter of a new idea. An encourager is none of these; he is rather an instigator of processes that call upon others to become innovators. He takes the initiative so that others will take the initiative.

In an age of change, the encourager hopes that people may learn to exercise more control over change, rather than to be its victims only. He expects people, through their experience with process, to discover many new ways of controlling change (that is, to innovate) in proposals that he himself has not brought forward, in proposals that are beyond his own ingenuity. He is free, in discussion, to offer his innovations, not to compel their adoption, but to stimulate the expression of ideas. He offers his suggestions as alternatives among many other alternatives, some of which he hopes will be created by the people he encourages.

Neither is the encourager a change agent, in the sense of an advocate of (to him) favorable changes. He is rather the expediter of the favorable changes that people have chosen.

Though the process may begin and continue without him, he is central to any planned and organized utilization of it. Professional nucleus-level workers of some sort become indispensable, and some institutional responsibility for employing and training them is called for, if community development is to have any impact upon the history that is lived. But if the professional workers do their job adequately, they can expect people to learn how to develop with less and less encouragement from themselves.

An encourager instigates a growth of initiative that may run away from him. For he takes the initiative in starting a process that increases people's independence from him. There is little precedent in American admiration for such a role; traditionally, those who take the initiative are expected to "sell" ideas, loyalties, programs, and merchandise, not to stir people to make decisions that meet their own perception of need.

This is the fine art of encouragement. It is carried on in the hope that each person will become more nearly the better self he could be. The process that expedites this becoming, carried out in an atmosphere of critical evaluation by ethical standards, starts from very small beginnings. Such small beginnings also run contrary to the American experience in such matters, in which the significance of a program is judged by its bigness, clamor, or the amount of printer's ink expended.

The paradoxes and dilemmas arise because the encourager's role runs counter to much of his habituated behavior and self-concept. The paradoxes and dilemmas seem less frightening, however, when the difficulties are expressed concretely and faced. Then the necessity for his changed behavior begins to make more sense.

The Institutional Dilemma

All helping professions face a dilemma posed by their institutionalization: Which shall come first—service to human beings or loyalty to employing organization? We have mentioned three kinds of institutions in social, religious, and educational work. There are many others, such as nursing, institutional medicine, public health, various kinds of government service, work for civic bodies, and even work for labor unions, corporations, and technical operations. All must confront and resolve, partially or wholly, this dilemma. But in community development, the dilemma reaches a high point. For the flexibility that is required to serve the people's needs is restricted by the pressure upon the developer to support the sponsoring institution and to follow its program prescriptions.

NOT A SEPARATE PROFESSION

Though we may have seemed to call for a new profession of community development, we must acknowledge the reality; at present the profession does not exist. For some time to come, community development will be no more than a social methodology that may be used by many helping professions. It has no institution of its own. Possibly it never will have. Perhaps it will be truer to its concern for people and their development if it is found in universities and schools, in social agencies and churches, and in various nonprofessional efforts of good will. And it might thus also remain more useful for fields of endeavor beyond those identified as "helping," such as planning, urban renewal, public relations, engineering, business, and politics, when any of these can look at people with hopeful compassion.

We would then plead that this social methodology be identified for what it is, a process distinct from the procedures used by these other professions and institutions. We would ask that those who work to bring about development of people locally be then designated as community developers, at least during the time when they are devoting themselves to the encouragement of the process. In this way the emerging field may become identified and its exponents articulate, even though they are operating within the framework of different institutions.

INSTITUTIONAL AGGRANDIZEMENT

When the social process is used by many institutions, there is an advantage in plurality and variety, but the institutional dilemma is multiplied. Each employing organization makes its own demands, many of which are incompatible with the processes of community development. For example, any institution may demand to be aggrandized, "played up," given credit; and, usually, there is pressure to follow its traditional rituals. But any nucleus may go off in pursuit of activities of its own choosing. It may make its own program; it may fail to give credit to the encourager or to the institution that employs him. Indeed, the community development encourager seeks such displays of independence as evidence of the growing initiative of the citizens. Whenever initiative is cultivated in people, there is always the hope that they will evolve their own good ideas. Part of the learning for participants comes through the making and correcting of mistakes. But such autonomy for a nucleus disturbs many institutions.

Closely related to the institutional dilemma is the problem of financial support. The employed encourager wants to keep his institution solvent, if only to preserve his salary. But if the work with community nuclei is so little heralded that the donors to the institution do not hear of it, this particular work may fall on evil days, or the institution itself be in jeopardy.

Most institutions, once they have received public recognition for their work, tend to identify with "the establishment." In the United States this usually means lining up with middle-class morality and values, with the ethic of "success," and so on. Indeed, most encouragers tend to come from such a background. Thus many encouragers must wrench themselves away from their accepted beliefs to accept the patterns of value that may grow in the nuclei. Uncomfortable as the encourager may be, an institution is even more uncomfortable when it discovers that its employees have identified with people other than those who accept middle-class values.

In addition, it is easy for the institutional demand for professional excellence among its staff workers to interfere with the flexibility that the workers require to meet citizens on their own grounds. Sometimes, indeed, the encourager who does come close to people's needs and thinking may be condemned for lowering his standards of excellence or for being disloyal to middle-class ethics.

In working with people through the community development process, it is easier for an encourager to be self-effacing than it is for him to reduce the prominence of his institution. But then, institutions, too, can change—in aspiration and in the nature of their programs. Sometimes they do this as a result of pressure (gently applied) from employees. There are some that are beginning to set up programs which call for the flexibility to meet people where they are and which will free employees to follow the stumbling yet hopeful development of ordinary people.

Over the years institutions that expedite and give permanence to a compassionate concern for people have developed. As these various institutions have become established, they have bred administrators, who, devoted to organizational maintenance and efficiency, have dominated policy. But other types of persons have also become necessary, those whose main characteristic is skill in serving human beings. In the institutions that support programs that help people, it would be wise to give recognition to both functions, the administrative and the compassionate. Sometimes the two can be combined in a single person, but typically they need to be separated. If the "organization men" can take the prominence and the responsibility for operational maintenance, then it might be possible to free others to carry the role of compassion. Community encouragers belong in this second category.

The institution's acceptance of community development as one of its responsibilities should allow its administrators to make a place for compassionate encouragers on the organization pay roll. In any large institution that serves people, there are numerous job assignments to be set up and coordinated into a total task. One of these assignments could be that of encourager of the community development process. Then a part of the administrators' obligation would be the making of arrangements that would allow the people who fill this role to do the necessary quiet job.

Nevertheless, it would be honest to admit that the institutional dilemma can never be completely escaped. It can be reduced when institutions make the community development process central to their responsibility. Then money can be raised for the support of such encourager-effacing activity, and the pressure on them to aggrandize the great organization can be minimized.

Personal Dilemma

To certain scientific purists, the relationship of the encourager to people seems undisciplined. The process and the desired results cannot be replicated by just any competently trained experimenter. There are uniquenesses of personal relationship that seem to effect outcomes favorably or unfavorably. The success of process seems to depend upon a mutual trust between the encourager and the encouraged. And then, as has already been mentioned, there comes the shock of diminishing dependence. The trust and friendship continue, but the need for the encourager's presence reduces. The experimenter begins to suspect that he is no longer necessary to the on-going process.

PERSONAL RELATIONSHIPS

There are precedents from other scientific disciplines pointing to the necessity of unique personal relationships. Psychiatrists and clinical psychologists have concluded that progress with disturbed people is dependent upon the establishment of a good rapport between the therapist and the person in need. Some doctors have reached similar conclusions even about physical disorders—many of which have a psychological component. In the same spirit, unless the encourager trusts and is trusted, unless he is acceptant [3] of people, the process cannot be expected to work.

The relationship (rapport) is one of warmth toward people, one

---

[3] The word "acceptant" is used in this connection by psychotherapist Carl R. Rogers. See especially his *On Becoming a Person* (Boston: Houghton Mifflin, 1961).

in which they come to trust him because he obviously believes in them. He is acceptant of them, as they are, but with the expectation that they will become better in a process that develops from friendship. He likes them as individuals and believes in their favorable potentials. His belief, expressed in manner, tone of voice, and activity, more than in words, tends to create an atmosphere of confidence—confidence in themselves and in the growing competence of other members of the group and in the group as a whole.

The encourager contributes to this social atmosphere by being the kind of person he is. He is imperturbable, nonshockable, quietly confident, patient, nonpartisan but devoted to people, and on the side of the good that can be shared by everyone.

There are some other points at which an encourager can learn from psychotherapeutic thinking. Some psychiatrists have adopted the concept of process (in people's lives) to replace the rigidity of older classifications of mental and emotional disorders. That is, people are no longer to be pigeonholed and subjected to the treatment prescribed for that classification. Both the disturbed person and the well adjusted person are in process of becoming. Even to classify them as abnormal and normal is to stultify some of their possibilities for development.[4] When an encourager (or anyone else who has reached a relationship of trust) treats human beings as though they were fixed and unchanging, they tend to remain enslaved to whatever inadequacies they presently exhibit—or to get worse. When an encourager assumes (and acts as though he assumes) that people are in process of changing for the better, they are more likely to improve. The opportunity for a psychiatrist, as well as for an encourager, is to create the conditions that help people to point themselves toward their improving concept of the good.

The people thus encouraged tend to discover that they are creative in ways they had not earlier expected.[5] Again, favorable outcomes seem to depend upon the relationships between the encourager and the encouraged, with favorable expectations providing the warmth that urges on to new experience.

---

[4] For a full-scale amplification of this point of view, see Karl Menninger, *The Vital Balance* (New York: Viking, 1963).

[5] Rogers, *op. cit.* See also Abraham Maslow, "Further Notes on the Psychology of Being," *Journal of Humanistic Psychology* (Spring 1963).

To the extent that an encourager starts or becomes part of a process of community development, he carries a responsibility for intervening in people's lives. He does not carry a responsibility for directing those lives, but for creating an atmosphere in which they learn to direct their own lives. The kind of person he is, and the evidence of faith in them that he exhibits, are key factors in a process that they learn to conduct.

SELF-CONCEPTS

But can an encourager be satisfied with such a self-effacing role? Most trained workers-with-people feel obligated to exhibit the skills in which they are expert. The teacher must instruct; the social worker must take care of people; the religious worker must conduct worship services; the sociologist must make community surveys; and so on down a long list. The trained person's concept of his own dignity rests upon his doing the job that is associated with his own sense of importance. Merely to understand people, to share their worries, to believe in them, and to create circumstances that will help them to solve their problems, may not give an encourager enough of a conviction of his contribution, a sense of his importance.

An encourager may even (we hope not) impose one of the process outlines we have given earlier in this book or may write and publish research monographs (as we have done). Is he not an expert, too? Yes, he is. But he is an expert in expediting a process, one that works only if the participants take the initiative away from him. As far as our outlines are concerned, these are idealized statements of what may be expected to happen. People seldom follow them point by point, because they are making the decisions. And as for writing monographs, well, some people are just incorrigible.

The desire for personal prominence tends to interfere with sensitivity to the people who are to develop. Hopes for recognition (conscious or unconscious) reduce the probability of learning along with the participants. It is better to seek the triumphs of success in the lives of those who develop. There is satisfaction in discovering such triumphs, but this is not likely to be apparent until the expectation of prominence has been cheerfully abandoned.

SENSITIVITY

An encourager needs great sensitivity to the people whom he is to encourage. He needs to understand both their frustrations and their aspirations. So important is this that the National Training Laboratories [6] make sensitivity the central core of their training for community development. Their training experience (which also serves other human relations professions) utilizes face-to-face contacts in especially created small groups. The participants, who are sophisticated (and wealthy enough to choose to come together for a week or two of residence away from their normal work and livelihood), are encouraged to become sensitive to each other and to become objective about their own idiosyncrasies.

Such training in sensitivity represents a good beginning. But it suffers from the limitations of having occurred in the environment of an artificial group, which will probably never meet again. The participants, who are necessarily among the economically privileged, report that they are better able to understand and be acceptant of their neighbors back home. But for effective operation in the context of a community-to-be, the sensitivity needs to be cultivated in many of the ordinary settings of life. Kindly and understanding relationships with a variety of people are not achieved by a single training experience. These relationships must be worked upon for the lifetime of an encourager, in various social environments and with various kinds of people.

A nucleus that addresses its attention to growing concepts of community is a most promising instrument for the continuous cultivation of sensitivity. The encourager may grow in the experience, but so may the participant citizens. Again, this is a matter for much more research. The keeping of records and the analysis and evaluation that follow the record keeping provide data and a procedure for such research.

No encourager ever reaches a sufficiently discriminating and wise sensitivity. He is concerned for his self-training for as long as he works with people. It is his responsibility also to help the participants in the nucleus to increase in the kind of nonsentimental

---

[6] Of Bethel, Maine, and Washington, D.C.

sensitivity that serves a broadening concept of the common good. All this represents a continuing self-discipline for the encourager and a kindly understanding addressed to participants.

In constantly seeking to increase his sensitivity, an encourager is faced with the necessity of abandoning an old human failing, the tendency to nominate scapegoats. He needs to discipline himself to seek out understanding rather than to assess blame. When things go wrong, his first inquiry should be, "Have I made some mistake?" And if there is any laugh, it is on him, on the pathetic human race, on unpredicted events that impede the process, but seldom on the nucleus members or on favorite villains in or outside the community. If the process falls short of the expected results, the fault is to be looked for in forces beyond the control of the encourager or in his own failure to be sufficiently sensitive, wise, and skilled.

We have insisted that an encourager's sensitivity needs to be discriminating and balanced. It should never lead him into total identification with the points of view and prejudices of the people whom he encourages. It is possible to be sympathetic and helpful without becoming involved in their fights. It is possible, but it is difficult. The sympathy he shows is one that has compassion for all suffering humanity but does not join in enmity against scapegoats (who are also part of the human race). The difficulty arises when the encouraged people conclude that the refusal to hate along with them means that the encourager is no longer accepted as a friend. It becomes necessary for him to hold to a nonpartisan empathy even in the midst of such misinterpretation, in hopes that an increase in the sensitivity of the participants will, in time, bring about a more accurate interpretation of his sympathies.

DO-GOODER IMPULSES

All community developers suffer from another dilemma, which is as old as the impulse to help people. This might be termed "the frustration of the do-gooder." Since encouragers have humanitarian motives, they have, or rapidly acquire, ideas about the "correct" improvements people "must" accept. They set out to bring the benefits they have chosen, and then they find the potential beneficiaries unwilling to acquiesce. In an extreme form, the do-gooder becomes desperate because he concludes that the people are so apathetic, stupid, or badly motivated that they will not or cannot do his bidding.

When the encouragers of community development make process central, however, the do-gooder frustration is diminished. Citizens learn to modify their motivations, but at their own pace and by their own choosing. Emphasis upon process makes less compulsory the improvements that encouragers "know" are good for people. But even so, the frustration is never wholly eliminated.

The emphasis upon predetermined improvements and the reliance upon process represent extreme poles of a scale of operational influence. Few community developers, including the writers, fully escape do-gooder impulses. The seeking of acquiescence to "my" good ideas is ever a temptation. But some developers, including the writers, have been attempting to make clearer a method that seeks the strengthening of problem-solving initiative among the beneficiaries of development.

HOW MUCH INFLUENCE?

A final paradox needs to be mentioned. It has to do with an encourager's concept of his influence. He may be instrumental in bringing about the fundamental changes in people's lives that make them more ethically competent citizens. At the same time he must recognize that his voice is a feeble one among the cacophony of influences that exist in modern life.

An encourager wields one very small influence in the midst of a confusing complex of forces. The process he hopes for may never start, may be stopped after starting, or may be diverted to undesirable purposes by extraneous events and circumstances. While almost miraculous changes may occur in people (we have seen them occur time and time again), he must also be prepared for the disappointment of poor response.

We have seen the process fail to start because no one on a local scene has had the time or the energy or the imagination to act. We have seen brave beginnings come to naught because early emergent leaders were transferred (a minister leaves for a distant church, an industrial manager is reassigned to another plant, and so on). Sometimes a too rapid rotation of personalities has hampered the continuation of process. Sometimes political events have discouraged people or have drawn their loyalty away from a non-partisan nucleus. Sometimes the sponsoring institution has interfered with the autonomy of citizen-directed processes. All these extraneous influences remind the encourager that he had best remain humble.

The humbleness is illustrated even in the successful episodes of a nucleus. At such moments of triumph, the participants will characteristically take the credit for themselves, rather than compliment the encourager. And this is as it should be. For any genuine accomplishment should come through the initiative of the citizens. To grow in responsibility, they should be conscious of their achievement.

A paradox of attitude can be stated with poignancy this way: Despite his awareness of his feeble influence and of the risk of failure, an encourager enters every new social situation with full confidence that the process will bring near-miraculous changes in the lives of the people. Frequently, the process does bring such changes, but favorable outcomes can never be guaranteed. When they fail to occur, the encourager retains his objectivity to analyze why. He makes renewed efforts through himself or through others. Or if the people or he himself is not ready, he may bow out. When favorable changes do occur, he should be insightful enough to recognize that these represent real achievements to the people involved, even though they may not be the outcomes he sought. And then he disciplines himself to accept the favorable changes calmly, with the assurance that he "knew" all along that they were going to happen.

An encourager, if he exhibits scientific objectivity, is even denied the satisfaction of self-congratulation. Even when the favorable changes appear in people's lives, he must acknowledge that these were not caused by his efforts. The people involved changed themselves. Or the triumphs of development came as a phase of the process. He was a participant in, but not a director of, that process.

Questions

Many questions are asked about the community development process, the answers to which can only be given in terms of the encourager's role.

Isn't there a difference between community development as the improvement of local facilities and as personal growth of people? Yes, but the second comes as a result of people working to accomplish the first.

Will the process work for all people? For all kinds of populations, from the most depressed to the most privileged, from the vicious to the ethical, from irresponsible and rootless folk to those with much local loyalty? As yet, we do not know what limitations may be set by the initial conditions and attitudes of those who are to develop. Most recorded experience comes from disadvantaged and rural people. But research data is beginning to be collected from economically favored folk and from urbanites. It comes from experience with slum dwellers, but also from comfortably fixed people. Today the need for growth through community experience is universal.

Among the populations for whom the experience with process is only beginning are the dwellers in slurbs (those sprawling exurban slums for the affluent), the residents in urban renewal projects (high-rise and low-rise, low-income and publicly subsidized, as well as luxury type), and such microclassifications among the general population as the aging, racial ghettos, school dropouts, and rootless refugees from somewhere else.

What about pathological people? Are there individuals in any population who will not respond to normal encouragement? Do not such people require the specialized services of psychiatrists, hospitals, and perhaps custodial care? Persons outside the normal range cannot be expected to join a process of development that attracts the average. But we do not know what the limits of the normal range are until we have had further experience with encouraged community development that improves individual lives.

We suspect that many people who have been hospitalized or institutionalized can benefit by nucleus experience after therapy or special education. We know of delinquents, blind persons, illiterates, those on relief, those suffering from mental disturbances, who have moved up the scale of development sufficiently to require special help no longer. There will always be a need for social welfare, health, and psychotherapeutic services. Many specialists who supply these services will welcome community development processes, in the hope that these processes will lighten their loads. But more experimentation is needed. Might the dividing line between normal and abnormal be changed by development experience?

What about transients? Is not community development dependent upon people who are more or less permanent residents in an area? It is difficult to provide an adequate answer. Some workers with agricultural migrants have found that some foot-loose people have a home to which they return for a few months of the year. There an encourager might start his work. In other instances, the encourager may be able to seek out a few more stable residents who could take responsibility for helping the transients become more permanent. More work with wanderers is needed. Privileged migrants need attention as well as victims of poverty.

What do you do if the initiative you stir turns against you? A personal attack upon the encourager is always a possibility. Every encourager should be prepared for such an eventuality. When it does happen, he must re-examine his own behavior. Has he made mistakes? Or are the people "taking out" on him their frustrations? Or are both explanations true?

Whenever people come anew to responsibility, they may blame their errors upon some convenient victim. They may resent anyone who can be interpreted, by their thinking, as an authority. They may transfer their irritations against historic dominators to an encourager who means to be kindly and flexible. The best recommendation for him is to bear the resentment cheerfully and wait until new events present an opportunity for the development of more favorable attitudes. Often a catharsis of past frustrations is a stage in the developmental process.

What do you do if people turn against your program? They should, if the encourager has a program he is trying to impose. Otherwise the program they turn against is their own. And they have every right to change their minds. This is one way they learn.

What do you do if people turn against the institution that employs you? This is more difficult, because the encourager's job and income may be jeopardized. Institutional policy should allow for such possibilities, but too often the policy makers are not that generous. The encourager can use his influence (feeble though it may be) to persuade his employers to allow for such episodes. And though nucleus members may make mistakes, if they can be encouraged to discuss freely and learn from experience, they usually come to have an enthusiasm for the expediting institution.

As institutional policy makers come to understand the processes of community development, the administrators tend to admit that all human beings (themselves included) are fallible. Then the people who develop can be allowed to criticize the specific actions taken. And why should they not? Such criticism of an institution is not incompatible with loyalty to it.

What if people choose to do immoral or antisocial things? Single isolated individuals or predatory small gangs may make such negative decisions. But nucleus groups that openly seek the responsibility for the common good seldom do. We have worked with many such groups and have yet to encounter one that consciously preferred a less moral act to a more moral one. Three provisos are necessary, however. First, the moral choice is always one that reflects the ethical understanding of the group members, rather than the preference of the encourager. Second, several alternatives for choosing need to be examined in open discussion. Finally, there is a greater assurance of a moral choice if the possible consequences of each alternative have been examined in the light of stated values. Hasty decisions may be unwise or immoral. They become more ethical as a result of discussion in which the encourager joins.

What if the people refuse to respond to encouragement? We have yet to find a population in which there were not at least two or three who wished to move ahead. An encourager starts with these, and hopes that others will join later.

Don't you have to "motivate" people? Yes, if an encourager believes it his obligation to persuade people to adopt his proposals or his institution's program. If he places reliance upon encouraging a process, he counts upon the participants to find motivation within themselves. His responsibility comes down to assuring the people that they can do some socially good thing they wish to do. He helps them find ways to carry their desires into action. If he finds himself "motivating" people, he had better be suspicious of his own motives.

In reality, the encourager should realize that the participants in nucleus processes go through periods of enthusiastic action and weariness. He tries to warn against hasty decision during the periods of great energy. He tries to curb his own impatience during the periods of quiescence, realizing that if he maintains his friendly contact to help the participants move when they choose to do so, they will overcome their reluctance after a time.

What do you do when the problems that interest the people are purely personal? When their interests reflect no concern for the common good? We have encountered this, too. An estimated 90 percent of the responses in the exploratory period will reflect only personal grievances. But perhaps 10 percent of the responses will have a tinge of respect for their concept of the all-inclusive good. An encourager draws attention to these prosocial motivations and treats the others as complaints to be listened to, but not to be utilized as a basis for process.

Is hatred of a common enemy necessary as a beginning for action? No. Certain encouragers use such a common indignation as a spur to cooperation. But our experience, and that of most community developers, leads one to believe that there is latent good will in any population. With skillful exploration for that good will, a process of positive development can be started. Community action that involves conflict against someone limits the spreading inclusiveness of the community. That which utilizes good will starts a process that anticipates no limits for cooperation.

Can a process start unless there is some crisis to spur it on? Often community development will begin as a result of a disaster or of some other emotion-stirring event. We believe, however, that if disaster-born initiative is the only motivation, the process will be short-lived and addressed to a single accomplishment. Our experience with many contrasting populations leads us to believe that the frustrations and the hopes for betterment accumulated from crises of the past are a sounder basis for process.

How can you tell when people are ready to start a community development process? There is no way to predict. The only way to discover readiness is to start the exploration and see what happens.

But don't you, as an encourager, have some objectives for the people other than the reliance upon process? Specific answers to specific problems, no. Objectives in terms of their growth as persons, yes.

Don't people ascribe false motivations to you? And aren't these usually uncomplimentary? Yes, this almost always occurs, often in the form of accepting a stereotype of how a teacher, a pastor, a social worker, a government bureaucrat, or a "do-gooder" is supposed to act. That an encourager should be interested in people, in their common good, in their development to self-control, is incomprehensible to many people. Many otherwise kindly people refuse to believe any such "unlikely" story. So they create all kinds of "explanations" of why the encourager is there, of why he is giving time to serve the good of everyone.

An encourager avoids becoming defensive when he encounters these ascriptions of unworthy motivations. He quietly corrects each one as it comes to his attention. The people may go through numerous uncomplimentary explanations of his conduct, some contradictory to earlier ones. Finally, they may accept him for what he is—provided he is generous in motivation and avoids self-congratulation or a better-than-thou attitude. He makes it clear, again and again, that he simply wants to help the people make progress in the solution of their problems.

Isn't there a danger that a (larger) nucleus will turn into an instrument of power? And then will it not attract the power-hungry rather than the potentially altruistic? Yes, this is a possibility that calls for vigilance. But it is not probable as long as the nucleus avoids becoming an operating agency, an institution, a part of government, or a supporter of partisan political causes. The ideal nucleus will be a voice of a local collective conscience, forever sensitive to the unmet problems of the people, forever appealing to the powerful with the persuasiveness of trying to be ethically intelligent.

Won't some people use the process as a means for gaining political ends or personal prominence? May not encouragers themselves be tempted? Yes, there is always a danger that a nucleus will be misused. The danger should be acknowledge openly so that the members of the nucleus can be alert to their own and even the encourager's temptations.

The final crusher is more frequently heard as an accusation than as a question: *"You, as an encourager, are just a manipulator. You are deviously inducing people to do as you wish, while you convince them that they are following their own decisions."* This is the accusation that infuriates conscientious encouragers, especially when their earnestness has overcome their sense of humor. The accusation comes from critics whose method of work with people is manipulative, from critics who find it difficult to believe that any initiative to cultivate initiative in others is possible.

Since encouragers, too, are human, they are prone (even as you and I) to welcome agreement with their beliefs more readily than decisions and actions that challenge these convictions. They are likely to accept agreement as evidence that they were right all the time. When the encourager is aware of this human frailty, it becomes easier to guard against it and to admire independent judgment as evidence of the success of process.

The Encourager as Person

In summary, we are trying to avoid a list of traits that an encourager should possess. Instead, we are seeking to state the characteristics he should seek to exemplify—and forever fall short of attaining.

An ability to put himself in other people's shoes, to see things from the other person's point of view—while retaining his own convictions.

A willingness to avoid prominence, or to start with it and then retire as other people grow in initiative and confidence.

An "inner directedness" of conviction that holds so surely to his own values that any emotional disturbances or demands for conformity are less likely.

An ability to listen with attention and empathy. The skill to adopt the manner, make the gestures, say the word that will invite the other person to examine his own inner thoughts and best motivations.

A deep and abiding faith in the probability that other people will become better if encouraged with sufficient skill—and this despite evidence that, at any given time, these people are apparently hopeless.

An unshakeable conviction that there are processes by which this better becomes more operative in the lives of the people. A faith in the people calls for a faith in the effectiveness of a process of growth that they carry on cooperatively.

A freedom from fear of new ideas or even "crazy" proposals.

A conviction that a group growing in responsibility will learn how to deal with such "far out" suggestions.

The skill to feed in ideas, questions, alternatives, without dominating or seeking credit. The purpose is to expedite the process of development for persons.

An acceptance of conflict as an inevitable aspect of development. A welcoming of differences of opinion that makes possible an invitation for others to be unafraid of conflict.

An ability to marvel at the unexpected, and not be upset by it.

A tendency to discover great significances in humble events.

A freedom from impatience when the people fail to take responsibility, coupled with tactful skill to draw the attention of a group-for-growth to the necessity for decision and action.

A willingness to work quietly with little or no publicity, yet to be skillful in helping people to gain publicity when they have decided that this will expedite the process they are helping to conduct.

More concern for the achievements of people than for the glory of the institution that employs him.

A willingness to find personal satisfaction in the achievements of other people—even though this may mean lack of credit to himself.

If these characteristics sound too idealistic—they are. No encourager we have ever encountered has exhibited all these virtues. But all who have been worthy of the name have found satisfaction in striving to attain them, and in cultivating a compensatory virtue:

A conviction that if other people are reluctant to change inappropriate habits and attitudes, so is he. This amused awareness of his own limitations should be sufficiently robust to allow for continued striving to become a better encourager of growth in others. That is, he forever experiments to strengthen the prosocial even in himself.

APPENDIX I

Community Development
in the United States

APPENDIX II

Bibliographies

appendix I

Community Development in the United States *
(AND IN CANADA AND PUERTO RICO)

Certain basic human processes are discoverable in descriptions of community development activities all over the world, whether addressed to the needs of the underprivileged or the privileged, whether to people in a non-Western cultural setting or to people in the United States.

Though these basic themes of human development are discoverable, they are not obvious. A discerningly patient search is required.

A first impression from the descriptions is one of great variety in methods and interpretation. Many authors of handbooks, of laudatory articles, of appeals for financial support, and even of research studies, write as though their particular methodology were the only one. Some refer vaguely to "the principles of community development," as though there were agreement amidst the confusion, but usually saying or implying that their outline of proce-

---

* The bulk of this article was originally published by the Department for Community Development, School of Social Work and Community Development, University of Missouri, in a pamphlet, "Currents in Community Development." Copyright by the University of Missouri, 1964; Library of Congress Catalog Card Number 64–64444. Used with permission of the University.

The first article in the pamphlet was entitled "Currents in Community Development in Newly Developing Countries," by Arthur Dunham. The second was the present article (with some modifications) by William W. Biddle.

dure embodies those principles. This isolation of programs and
authors from each other is especially observable in the description
of work in the United States.

A second impression is that community development is immensely popular. "Everyone" pushing for social improvement
seems to be eager to utilize this methodology, or at least to apply
the term to the work he or she is doing or advocating.

We shall try to classify a great many programs operating in the
United States as a preliminary to making the common themes of
human development more explicit.

The Penalty of Popularity

If community development (variously defined) is popular, it suffers
from the confusions of popularity. Consider a few of the meanings
with which it is used. Community development may refer to:

The acquiring of visible installations (homes, apartments, stores,
highways, schools, churches, hospitals, sewage disposal plants,
water systems, parks, and so on) that would supposedly improve
local life.

The providing of better services for people (improved teaching
in schools, social welfare, police and fire protection, library services,
recreation supervision, and so on).

A raising of economic levels, usually average incomes, by improved farming practices, the introduction of new industry or
tourist trade, and the acquiring of skill to be employed in the bet-
ter-paid occupations.

A means for developing people to higher levels of cooperative
competence, an actualization of good personal potentials through
the experience of working together.

A means of conflict for the underprivileged to put pressure upon
the powerful, in order to gain their rights or new privileges.

A methodology of conciliation that maximizes cooperative good
will. People of different privilege levels learn to work with each
other in mutual helpfulness.

A means for enhancing the privileged position of those who
already enjoy privilege. The local scene is improved in such a way
as to benefit the wealthier and more powerful elements in a population.

A type of activity best adapted to rural life and towns or small cities.

A type of activity necessary in metropolitan areas, in city neighborhoods, urban renewal developments, urban area rehabilitation programs, and so on.

An activity that utilizes a social system called a community. This entity, "the community," makes decisions, assumes the initiative, can be called upon to participate in development.

A process by which people learn to create their own experience of and sense of community, because these have been or are being lost in modern times.

An activity that is task-oriented. That is, it serves some job-to-be-done that is chosen to meet a specific need.

An activity which is education-oriented. It is one kind of adult education. The task is incidental. The education of the participants is central. Education may call for instruction, or learning from experience, or some of each.

An activity that is propaganda-oriented. Its main purpose is to win people over to some good point of view or practice (that is, good nutrition, better health habits, learning to read if illiterate, or learning new vocational skills to become employable). CD is then thought of as a tool to serve good purposes.

A process that is research-oriented. Research may be thought of as primarily an accumulating of data about problems or about people, or it may be looked upon as action research that both expedites the development and provides information about processes of change in people.

A process that can be reduced to a formulalike outline and put into a handbook-to-be-followed.

A process that is free-flowing and unique to each social situation. Any outline of a development pattern must allow for flexibility, depending upon decisions made by the participants.

Those differing interpretations are not all contradictory of each other. Some are mutually exclusive, but others can be combined for a broadened understanding. Practitioners are usually so unaware of each other that they fail to seek the broadened scope that would increase usefulness. An examination of the wide spectrum of programs and points of view may help practitioners to discover what CD could be at least upon the domestic scene.

Contrasting Programs

There are various ways to classify domestic CD programs and writers about them. Most such categorizations are likely to reflect the bias of the classifier. The one that follows was chosen in the hope of minimizing that bias.

Bias will also be reflected in the selection for inclusion and exclusion. There are no clearly defined boundaries between the emerging field of community development and other "helping" professions and services. In general, the justification for inclusion in our list is that those who conduct the work say that their programs are community development (or study or service or education)—either because they have an organization or section of an organization with such a title or because they claim to use CD to expedite whatever else they are doing.

Academic Connections

There are approximately thirty academic institutions or systems that carry on some kind of community development, as defined. The number cannot be made more exact at this time because programs fade in and out, depending upon who heads them at any given time, the decisions made by administrators, and the availability of funds (often from some source outside the regular budget, from foundations or other special donors). And emphasis may shift into or away from CD.

Most universities that are active in this field offer a consultation service. The institution makes available the field services of experts (either those wise in subject matter, or expediters of process), handbooks or guides for development, and such items as newsletters or library materials.

Among the universities offering such help are:

University of Arizona, graduate study with emphasis upon Anthropology, Sociology, and Public Administration.

University of California (Berkeley), general consultation with special emphasis upon public health and certain urban improvement projects. Offers annual seminar on "Principles and Practices of Community Development" for foreign participants.

University of Chicago, Industrial Relations, Human Development and Action Anthropology. (This latter carries on projects similar to those ordinarily clasifsied as CD.) Some time ago, the university carried on neighborhood CD activities, but these have tended to disappear in recent years.

Columbia University, Teachers College, Adult Education emphasis.

Cornell University, research on the economics of rural life. Ph.D. degree in Rural Sociology with emphasis on CD.

Earlham College, services that led to research for undergraduate and graduate students. Program terminated. Now service-centered.

University of Georgia, generalized Area and Community Development.

Glenville State College (West Virginia), area and community improvement, with emphasis upon developing underdeveloped regions.

Goddard College (Vermont), services to smaller centers in New England and undergraduate training.

Harvard University, The Department of Psychiatry (The Laboratory of Community Psychiatry) and The Department of Social Relations.

Illinois College, services related to undergraduate courses in Sociology.

University of Illinois, strong emphasis upon architecture, engineering, and physical structures, with some human-centered material in agricultural extension work. Emphasis upon small towns.

Kansas State University, community services, continuing education, and area development.

University of Kentucky, community survey research and on-campus conferences.

Merrill Palmer Institute (Detroit), CD related to childhood and family development.

University of Michigan, Program of Community Adult Education. Graduate work for degrees with emphasis upon CD. Institute for Social Research includes Group Dynamics and Action Research. School of Social Work previously offered summer seminars in CD.

Michigan State University, Continuing Education and attention to physical construction and governmental problems. Sociological and Economic Research. Extension focus upon social conflict and land-use. Graduate degrees in Sociology and Anthropology with area of concentration in CD.

University of Nebraska, CD related especially to improvement of schools.

University of New Mexico, service in connection with training for young people entering the Peace Corps.

City College, The City University of New York, research into problems of city neighborhoods.

New York University, graduate programs in urban and regional planning. Leadership training for community action.

Northern Michigan University, health and community improvement in a less developed section of the state.

Ohio State University, school services mainly, with also some emphasis upon physical improvement.

San Bernardino Valley College (California), Adult Education with emphasis upon community discussion.

University of Saskatchewan (Canada), services to communities in a province that is developing economically and in other ways.

University of Utah, work with Indians. Urban emphasis; sociological research.

University of Virginia, services to communities in Virginia and neighboring states. A pioneer program originally guided by the husband and wife team of Jess and Jean Ogden.

Virginia Polytechnic Institute, one of several universities in Agricultural Extension that have pushed CD. Some others are Arkansas, Wisconsin, West Virginia, and Missouri.

University of Washington, general consultation to meet community requests. Emphasis upon community self-study.

University of West Virginia, Appalachian Studies and Development, in addition to agricultural extension.

University of Wisconsin (Madison), in addition to Agricultural Extension. Economic improvement under General Extension and Urban Studies.

University of Wyoming, Adult Education emphasis.

Several graduate schools of social work have been edging over toward community development. The problem they face is a nostalgic loyalty to community organization.

Special mention should be made of two universities that combine consultation service with graduate (master's) degrees specifically in CD. These are the *University of Southern Illinois* and the *University of Missouri*. At SIU, the academic and the field services are separate programs. At Missouri, the academic, research, and field and international training for CD are embodied in the Department for Community Development, School of Social Work and Community Development.

Some others need mention because of a new stress upon Urban CD or the training of urban agents to carry on development work in metropolitan centers. Some are the *University of Oklahoma, Rutgers University,* the *University of Wisconsin* (Milwaukee), and the *University of Delaware.*

Still another program needs special attention because it is such an outstanding demonstration of good CD consultation and encouragement. It has produced process research. It lacks a university or college connection but belongs within the academic classification since it is affiliated with a department of public schools. This is the *Bureau of Community Education* on the *Island of Puerto Rico.* The population served is largely rural, but the people are developing rapidly into an industrial economy, with rising economic and social standards. The CD program represents the human development phase of one of the most successful improving areas of North America, if not of the world.

Then there are two national academic organizations with active CD sections, the *Adult Education Association* and the *National University Extension Association.* Representatives from CD departments of many educational institutions will be found as members of these national bodies.

The academic classification would not be complete without referring to the work of the *National Training Laboratories* (Bethel, Maine, and Washington, D.C.). This organization, formerly affiliated with the National Education Association, does not offer direct services to communities, but trains community leaders and professionals in CD skills. It is not affiliated with any single university, but offers group laboratory experience to academicians and community leaders and carries on group dynamics research that serves CD. Numerous faculty people from the universities and colleges already mentioned have benefited from the training carried on by this independent organization. Its training stresses the increase of sensitivity to other people and objectivity toward one's own weaknesses, in small-group context.

Other Services That Encourage Local Development

1.   There are many organizations and agencies that contribute importantly to CD. Some have been set up for this purpose only; others have taken on the service as an aspect of other purposes.

First are those that focus on economic health and the improvement of the business atmosphere. In addition to some educational programs already mentioned above are a number of nonacademic services.

The *Chamber of Commerce of the United States* publishes an extensive and excellent series of "how to" pamphlets addressed to a national audience. In addition, various state chambers put out material and even carry on some such local projects as community surveys, which might lead toward developmental activities. The *United States Junior Chamber of Commerce* has a U.S. "Jaycee" Community Development Program (with American Motors). This program works through state offices on down to the local level, providing practical useful guides and advice. The *Junior Chamber of Commerce International* (with the help of Pepsi Cola International) also has a series of pamphlets and an advisory service for communities that seek improvement. Although addressed mainly to nations other than the United States, the help is useful on the American scene.

Then there is the *National Clean Up, Paint Up, Fix Up Bureau* (with the Paint, Varnish and Lacquer Association), which publishes "how to" guides. These are not limited to the kind of improvement mentioned in the title of the Bureau; they include recommendations for a Year-Round Community Development Program.

Various corporations carry on programs of encouragement for community improvement. The interest for some of these is regionally oriented, as is the case with electric utility companies, especially in rural areas. Some have offices with national interest, *General Electric Company, Kroger Supermarkets, Sears Roebuck.* Some of these do no more than give financial grants; some offer prizes for achievement; some have bureaus that offer consultation help, or build up local community loyalty.

2. A second classification includes organizations of more general civic interest. There are community councils throughout the country, inspired by universities, councils of churches, state CD bureaus, social welfare organizations. Or some arise spontaneously. Sometimes such local groups as Parent-Teachers Associations, or YMCAs or YWCAs become the originators of local community councils. The YWCA has given national attention to such efforts.

There are more specific national organizations which have programs of encouragement. There is *ACTION, the American Council to Improve Our Neighborhoods,* which issues literature helpful especially for metropolitan areas. Then there is the *General Federation of Women's Clubs,* which carries on an annual contest that gives awards to communities for making the most progress in development during the preceding year (with the aid of the *Sears Roebuck Foundation*).

3. Another characteristic form of CD is found in services to disadvantaged people. This takes several forms, some of which are quite incompatible with each other, though all stress the principle of self-help for the underprivileged.

One point of view emphasizes conflict. Organizations which stress conflict such as the *Industrial Areas Foundation* usually classify themselves under the term "community organization." But certain of their followers describe this emphasis as community development. The confusion arises out of poor definitions. There are other conflict organizations with even less of a community-building purpose, *CORE (The Congress of Racial Equality), NAACP (National Association for the Advancement of Colored People),* and some others.

Special mention should be given to the *SCLC* (Southern Christian Leadership Conference) which teaches methods of nonviolent conflict to the end of achieving community reconciliation.

In contrast, are the national programs that stress self-help through cooperation. There is the *Save the Children Federation* and the *Community Development Foundation* (an affiliate of the Federation). These encourage local programs of community development in order to benefit children—especially in areas of poverty, overseas and in the U.S.A. The *Board for Fundamental Education* also serves people in less-privileged areas, but with more stress upon directive instruction. One of its greatest triumphs has been the cooperative building of better homes, which called for the teaching of construction skills.

Certain American Indian organizations have been turning their energy less toward pressure lobbying to gain their rights and more toward the self-help that calls for community development. Among these are the *National Congress of American Indians* and *American Indian Development, Inc.* The *Federal Bureau of Indian Affairs* has welcomed this shift of emphasis but has not offered much in the way of consultation or guidance material to expedite the CD. Certain tribal groups have moved ahead with their own initiative, especially among the Navajo. Their progress in self-development has been noteworthy.

The *Council for the Southern Mountains* carries on some work in CD. This usually takes the form of advice to local people and of laudatory descriptions of local initiative.

The *Ford Foundation* has stressed an urban emphasis that gives support to CD. In addition to universities, several cities and one state have received grants for programs. Among these are *ABCD, Action for Boston Community Development,* a mobilization of public and private agencies that seeks new approaches; *New Haven,* a neighborhood program that rests upon schools, employment opportunities, and social well-being; *Oakland* (California), another neighborhood cooperation among agencies, involving also the University of California; and *Philadelphia,* agency work upon youth development and delinquency control. The state program is in *North Carolina,* stressing economic betterment and (probably) encouragement of citizen self-help. An additional grant has been made to the *National Council of Churches* to stimulate the training of ministers, priests, and rabbis in city work.

Various religious organizations have been giving attention to CD, through the work with migrants of several denominations and of the *National Council of Churches.* The National Council and the *Presbyterian (U.S.A.) Board of National Missions* have set up offices of CD. The *American Friends Service Committee* has given attention to community programs, often without identifying the work as CD. This is true also of the *Brethren Service Commission.*

Certain social workers are turning to CD in the hope of finding ways for stirring the initiative of self-help among the clients who have too often waited to be helped. The tendency can be noted. No specific program can be singled out as yet, beyond those mentioned under Ford Foundation grants.

Government Programs—Direct and Indirect Participation in CD

Many existing Federal, and some state, programs of social and economic improvement have, or are coming to have, CD aspects. New proposed programs are even more explicit in calling for this emphasis as necessary to the success of the endeavor. So rapidly are changes occurring here that any listing will be quickly out of date. Nevertheless, several governmental programs are mentioned to give some idea of the scope of activity.

Certain state and provincial (Canada) offices have bureaus with greater or lesser amounts of CD responsibility. These have various names, Community Development, or just Development (frequently meaning the wooing of industry), Adult Education, Economic Planning, or just Planning, and so on.

An early use of CD was found in the work of the *TVA* (*Tennessee Valley Authority*). Local residents were stirred to a self-help that fitted into and supplemented the large-scale construction of dams, waterways, hydroelectric installations, and so on.

Another federal use came shortly after the Second World War. This was a Community Development section in *"Point Four" Programs,* then later *ICA* (*International Cooperation Administration*), and finally *AID* (*Agency for International Development*). Community Development work under these changing organizations has been variously named and variously classified in the structural charts. And although the target population has been overseas, there has been considerable influence upon domestic CD, in universities that put on training programs for foreign operation and in publications that gave form to the emerging new specialty.

A similar influence has been exerted through the training of Americans for service in the *Peace Corps.* Certain universities have been induced either to expand CD work or to introduce it for the first time. And since some activities in communities were necessary as field experience for trainees, the universities found themselves serving a CD service function.

The *Urban Renewal Administration* has turned more and more toward CD. It early became apparent that the demolition of old houses and the building of new would not solve the problems. The people who moved out (or protested moving out) of the old, the people who moved back into the new, needed a personal development to accord with the changes in structures. But in this, as in other matters, the federal government has been reluctant to undertake educational programs. Such efforts could easily be interpreted as propaganda for particular administrations or their policies. Therefore the responsibility for human development has been turned over to locally directed social, educational, or religious agencies, sometimes with federal subvention. When the emphasis changed to rehabilitating some deteriorated sections of cities, the need for CD became even more apparent. Residents would not take the initiative for the improvement of their housing unless encouraged—by some of the CD services from educational, religious, or social work agencies.

Area Redevelopment programs have encountered similar difficulties that demand CD. Local committees are usually called for when federal legislation allocates funds for county or small regional improvement. When such indigenous committees proved to be no more than paper organizations, the funds have often been ill spent. When some local organization has been built up through a CD process, the area redevelopment has been much more promising. Federal legislation has presupposed, but has not set up, the means for encouraging the process.

A more direct involvement of federal funds is found in the changing emphases of the *Agricultural Extension Service*. This is administered through the land-grant colleges (universities), but much urging toward CD activities has come from Washington. There has been a broadening of emphasis from the improvement of agricultural practices to a concern for the improvement of total local life (usually on a county basis). Inevitably, Agricultural Extension has become involved in CD processes. Efforts in regional planning and services that cross county lines are becoming increasingly evident.

Even more directly is the federal government involved in proposals for new programs, the recommendation for a *Cabinet Department of Housing and Community Development,* the *National Service Corps,* and the *Economic Opportunity Act of 1964.* The latter is vaguely referred to as a "War on Poverty," embodying many other improvement efforts (area redevelopment, urban rehabilitation, improved employment information and better job opportunities, better health programs, adult education, better conditions for the aging, and so on) but is openly based upon some kind of community development. How the CD is to be set up and the process expedited is not made clear.

Federal legislation is usually drafted to call for indigenous committees or community coalitions to propose local programs which, when approved, will receive federal financial support. Sometimes, however, training is provided in the national setup, often including CD—as in the case of *VISTA* (*Volunteers in Service to America*).

The success of those mentioned and some other federal programs depends in part upon the vitality of local CD processes. Will provision be made in the programs that are administered from Washington, or will the responsibility be left to other agencies? And if so, will Federal funds be made available to subsidize work of the other agencies?

Related Enterprises

Finally, there is a vast array of organizations that serve CD, or attempt to move their programs toward it. Some offer helpful materials; some discuss this new field in publications or at conventions; some offer services; some insist that they have been carrying on CD for years under other names. Among these more or less related organizations are

> *American Institute of Planners*
> *American Society of Planning Officials*
> *American Jewish Committee, Institute of Human Relations*
> *American Public Health Association*
> *American Public Welfare Association*
> *Association for International Development* (a private religious organization, not to be confused with the federal Agency for International Development)

B'nai B'rith
Center for the Study of Liberal Education for Adults
Community Research Associates, Inc.
Community Services, Inc.
Community Services to International Visitors
Grail Movement
Institute for the Christian Apostolate
League of Women Voters
National Association of Housing and Redevelopment Officials
National Association of Social Workers
National Catholic Welfare Conference
National Conference of Christians and Jews
National Conference on Social Welfare
National Social Welfare Assembly
National Urban League
United States Conference of Mayors

Some writers list such programs as the *AFL-CIO Community Services Activities,* or the *Junior League* training to serve the community (for new members). But these programs, and some others that stress good citizenship, are only remotely related to planned and organized CD.

Preliminary Summary of Trends

We realize that many readers will be dissatisfied with the classification of CD programs we have made. Some will insist that we have put their programs into incorrect categories. Some will complain because we have included them, others because we have failed to include them.

Two categories have been omitted. One is a listing of writers contributing to the field (this is covered in bibliographies [1] which must be revised every year in order to keep up to date). The other is a listing of foundations and other sources of financial support (this is subject to constant change as the policies of financial decision makers shift).

Are there trends discernible amidst the confusion of popularity?

---

[1] See App. II.

Any summary must also be based upon the biases of the summarizer, as well as upon information about the various programs and points of view.

1. It must be clear that community development is being used as a vaguely defined touchstone of progress. Many people and (new or old) organizations are using the term, or the idea:
   a. As a source of hope for the future in a period of uncertainty, fear, and loss of trust in neighbors or in experience of the common good.
   b. As an instrument for gaining support for the purposes they regard as worthy.
   c. As a means for rejuvenating programs about which social service practitioners have come to have doubts.

None of these uses should call for cynical comments. All may have positive purpose. But every use should be evaluated in view of the next item.

2. Most practitioners of CD, overly conscious of their own outline of procedure, are only dimly aware of the basic processes by which adult-aged people can learn to take the initiative, make progress on the solution of self-defined problems, and relate themselves to sources of help that can be used in such a way as to strengthen their dignity of decision.
3. All these positive outcomes in terms of personal maturation are potential, in almost all the programs mentioned. This potential will become more clear to community developers when they accept some of the following:
4. Although concerned with the total improvement (economic, social, cultural, political, and so on) of a geographic area, CD focuses upon the development of people.
5. It is inherently unspectacular. It deals with developmental processes in human beings and their achievement of a sense of responsibility for community welfare. This growth is slow and undramatic.
6. The participation of all citizens is sought at several levels of sophistication, education, and wealth. An attempt should

be made to provide participation activities for all residents of the area served.

7. CD seeks to serve some concept of total community, not just some specialized interest, such as schools, housing, city planning, health, or social welfare.

8. Total community also means serving the welfare of all the people in the area, not just some one faction.

9. Nevertheless, the number active at any given time will represent a small fraction of the total population.

10. The CD process continues over a substantial period of time. It is an on-going process, not a single great endeavor with a termination date. The slow growth and the permeation of influence throughout the area are dependent upon a growth that continues over the years.[2]

11. Although many programs have produced "how to" handbooks, a study of these leads to the conclusion that there is no universally useful formula. For best CD, local participants work out their own pattern, following an action research methodology.

---

[2] Items 4 through 10 were adapted from Arthur Dunham, "Social Work and Its Relationships in Community Development in the United States," a working paper for a workshop on Community Development at Brandeis University, April 1962.

appendix II

Bibliographies [1]

A. Social Scientific Theory and Background (*A Selected List*)

BOOKS

ALLPORT, GORDON, *Personality and Social Encounter*. Boston: Beacon Press, 1960. Chapter II, "The Psychological Nature of Personality."

* ANDERSON, NELS, *The Urban Community: A World Perspective*. New York: Holt, Rinehart and Winston, Inc., 1959. Especially good on aspects of "dynamic planning."

ARENSBERG, CONRAD M., AND SOLON T. KIMBELL, *Culture and Community*. New York: Harcourt, Brace & World, Inc., 1965. A health survey as a community building project.

ARONOVICI, CAROL, *Community Building*. New York: Doubleday and Company, Inc., 1956. Democratic community planning in an age of change.

ASHER, ROBERT E., AND OTHERS, *Development of the Emerging Countries: An Agenda for Research*. Washington, D.C.: The Brookings Institute, 1962. See especially "The Role of Education in Development," Mary Ann Bowman and C. Arnold Anderson; "Conclusion," Robert E. Asher.

---

[1] Items marked with an asterisk (*) appear in footnotes in the text.

BAKER, GEORGE W., AND DWIGHT W. CHAPMAN, *Man and Society in Disaster*. New York: Basic Books, 1962. An exploration of "human behavior under stress," by seventeen leading behavioral scientists.

* BENNIS, WARREN G., KENNETH D. BENNE, AND ROBERT CHIN. *The Planning of Change; Readings in the Applied Behavioral Sciences*. New York: Holt, Rinehart and Winston, Inc., 1961. *Part Three*, "Dynamics of the Influence Process," and *Part Four*, "Programs and Technologies of Planned Change."

* BIDDLE, WILLIAM W., *The Cultivation of Community Leaders*. New York: Harper and Row, Publishers, Inc., 1953. Chapter I, "Where Shall We Find Our Leaders?" and Chapter VII, "The Method of Encouragement," through Chapter XII, "A Practitioner's Handbook."

———— AND LOUREIDE J. BIDDLE, *Growth toward Freedom*. New York: Harper and Row, Publishers, Inc., 1957. Chapter III, "A Community for Growth," and Chapter V, "Teaching Methods for Citizens."

BONNER, HUBERT, *Group Dynamics, Principles and Application*. New York: The Ronald Press Company, 1959. Chapter X, "Group Dynamics in Community Relations."

* BRADFORD, LELAND P., JACK R. GIBB, AND KENNETH D. BENNE, *T-Group Theory and Laboratory Method*. New York: John Wiley and Sons, Inc., 1963. Chapter XII, "Studying Group Action," Chapter XIII, "Training in Conflict Resolution," Chapter XIV, "Explorations in Observant Participation," and Chapter XVIII, "A Look to the Future."

BROWNELL, BAKER, *The Human Community*. New York: Harper and Row, Publishers, Inc., 1950. Based on the author's work in the "Montana Study."

* BRUNNER, EDMUND DE S., AND OTHERS, *An Overview of Adult Education Research*. Washington, D.C.: Adult Education Association, 1959. Chapter 12, "Group Research and Adult Education," David E. Wilder.

CARTWRIGHT, DORWIN, AND ALVIN ZANTER, eds., *Group Dynamics: Research and Theory*. New York: Harper and Row, Publishers, Inc., 1953 (Second Edition, 1960). An encyclopedia presentation of group dynamics. See especially Part III, "Studies in Group Decision," Kurt Lewin.

CHASE, STUART, *Roads to Agreement*. New York: Harper and Row, Publishers, Inc., 1951. An excellent summary of methods of conciliation.

* COLEMAN, JAMES C., ed., *Personality Dynamics and Effective Behavior.* Chicago: Scott, Foresman and Company, 1960. See Prologue, "Science and Personal Adjustment"; "A Theory of Personality and Behavior," Carl R. Rogers; "Deficiency Motivation and Growth Motivation," Abraham Maslow; "Values, Psychology, and Human Existence," Erich Fromm; and "Science and Ethical Behavior," Nicholas Hobbs.

COMMUNITY DEVELOPMENT ABSTRACTS, Rural and Community Development Service, Office of Technical Cooperation and Research, Department of State, Agency for International Development, Washington, D.C., 1964. Prepared for Agency for International Development by Sociological Abstracts, Inc., New York.

DAS, RAM, *Action Research and Its Importance in an Under-developed Economy.* Lucknow, India: Planning Research and Action Institute, Planning Department, Uttar Pradesh, 1962. A theory of action research coming from community development work in India.

DEAN, JOHN P., AND ALEX ROSEN, *A Manual of Intergroup Relations.* Chicago: University of Chicago Press, 1955. The principles of group dynamics applied to community conflict situations of minorities.

* DRUCKER, PETER F., *Landmarks of Tomorrow.* New York: Harper and Row, Publishers, Inc., 1957. Summary of recent changes in scientific theories.

* ENGLISH, AVA C., AND HORACE B. ENGLISH, *A Comprehensive Dictionary of Psychological and Psychoanalytical Terms.* New York: Longmans, Green and Co., Inc., 1958. A valuable reference dictionary.

ESSERT, PAUL L., *Creative Leadership of Adult Education.* Englewood Cliffs, N.J.: Prentice-Hall, Inc., 1954. Chapter 8, "Creative Leadership for Community Development Analyzed and Applied."

FOSTER, GEORGE M., *Traditional Cultures and the Impact of Technological Change.* New York: Harper and Row, Publishers, Inc., 1962. See especially Chapter 13, "The Ethics of Planned Change," and Chapters 5, 6, and 7 through 10.

FRIED, MORTON H., *Readings in Anthropology.* New York: Thomas Y. Crowell Company, 1959. Vol. II, "Cultural Anthropology," Reading #24, "American Communities."

FROMM, ERICH, *The Art of Loving.* New York: Harper and Row, Publishers, Inc., 1962. (Bantam Books Edition, 1963) Chapter IV, "The Practice of Love."

————, *The Dogma of Christ and Other Essays on Religion, Psychology, and Culture*. New York: Holt, Rinehart and Winston, Inc., 1963. See especially "On the Limitations and Dangers of Psychology."

* ————, *The Sane Society*. New York: Holt, Rinehart and Winston, Inc., 1941. The problem of contemporary alienation.

GAILBRAITH, JOHN KENNETH, *The Affluent Society*. Boston: Houghton Mifflin Company, 1958. Background material on the contemporary economic scene.

————, *Economic Development*. Cambridge, Mass.: Harvard University Press, 1964. Chapter IV, "Development as a Process," Chapter V, "Developing and Developed," and Chapter VI, "Development Planning and Practice."

GOODMAN, PERCIVAL, AND PAUL GOODMAN, *Communitas, Means of Livelihood and Ways of Life*. New York: Alfred A. Knopf, Inc., 1947. Chapter 6, "A New Community," and Chapter 7, "Planned Security and Minimum Regulations."

GORDON, THOMAS, *Group Centered Leadership*. Boston: Houghton Mifflin Company, 1955. Especially Part I, "A New Leadership Approach."

GREER, SCOTT, *The Emerging City, Myth and Reality*. New York: The Free Press of Glencoe, 1962. See "The Metropolitan Area as a Power Structure."

HAMBIGE, GOVE, ed., *Dynamics of Development: An International Reader*. New York: Frederick A. Praeger, 1964. Thirty-two selected essays from the *International Development Review*.

* HARE, A. PAUL, *Handbook of Small Group Research*. New York: The Free Press of Glencoe, 1962. Summary of small group research, to date.

* HARPER, ERNEST, AND ARTHUR DUNHAM, *Community Organization in Action*. New York: Association Press, 1959. Part Six, "Community Development in the United States and Elsewhere."

HARTLEY, EUGENE L., AND GERHART D. WIEBE, *Casebook in Social Processes*. New York: Thomas Y. Crowell Company, 1960. Mainly sociological studies.

HYMAN, HERBERT H., CHARLES R. WRIGHT, AND TERENCE K. HOPKINS, *Applications and Methods of Evaluation*. Berkeley, Calif.: University of California Press, 1962. Preface and Part I, Chapter I, "Principles of Evaluation."

* JAHODA, MARIE, MORTON DEUTSCH, AND STUART W. COOK, *Research Methods in Social Relations*. New York: Holt, Rinehart and Winston, Inc., 1951. Part I, "Basic Processes," and Part II,

"Selected Techniques." (See also Revised, one-volume edition. Claire Selltiz, Marie Jahoda, Morton Deutsch, and Stuart W. Cook. New York: Holt, Rinehart and Winston, Inc., for the Society for the Psychological Study of Social Issues, 1959).

* JANOWITZ, MORRIS, *The Community Press in an Urban Setting.* New York: The Free Press of Glencoe, 1962. A research study of press media on the urban scene.

KLUCKHOHN, RICHARD, ed., *Culture and Behavior: The Collected Essays of Clyde Kluckhohn.* New York: The Free Press of Glencoe, 1962. See Chapter 2, "The Concept of Culture."

KNOWLES, MALCOLM, AND HULDA KNOWLES, *Introduction to Group Dynamics.* New York: Association Press, 1959. A brief but adequate introduction to group dynamics.

LEWIN, KURT, *A Dynamic Theory of Personality.* New York: Mc-Graw-Hill, Inc., 1935, Series in Psychology. Chapter II, "On the Structure of the Mind."

* ———, *Field Theory in Social Science,* Dorwin Cartwright, ed. New York: Harper and Row, Publishers, Inc., 1951. Chapter VIII, "Psychological Ecology," "The Field Approach: Culture and Group Life as Quasi-Stationary Processes."

———, *Principles of Topological Psychology,* Series in Psychology. New York: McGraw-Hill, Inc., 1935. Chapter II, "Formulation of Law and Representation of Situation," and Chapter III, "General Considerations about Representing Life Space."

* ———, *Resolving Social Conflict.* New York: Harper and Row, Publishers, Inc., 1948. Chapter XIII, "Action Research and Minority Problems."

* LIPPITT, RONALD, JEANNE WATSON, AND BRUCE WESTLEY, *The Dynamics of Planned Change.* New York: Harcourt, Brace and World, Inc., 1958. ". . . a comparative study of principles and techniques."

* LORING, WILLIAM C., JR., FRANK L. SWEETSER, AND CHARLES F. ERNST, *Community Organization for Citizen Participation in Urban Renewal.* Boston: Housing Association of Metropolitan Boston, 1957. See Section VII, "Citizen Participation and the Social Work Profession."

MASLOW, ABRAHAM M., *Motivation and Personality.* New York: Harper and Row, Publishers, Inc., 1954. Chapter 13, "Love in Self-Actualizing People."

* MENNINGER, KARL, *The Vital Balance.* New York: The Viking Press, Inc., 1963. Psychiatric background for change in people.

MERRILL, FRANCIS E., ed., *Society and Culture,* 2d ed. Englewood Cliffs, N.J.: Prentice-Hall, Inc., 1961. Part Six, "Methods of Studying Society and Culture," Pauline V. Young; Chapter 27, "The Techniques of Social Research."

MERTON, ROBERT K., LEONARD BROOM, AND LEONARD S. COTTRELL, JR., eds., *Sociology Today: Problems and Prospects.* New York: Basic Books, Inc., 1959. Chapter XIII, "Small-Group Theory and Research," Robert F. Bales, Chapter XII, "The Study of Consensus," Theodore M. Newcomb.

MURPHY, GARDNER, *Human Potentialities.* New York: Basic Books, Inc., 1958. Psychological background for potentiality of human development.

————, *In the Minds of Men: The Study of Human Behavior and Social Tensions in India.* New York: Basic Books, Inc., 1953. Chapter 13, "An American Opportunity."

MURRAY, CLYDE E., MARX G. BOWENS, AND RUSSELL HOGREFE, *Group Work in Community Life.* New York: Association Press, 1954. A social work approach.

* NEWCOMB, THEODORE M., *The Acquaintance Process.* New York: Holt, Rinehart and Winston, Inc., 1961. How a group of strangers in a university setting become acquainted. A study of the process involved.

———— AND EUGENE L. HARTLEY, eds., *Readings in Social Psychology.* New York: Holt, Rinehart and Winston, Inc., 1947. See "Group Decisions and Social Change," Kurt Lewin. (See also Third Edition, Eleanor E. Maccoby, Theodore M. Newcomb, and Eugene L. Hartley, eds. New York: Holt, Rinehart and Winston, Inc., 1958).

NIEBUHR, H. RICHARD, *The Responsible Self: An Essay in Christian Moral Philosophy.* New York: Harper and Row, Publishers, Inc., 1963. Religious imperatives in work with people.

POLLARD, FRANCIS E., BEATRICE E. POLLARD, AND ROBERT S. W. POLLARD, *Democracy and the Quaker Method.* London: Bannisdale Press, 1949. See especially pp. 28 ff.

ROGERS, CARL R., *Client-centered Therapy.* Boston: Houghton Mifflin Company, 1951. The well-documented point of view of a clinical "developmental psychologist." Especially Parts II and VII.

* ————, *On Becoming a Person.* Boston: Houghton Mifflin Company, 1961. Part II, "How Can I Be of Help?" and Part VII, "The Behavioral Sciences and the Person."

Ross, Murray G., *Community Organization, Theory and Principles.* New York: Harper and Row, Publishers, Inc., 1955. Social work point of view.

Sanders, Irwin T., *The Community: Introduction to a Social System.* New York: The Ronald Press Company, 1958. Part Three, "Community Action," Classic sociological description.

Social Welfare Forum, Proceedings of the National Conference on Social Welfare, 1962. New York: Columbia University Press, 1962. See "Perspectives on Urban Community Development and Community Organization," Marshall B. Clinard.

Spicer, Edward H., *Human Problems in Technological Change: A Casebook.* New York: Russell Sage Foundation, 1952. Part IV, "Conceptual Tools for Solving Human Problems."

Sussman, Marvin B., ed., *Community Structure and Analysis.* New York: Thomas Y. Crowell Company, 1959. See "The Developmental Concept," William W. Biddle. A symposium of contemporary writers on the community.

Tax, Sol, ed., *Horizons of Anthropology.* Chicago: Aldine Publishing Co., 1964. Chapter 21, "The Uses of Anthropology," Sol Tax.

Thelen, Herbert A., *Dynamics of Groups at Work.* Chicago: University of Chicago Press, 1954. See Chapter I.

United Nations International Children's Emergency Fund, *Children of the Developing Countries.* New York: The World Publishing Company, 1963. Chapter I, "Programs for Children," and Chapter II, "Family and Child Welfare."

Warren, Roland L., *The Community in America.* Skokie, Ill.: Rand McNally Company, 1963. Chapter X, "Community Action and Community Development." A systematic, sociological approach to the study of "the community" in America.

————, *Studying Your Community.* New York: Russell Sage Foundation, 1955. A sociological treatment, with some practical suggestions as to what to look for and how to get an accurate picture of conditions at the time of a survey.

PERIODICALS, PAMPHLETS, AND UNPUBLISHED MANUSCRIPTS

American Psychological Association, "Ethical Standards of Psychologists," *American Psychologist,* Vol. 18, No. 1, January 1963.

Babchuk, Nicholas, "Participation and Observation in the Field Situation," *Human Organization,* Vol. 21, No. 3, Fall 1962.

BAUMRIND, DIANA, "Some Thoughts on the Ethics of Research," *American Psychologist,* Vol. 19, No. 6, June 1964.

BENNIS, WARREN G., "Goals and Meta-Goals of Laboratory Training," National Training Laboratories *Training News,* Vol. 6, No. 3, Fall 1962.

* BIDDLE, WILLIAM W., "The Challenge of Major Research," *Adult Leadership,* Vol. 7, No. 5, November 1958.

* ———, "A Major Breakthrough for the Social Sciences," University of Wisconsin, June 1958. Mimeographed.

———, "Varieties in Community Work," An abstract of a speech presented before a conference on urban problems at Milwaukee, Wisconsin, November 1961. Mimeographed.

BOULDING, KENNETH E., "Conflict and Defense: A General Theory," *Contemporary Psychology,* Vol. VIII, No. 1, January 1963.

———, "Where Are We Going If Anywhere?" *Human Organization,* Vol. 21, No. 2, Summer 1962.

* BRUYN, SEVERYN T., "The Methodology of Participant Observation," *Human Organization,* Vol. 22, No. 3, Fall 1963.

* BUGENTAL, J. F. T., "Humanistic Psychology: A New Break-Through," *American Psychologist,* Vol. 18, No. 9, September 1963.

CHEIN, ISIDOR, "The Image of Man," *Journal of Social Issues,* Vol. XVIII, No. 4, October 1962.

———, STUART W. COOK, AND JOHN HARDING, "The Field of Action-Research," *American Psychologist,* Vol. III, 1948. Pages 43-50.

"Cities Are for Living," *Social Progress,* Special Issue, December 1962.

"Citizen Participation," *Journal of Housing,* Special Issue, October 1963.

CLINARD, MARSHALL B., "Evaluation and Research in Urban Community Development," *International Review of Community Development,* No. 12, 1963.

COHEN, OSCAR, "Implications of Inter-Group Relations for Research," *Review of Religious Research,* Vol. 4, No. 1, Fall 1962.

* COMMISSION OF THE PROFESSORS OF ADULT EDUCATION ASSOCIATION, *Adult Education: A New Imperative for Our Times,* Washington, D.C.: Adult Education Association, 1961.

* DODDY, HURLEY H., *Informal Groups and the Community,* A Research Study of the Institute of Adult Education, Teachers College, Columbia University. New York: Teachers College Bureau of Publications, 1952.

* DuBois, Philip H., and King M. Weintge, *Objectives and Methods of Research in Adult Education,* St. Louis, Mo.: Washington University, May 1962.

Franklin, Richard, "A Functional Harmony for Adult Education," *Adult Education,* Vol. XIII, No. 1, Autumn 1962.

Freeman, Linton C., Thomas J. Fararo, Warner Bloomberg, Jr., and Morris H. Sunshine, "Locating Leaders in Local Communities," *American Sociological Review,* Vol. 28, No. 5, October 1963.

"The Future of the American City," *Current,* Special Issue, October 1963.

Goodwin, Leonard, "The Historical-Philosophical Basis for Uniting Social Science with Social Problem-Solving," *Philosophy of Science,* Vol. 29, No. 4, October 1962. (reprinted)

———, "Religion and the Behavioral Sciences: A Challenge to the American College," *Religious Education,* July-August 1960.

Hackenberg, Robert A., "Process Formation in Applied Anthropology," *Human Organization,* Vol. 21, No. 3, Fall 1962.

* Hayes, Samuel P., Jr., *Measuring the Results of Development Projects: A Manual for the Use of Field Workers.* UNESCO, 1959.

* Hayes, Wayland J., "The Problem of Community Intelligence," *International Review of Community Development,* No. 10, 1962.

Haygood, Kenneth, *The Impact of Urbanization on University Extension,* Proceedings of the Community Development Division, National University Extension Association (1962). Washington, D.C.: National University Extension Association, 1962.

Holik, John S., and V. Wayne Lane, "A Community Development Contest as a Catalytic Agent in Social Action," *Rural Sociology,* Vol. 26, No. 2, June 1961.

Holmberg, Allan R., and Henry F. Dobyns, "The Process of Accelerating Community Change," *Human Organization,* Vol. 21, No. 2, Summer 1962.

"International Conference of Social Work," *Community Development Review,* Vol. 7, No. 1, June 1962.

Katona, Arthur, "Approaches to Action Research," *Journal of Higher Education,* Vol. XXIV, No. 6, June 1953.

Kindelsperger, Kenneth W., reporter, *Community Development and Community Organization,* Proceedings of a Workshop at Brandeis University. New York: National Association of Social Workers, 1961.

* Kluckhohn, Florence R., "The Participant-Observer Technique in

Small Communities," *American Journal of Sociology,* Vol. XLVI, No. 3, 1940.

KNEELAND, NATALIE, *A Guide to Practical Research,* Office of Education, U.S. Department of Health, Education, and Welfare. Washington, D.C.: Government Printing Office, 1963.

"Leadership and Participation in a Changing Rural Community," *Journal of Social Issues,* Vol. XVI, No. 4, 1960. Issue edited by John Harding, Edward C. Devereux, Jr., and Urie Bronfenbrenner.

LEWIN, KURT, RONALD LIPPITT, AND RALPH K. WHITE, "Patterns of Aggressive Behavior in Experimentally Produced Social Climates," *Journal of Social Psychology,* Number 25, 1939.

* LOEVINGER, JANE, "Conflict of Commitment in Clinical Research," *American Psychologist,* Vol. 18, No. 5, May 1963.

MCKEE, JAMES B., *Community Power and Strategies in Race Relations.* East Lansing: Institute for Community Development and Services, Michigan State University, 1960–1961. Reprint Series (Reprinted from *Social Problems,* Vol. 6. No. 3, Winter 1958–1959). (pamphlet)

* MASLOW, ABRAHAM H., "Further Notes on the Psychology of Being," *Journal of Humanistic Psychology,* Spring 1963.

———, *Lessons from Peak Experience,* Western Behavioral Sciences Institute, Report No. 6, La Jolla, Calif., 1961.

———, *Notes on the Psychology of Being,* Western Behavioral Sciences Institute, Report No. 7, La Jolla, Calif., 1961.

"Metropolis in Ferment," The *Annals* of the American Academy of Political Science, Special Issue, November 1957.

* MIDDLETON, RUSSELL, "Alienation, Race and Education," *American Sociological Review,* Vol. 28, No. 6, December 1963.

MORGAN, ARTHUR E., *The Great Community,* Chicago: Human Events Association, 1946. Distributed by Community Services, Inc., Yellow Springs, Ohio.

MORGAN, GRISCOM, ed., *The Heritage of Community,* Yellow Springs, Ohio: Community Services, Inc., 1955.

MURPHY, GARDNER, *Where Is the Human Race Going?* Western Behavioral Sciences Institute, Report No. 2, La Jolla, Calif., 1961.

NIEHOFF, ARTHUR H., AND J. CHARNEL ANDERSON, "The Process of Cross-Cultural Innovation," *International Development Review,* Vol. VI, No. 2, June 1964.

"Planning and Politics: Citizen Participation in Urban Renewal,"

Journal of the American Institute of Planners, Special Issue, November 1963.

PLATT, WILLIAM J., "Individuals: Neglected Elements in Planning," *International Development Review,* Vol. V, No. 3, September 1963.

PYE, LUCIEN W., "The Political Implications of Urbanization and the Development Process," *Social Problems of Development and Urbanization,* Vol. VII, *Science, Technology, and Development.* U.S. Papers prepared for the United Nations Conference on the Application of Science and Technology for the Benefit of Less Developed Areas. Washington, D.C.: Government Printing Office, 1963.

* ROGERS, CARL R., "A Therapist's View of the Good Life," *The Humanist,* No. 5, 1957.

———, "Toward a Science of the Person," *Journal of Humanistic Psychology,* Fall 1963.

Rural and Urban Community Development in the U.S.A., International Conference of Social Work, Report of the 11th Annual Conference, Rio de Janeiro, Brazil. New York: U.S. Committee on the International Conference of Social Work, 1962.

SANDERS, IRWIN T., "Stages of a Community Controversy," *Journal of Social Issues,* Vol. XVIII, No. 4, October 1962.

———, "Theories of Community Development," *Rural Sociology,* Vol. 23, No. 1, March 1958.

* SANFORD, NEVITT, "Social Science and Reform," Address given at the annual meeting of the American Psychological Association, Washington, D.C., August 28, 1958.

SCHILLING, HAROLD K., "A Contemporary Macedonian Plea," Union Seminary *Quarterly Review,* Vol. XVII, No. 2, January 1963.

SCHLESINGER, ARTHUR, JR., "The Humanist Looks at Empirical Social Research," *American Sociological Review,* Vol. 27, No. 6, December 1962.

SCHLITZ, MICHAEL E., "Social Action for the Good Urban Life," *Current,* October 1963.

"Statement on Ethics of the Society for Applied Anthropology," *Human Organization,* Vol. 22, No. 4, Winter 1963–1964.

"The Study and Practice of Planning," *International Social Science Journal,* Vol. XI, No. 3, 1959.

* TAX, SOL, "Action Anthropology," Address given at the University of Michigan, March 20, 1958. Processed.

"Trigger for Community Conflict, The Case of Fluoridation," *Journal of Social Issues,* Entire Issue, Vol. XVII, Number 4, 1961.

"Understanding How Groups Work," Leadership Series, Pamphlet No. 4. Washington, D.C.: Adult Education Association, 1956. One of several pamphlets in this series.

"Urban Studies," Entire Issue, *American Behavioral Scientist*, Vol. VI, No. 6, February 1963.

WARREN, ROLAND L., ed., *Community Development and Social Work Practice*, Report of the Workshop on Community Development in the U.S.A., held at Brandeis University, April 8-12, 1962. New York: National Association of Social Workers, 1962.

WILSON, JAMES Q., "Is Urban Renewal a Class Struggle?" *Current*, January 1964.

WOLFINGER, RAYMOND E., "Reputation and Reality in the Study of Community Power," *American Sociological Review*, Vol. 25, No. 5, October 1960.

* WRONG, DENNIS H., "Political Bias and the Social Sciences," *Columbia University Forum*, Vol. II, No. 4, Fall 1959.

YOUNG, FRANK W., AND RUTH C. YOUNG, "Toward a Theory of Community Development," *Social Problems of Development and Urbanization*, Vol. VII. Geneva Conference on the Application of Science and Technology for the Benefit of Less Developed Areas. Washington, D.C.: Government Printing Office, 1963.

B.   Community Development in the U.S.A. and around the World

BOOKS

* ABRAHAMSON, JULIA, *A Neighborhood Finds Itself*. New York: Harper and Row, Publishers, Inc., 1959. The story of the Hyde Park-Kenwood Community Conference in Chicago.

APTHORPE, RAYMOND, ed., *Social Research and Community Development*. Lusoka, Northern Rhodesia: Rhodes-Livingstone Institute for Social Research, 1961. Uses community development in Africa as prototype for development of theory.

BATTEN, T. R., *Communities and Their Development: An Introductory Study with Special Reference to the Tropics*. London: Oxford University Press, 1957. A comparative study of the aims, methods, and organization of various community development projects.

————, *Problems of African Development*, 3d ed. London: Oxford

University Press, 1960. See Parts I, "Land and Labour," and II, "Government and People."

* ———, *Training for Community Development,* A Critical Study of Method. London: Oxford University Press, 1962. A scholarly presentation of overseas training for community development, with excellent insights based upon both field and academic experience.

* BIDDLE, WILLIAM W., *The Cultivation of Community Leaders.* New York: Harper and Row, Publishers, Inc., 1953. Some practical, down-to-earth recommendations on how to deal with people in community situations; more than a handbook; it puts the processes of human development in a philosophical and religious setting.

——— AND LOUREIDE J. BIDDLE, *Growth toward Freedom.* New York: Harper and Row, Publishers, Inc., 1957. A challenge to universities and colleges to make community development a regular part of their work. It outlines ways in which students and faculty members can carry on activities off the campus to benefit themselves and the citizens with whom they associate.

BINGHAM, JONATHAN B., *Shirt-Sleeve Diplomacy: Point Four in Action.* New York: The John Day Company, Inc., 1953. Examples of Point Four programs in various local settings.

BOLLENS, JOHN C., ed., *Exploring the Metropolitan Community.* Berkeley, Calif.: University of California Press, 1961. An analysis of the metropolitan complex of the St. Louis City-County Area. Good sociological research, descriptive and dynamic.

BROWNELL, BAKER, *The Human Community.* New York: Harper and Row, Publishers, Inc., 1950. A philosophical treatise on various aspects of small community life based upon the author's work in the "Montana Study." A classic of fundamental theory, especially for thoughtful readers.

BRUYN, SEVERYN T., *Communities in Action.* New Haven, Conn.: College and University Press, 1963. "A sociological study of what happened in four communities when citizens followed ... models of community action to solve their problems."

BURKE, L., AND J. McCREANOR, *Training Missionaries for Community Development.* Princeton, N.J.: National Conference of Catholic Charities, 1960. An exploration by Roman Catholics of the role of the missionary in the community development movement, with Ghana as prototype.

CHERMAYOFF, GEORGE, AND CHRISTOPHER ALEXANDER, *Community and Privacy: Toward a New Architecture of Humanism.* New

York: Doubleday and Company, Inc., 1963. Outlines ways that architecture can contribute to the "humanization" of cities, in text and photographs.

COADY, M. M., *Masters of Their Own Destiny*. New York: Harper and Row, Publishers, Inc., 1939. Through stimulation by a Catholic priest, local people in Nova Scotia learned to lift themselves by their own bootstraps through community cooperation. An inspiring story told by the priest who was the most active stimulator.

Community Development: A Handbook. London: Her Majesty's Stationery Office, 1958. Paperback. Prepared by a Study Conference on Community Development, involving numerous community development workers, from seventeen territories, all of whom contributed to this concise little manual.

* CROUCH, WINSTON W., AND BEATRICE DINERMAN, *Southern California Metropolis: A Study in Development of Government for a Metropolitan Area*. Berkeley: University of California Press, 1963.

DAYAL, RAJESHWAR, *Community Development Program in India*. Allahabad, India: Kitab Nahal, Publishers, 1960. An account of the national community development program in India, up to 1960, the date of publication.

DEAN, JOHN P., AND ALEX ROSEN, *A Manual of Intergroup Relations*. Chicago: University of Chicago Press, 1955. The principles of group dynamics, applied to community conflict situations. A very practical "how to do it" approach.

DUBE, S. C., *India's Changing Villages: Human Factors in Community Development*. Ithaca, N.Y.: Cornell University Press, 1958. How the Indian people are meeting their common needs, through the process of community development.

DU SAUTOY, PETER, *Community Development in Ghana*. London: Oxford University Press, 1958. An earlier account of the work in Ghana.

———, *The Organization of a Community Development Programme*. London: Oxford University Press, 1962. A description of a practical community development program, in Ghana.

* EDITORS OF FORTUNE, *The Exploding Metropolis*. New York: Doubleday and Company, Inc., 1958. A very descriptive look at the metropolis.

FOSTER, GEORGE M., *Traditional Cultures and the Impact of Technological Change*. New York: Harper and Row, Publishers, Inc., 1962. This book is primarily concerned with rural communities undergoing changes through development programs such as those offered by the United Nations, the Peace Corps, and certain private organizations. Chapter XIII, "The Ethics of Planned Change," is especially recommended.

GEEN, ELIZABETH, JEANNE R. LOWE, AND KENNETH WALKER, *Man and the Modern City*. Pittsburgh: University of Pittsburgh Press, 1963. A series of essays by various "urban specialists" examining the "implications of urbanism for modern man."

* GOODENOUGH, WARD H., *Cooperation in Change: An Anthropological Approach to Community Development*. New York: Russell Sage Foundation, 1963. Deals with the practical and theoretical implications of the relationship between the "change agent" and the people in overseas development.

* GOODMAN, PAUL, *Utopian Essays and Practical Proposals*. New York: Random House, Inc., 1962. It is especially recommended that community developers read Part I, entitled "Utopian Thinking."

Guide to Community Development. Ministry of Community Development, Government of India, 1957. Delhi: Coronation Printing Works. A handbook on the subject by the government offices of community development in India.

HALL, D. M., *The Dynamics of Group Discussion*. Danville, Ill.: Interstate Printers, 1950. A pamphlet offering practical guidance to discussion leaders.

* HARPER, ERNEST, AND ARTHUR DUNHAM, *Community Organization in Action*. New York: Association Press, 1959. Part Six, "Community Development in the U.S.A. and Elsewhere."

HAYES, WAYLAND J., *The Small Community Looks Ahead*. New York: Harcourt, Brace and World, Inc., 1947. An early sociological treatment of community life and the development of local leadership. Some good examples are given of progress in the Tennessee Valley Authority and in Virginia.

HOIBERG, OTTO, *Exploring the Small Community*. Lincoln, Neb.: University of Nebraska Press, 1955. A more recent sociological treatment, from the midwest. The author has had much practical experience in Nebraska, yet has a theoretical point of view as well. He discusses ways of undertaking work in a number of special fields—industry, recreation, schools, churches, and so forth.

JACKSON, I. C., *Advance in Africa*. London: Oxford University Press, 1956. The former principal of the Awgu community development training center in Eastern Nigeria gives his views of community development.

* JACOBS, JANE, *The Death and Life of Great American Cities*. New York: Random House, Inc., 1961. An analysis of current practices in city planning; the latter comes up short, according to Miss Jacobs' analysis.

* JANSSEN, LAWRENCE H., *These Cities Glorious*. New York: Friendship Press, 1963. A small but excellent background and resource book on the city.

LIPMAN, RABBI E. J., AND ALBERT VORSPAN, *Tale of Ten Cities*. New York: Union of American Hebrew Congregations, 1962. The relationships of Protestants, Catholics, and Jews in ten American cities.

* LORING, WILLIAM C., JR., FRANK L. SWEETSER, AND CHARLES F. ERNST, *Community Organization for Citizen Participation in Urban Renewal*. Boston: Housing Association of Metropolitan Boston, 1957. Experiences of the community organization program in Boston, Massachusetts.

* McKEE, ELMORE, *The People Act*. New York: Harper and Row, Publishers, Inc., 1955. Democracy in action in the present-day U.S.A. A collection of stories from all over the country, telling how local citizens worked together to solve their problems and became stronger persons in the process. A book that grew out of the "People Act" radio program of several years ago.

* MAYER, ALBERT, AND ASSOCIATES, *Pilot Project, India*. Berkeley, Calif.: University of California Press, 1959. The story of the rural development project in Etawah, Uttar Pradesh, told by one of the principal planners of that project.

MEAD, MARGARET, *Continuities in Cultural Evolution*. New Haven, Conn.: Yale University Press, 1964. A significant contribution to the human sciences.

———, *Cultural Patterns and Technical Change*. New York: UNESCO, 1953. The famous anthropologist explains how modern technical changes are affecting the lives of people accustomed to simple rural life. Although she tells most about people overseas, her conclusions apply to the domestic scene as well.

———, *New Lives for Old*. New York: William Morrow and Company, Inc., 1956. Case study of rapid cultural and social change, among the Manus of New Guinea.

MEZIROW, J. D., *The Dynamics of Community Development*. New York: Scarecrow Press, Inc., 1963. Especially Chapter I; remaining chapters deal with Pakistan's AID program, in which the author participated.

MIAL, CURTIS, AND DOROTHY MIAL, *Our Community*. New York:

New York University Press, 1960. A summary of much thinking and practice in the community development field, brought up to date.

* MILLER, HASKELL M., *Compassion and Community*. New York: Association Press, 1961. A history of the churches' concern for, and role in, community welfare.

MILLSPAUGH, MARTIN, AND GURNEY BRECKENFELD, *The Human Side of Urban Renewal*. Baltimore, Md.: Baltimore Fight Blight, Inc., 1958. Surveys of the attitudinal changes resulting from programs of neighborhood rehabilitation.

MONROE, DONALD, AND KEITH MONROE, *How to Succeed in Community Service*. Philadelphia: J. B. Lippincott Company, 1962. A practical guide on working with existing organizations, committees, and so on.

MORGAN, ARTHUR, *The Community of the Future and the Future of the Community*. Yellow Springs, Ohio: Community Services, Inc., 1957. Arthur Morgan's look into what the future might be with intelligent choosing, reflecting his enthusiasm for the small town.

———, *The Small Community*. New York: Harper and Row, Publishers, Inc., 1942. A pioneering work in the field of community development. See especially the last chapter.

MUKERJI, B., *Community Development in India*. Bombay: Orient Longmans Ltd., 1961. The story of the national program of community development in India, told by a native of that country.

NAIR, KUSUM, *Blossoms in the Dust: The Human Element in Indian Development*. New York: Frederick A. Praeger, Inc., 1962. An incomplete but provocative story of community development in India as seen through the eyes of a sympathetic and sensitive reporter.

NATIONAL SOCIETY FOR THE STUDY OF EDUCATION, *Community Education*. Chicago: University of Chicago Press, 1959. A symposium on community education processes that leans heavily upon overseas experience and work with disadvantaged people.

O'CONNOR, ELIZABETH, *Call to Commitment*. New York: Harper and Row, Publishers, Inc., 1963. The story of how a large church (in Washington, D.C.) has adapted its ministry to serving people in an urban community setting.

OGDEN, JEAN, AND JESS OGDEN, *Small Communities in Action*. New York: Harper and Row, Publishers, Inc., 1946. Thirty-four stories from small communities.

—— AND ——, *These Things We Tried.* New York: Harper and Row, Publishers, Inc., 1947. More of the experiences of the Ogdens.

* POSTON, RICHARD W., *Democracy Is You.* New York: Harper and Row, Publishers, Inc., 1953. A "how to" book on community development.

——, *Democracy Speaks Many Tongues.* New York: Harper and Row, Publishers, Inc., 1962. This book describes some examples of community development around the world. The conclusions reached in regard to community development are stimulating.

RAMIREZ, EMILIANO C., *Community School Practices.* Pasay City, Philippines: National Publishing House, 1954. A look at the American scene through the eyes of a Philippine educator. See especially pages 75 through 93.

ROSSI, PETER, AND ROBERT A. DENTLER, *The Politics of Urban Renewal.* New York: The Free Press of Glencoe, 1961. See especially Chapter VII; the central problem of the study is to "assess the contributions of citizen participation to urban renewal planning." Uses concrete examples of the Hyde Park-Kenwood Community Conference in Chicago and Morningside Heights, Inc., in New York City, covering many subjects of interest regarding the "human components" of urban planning.

* SANDERS, IRWIN T., *Making Good Communities Better.* Lexington, Ky.: University of Kentucky Press, 1950. A small but concise handbook of community stimulation, with brief quotations from seventeen "authorities" on specific steps of organization. Many helpful suggestions.

SILBERMAN, CHARLES E., *Crisis in Black and White.* New York: Random House, 1964. Race conflict in American cities.

STALEY, EUGENE, *The Future of Underdeveloped Countries.* New York: Frederick A. Praeger, Inc., 1961. An economist, analyzing development in newly developing countries, finds human development central.

TATE, H. CLAY, *Building a Better Home Town.* New York: Harper and Row, Publishers, Inc., 1954. Editor of a small-town newspaper, Tate believes in the decentralized way of life; he finds much that makes existence attractive in a small place, and discovers more that can be done to make it even more so.

* THELEN, HERBERT A., AND BETTIE BELK SARCHET, *Neighbors in Action.* Chicago: University of Chicago Press, 1954. A manual approach to local community action.

TURNER, ROY. ed., *India's Urban Future.* Berkeley, Calif.: University of California Press, 1962. See especially Kingsley Davis, "Urbanization in India: Present and Future."

UNITED NATIONS, *Social Progress through Community Development.* New York: United Nations, 1955. Brief, matter-of-fact and impersonal, although some examples from overseas operation are given. Useful for clarifying concepts.

PAMPHLETS, ARTICLES, AND REPRINTS

AGENCY FOR INTERNATIONAL DEVELOPMENT, *Community Development Training Materials, Series A.* Washington, D.C.: Agency for International Development, 1962. Pamphlets as follows:

1. *An Introduction to CD for Village Workers*
2. *Making Council Meetings More Effective*
3. *Community Development in Urban and Semi-urban Areas*
4. *Community Development and Social Change*
5. *Community Development, Extension, and the Village AID Synthesis*
6. *Conference on Conference Planning*
7. *The Village AID Worker and Democratic Program Planning*

ALCHIN, EDMOND JOHN DONOGHUE, IWAO ISHINO, AND STEWART MARQUIS, *A Holistic Approach to Community Development: A Working Paper,* Michigan State University, Institute for Community Development and Services, Technical Bulletin B-41, East Lansing, April 1964.

ALINSKY, SAUL D., "Citizen Participation and Community Organization in Planning and Urban Renewal," A presentation before the Chicago Chapter of the National Association of Housing and Redevelopment Officials, Chicago, Illinois, January 29, 1962. Chicago: Industrial Areas Foundation, 1962.

BEERS, HOWARD W., "Application of Sociology in Development Programs," *Community Development Review,* Vol. 8, No. 1, March 1963.

BIDDLE, WILLIAM W., *Adult Development: Some Guidelines for Community Educators.* Annual Report #10, Program of Community Dynamics, Earlham College, Richmond, Indiana, 1958.

———, *A Pattern of Fundamental Education: A Puerto Rican Project Report.* Annual Report #8, Program of Community Dynamics, Earlham College, Richmond, Indiana, 1956.

———, *People Grow in Communities: A Case Study from a Small Town.* Annual Report #9, Program of Community Dynamics, Earlham College, Richmond, Indiana, 1957.

————, *Training of Community Educators: Some Suggestions for Training.* Annual Report #11, Program of Community Dynamics, Earlham College, Richmond, Indiana, 1959.

* ———— AND LOUREIDE J. BIDDLE, *Community Dynamics Processes: Two Case Studies of People in Development.* New York: Emil Schwarzhaupt Foundation, 1962.

BOWLES, CHESTER, "Administration of Rural Development in the Underdeveloped Countries," *Community Development Review,* Vol. 8, No. 1, March 1963.

* CITY OF CHICAGO, HOUSING AND REDEVELOPMENT COORDINATOR, "Neighborhood Conservation," April 1956.

CLINARD, MARSHALL B., "The Delhi Pilot Project in Urban Community Development," *International Review of Community Development,* Number 7, 1961.

————, "Perspectives on Urban Community Development and Community Organization," *The Social Welfare Forum,* 1962, Official Proceedings, 89th Annual Forum, National Conference on Social Welfare. New York: Columbia University Press, 1962.

* COMMUNITY CONSERVATION BOARD, *The Chicago Conservation Program.* Chicago: Community Conservation Board, n.d.

Community Development and Its Role in Nation Building. Report of the Inter-Regional Conference, Seoul, Korea, May 6-12, 1961. United States International Cooperation Administration (now the Agency for International Development)

Community Organization, Community Planning, and Community Development: Some Common and Distinctive Elements. New York: Council on Social Work Education, 1962. Papers presented at the meeting of the Council in Montreal, February 1961.

CONSIDINE, JOHN J., M.M., ed., "The Missionary Approach to Urban Problems," *Community Development Review,* Vol. 8, No. 2, June 1963.

COUSINS, WILLIAM J., "Community Development: Some Notes on the Why and How," *Community Development Review,* No. 7, December 1957.

DE VRIES, E., "Community Development and Development," *International Review of Community Development,* Number 5, 1960, Theories and Values. Pages 87 *ff.*

* DUNHAM, ARTHUR, "Community Development," *Social Work Yearbook,* 1960. New York: National Association of Social Workers, 1960.

* ————, "Social Work and Its Relationships in Community Development in the United States," School of Social Work, University

of Michigan, Ann Arbor, April 1962. Mimeographed, paper presented at the workshop on community development in the United States, Brandeis University, April 1962.

————, "Some Principles of Community Development," *International Review of Community Development,* Number 11, 1963.

* du SAUTOY, PETER, AND ROSS D. WALLER, "Community Development and Adult Education in Urban Areas," *International Review of Community Development,* Number 8, 1961, "Current Problems in Community Development."

————, *Some Problems of Communication in Extension and Community Development Campaigns,* Booklet: Overseas Visual Aid Center 1964, London, England.

Erie Workbook for Community Development Action. U.S. Chamber of Commerce, 1960, compiled by Howard Evans. Also see *Community Development Pamphlet Series,* Chamber of Commerce of the U.S.A., Washington, D.C., 1960.

FRANKLIN, RICHARD, "Community Development: An American's Perspective," from Proceedings of *The International Seminar on the Role of Community Development,* University of New England, Armidale, N.S.W., Australia, February 4-18, 1964.

GALES, EDWIN A., "Political Implications of Community Development Programs in the Newly Developing Areas of the World," *Community Development Review,* Vol. 6, No. 3, September 1961.

HAIGH, GERARD V., "Competing Strategies for the Community Development Function in the Peace Corps," *International Review of Community Development,* Number 12, 1963.

HAWLEY, JOHN B., "Recruitment, Selection and Training for International Community Development," *International Review of Community Development,* Number 12, 1963.

"How" of Community Development. Community Development Bulletin, No. 2, September 1956. (now the *Community Development Review*)

INTERNATIONAL CONFERENCE OF SOCIAL WORK, *Rural and Urban Community Development in the U.S.A.,* Report of the 11th Annual Conference, Rio de Janeiro, Brazil, 1962. New York: International Conference of Social Work, 1962.

————, "Social Progress through Social Planning," Report of the U.S. Committee to the 12th Annual Conference of Social Work, Athens, Greece, September 1964.

LaGASSÉ, JEAN H., "Community Development in Manitoba," *Human Organization,* Vol. XX, No. 4, Winter 1961–1962.

"Leadership Library," Association Press, New York. A series of booklets on various aspects of groups and group leadership.

LEET, GLEN, *The Analysis and Evaluation of Community Development Project Proposals,* New York: Community Development Foundation, 1962. See also other papers by the same author, published by the Community Development Foundation.

* ———, *Partnerships Available in the Community Development Foundation Counselor Corps.* New York: Community Development Foundation, n.d.

MAYO, SELZ C., "Understanding Rural Community Development," *Social Forces,* Vol. 37, No. 2, December 1958.

MEZIROW, J. D., "Community Development as an Educational Process," *International Review of Community Development,* Number 5, 1960, Theories and Values.

MIAL, CURTIS, "Community Development: A Democratic Social Process," *Adult Leadership,* April 1958.

——— AND DOROTHY MIAL, "The Development, Training, and Use of Leadership Resources in Community Development Programs," *Community Development Review,* Vol. 7, No. 1, June 1962.

——— AND ———, "Observations on Community Development in Europe," *International Review of Community Development,* Number 6, 1960.

* MINICLIER, LOUIS M., "Community Development Defined," *Community Development Review,* No. 3, December 1956.

———, "Community Development in the World Today: Ten Years of Progress," *Community Development Review,* Vol. 7, No. 1, June 1962.

———, "Economic Development and Community Development," *Community Development Review,* Vol. 8, No. 2, June 1963.

———, "Social Group Work in Community Development Programs," *Community Development Review,* Vol. 7, No. 1, June 1962.

MOE, EDWARD O., "Utah Community Development Program," *Community Development Review,* Vol. 8, No. 2, June 1963.

* MURPHY, GARDNER, AND LOIS MURPHY, "The Ego at Work in India," *Contemporary Psychology,* Number 4, September 1959.

* NATIONAL TRAINING LABORATORIES, *Community Development,* Selected Reading Series Four. Washington, D.C.: National Training Laboratories, 1961.

NATIONAL UNIVERSITY EXTENSION ASSOCIATION, *Proceedings of the Third Annual NUEA Community Development Seminar,* Southern Illinois University, June 9-13, 1963. Community Development Publication #8, Southern Illinois University, Carbondale, Illinois.

OGDEN, JESS, "A Philosophy of Community Development," *Adult Leadership,* April 1958.

PERPETUA, ANTONIÓ A., "Training in Community Development," Paper presented before the SEATO Conference on Community Development, Baguio City December 7-16, 2960, Manila: Presidential Assistant on Community Development, 1961, 36 pp.

PONSIOEN, J. A., "Community Development as a Process," *International Review of Community Development,* Number 6, 1960, Europe.

POSTON, RICHARD W., "Comparative Community Organization," *Community Development Review,* Vol. 8, No. 1, March 1963.

* *Proceedings of the Seminar on Community Development,* Department of Health Education, University of North Carolina, Chapel Hill, 1963.

RIVKIN, MALCOLM D., "Let's Think Small for Development," *International Development Review,* Vol. V, No. 1, March 1963.

* ROSECRANCE, FRANCIS C., *You and Your Community,* New York University, American Community Project, "The Community Then and Now." New York University Press, 1954. One of a series.

SEHNERT, FRANK H., *A Functional Framework for the Action Process in Community Development.* Carbondale, Illinois: Community Development Department, Southern Illinois University, 1962. Draft edition, mimeographed.

STENSLAND, PER G., "Urban Community Development," *Community Development Review,* No. 8, March 1958.

THEOBALD, ROBERT, "Needed: A New Development Philosophy," *International Development Review,* Vol. VI, No. 1, March 1964.

UNITED NATIONS BUREAU OF SOCIAL AFFAIRS, *Social Progress through Community Development.* New York, 1961.

UNITED NATIONS, DEPARTMENT OF ECONOMIC AND SOCIAL AFFAIRS, *Community Development and National Development,* Report of the Ad Hoc Group of Experts on Community Development, March 1963.

———, *Community Development and Related Services.* New York, 1960.

———, *Community Development in Urban Areas.* Report by the Secretary-General. New York, 1961.

———, *The Social Training of Front-Line Rural Development Workers.* New York, 1962.

* United Presbyterian Church U.S.A., Board of National Missions, *The City, God's Gift to the Church.* New York, 1963.

United States Army, Civic Affairs School, *Training Manual for Village Level Workers.* Fort Gordon, Georgia, n.d. "Special Text," originally published by the Community Projects Administration, Planning Commission, Government of India.

United States Department of Commerce, "Handbook of Federal Aids to Communities." Washington, D.C.: Government Printing Office, 1963. A reference to the various types of government aids available to communities.

* Wale, Fred, "Education in Community Development," *Community Development Seminar Proceedings,* University of North Carolina, Department of Health Education, 1963.

Warren, Roland L., *Community Development and Social Work Practice.* Report of a Workshop on Community Development in the U.S.A. at Brandeis University (1962). New York: National Association of Social Workers, 1962.

PUBLISHED BIBLIOGRAPHIES

Bester, George C., and Holway R. Jones, *City Planning: A Basic Bibliography.* Sacramento, Calif.: California Council of Civil Engineers and Land Surveyors, 1962. See especially page 98 and following, "Citizen Participation."

Community Development Bibliography. University of London, Institute of Education, Malet Street, W.C. 1, London, England. In Bulletin of Acquisitions, April 1964, and previous issues.

Dunham, Arthur, *Community Development, Rural and Urban: A Selective Bibliography.* New York: International Conference of Social Work, May 1961.

———, and Rameshwar Nath Paul, "Community Development: A Working Bibliography," *Community Development Review,* March 1959.

Foster, Robert J., *Human Factors in Civic Action: A Selected Annotated Bibliography.* Washington, D. C.: George Washington University Human Resources Research Office and the Department of the Army, June 1963.

Lackey, Alvin S., "A Working Bibliography in Community Development," *Community Development Review,* Vol. 8, No. 2, June 1963.

The Literature of Community Development: A Bibliographic Guide. Prepared by J. D. Mezirow for the Agency for International

Development and The Peace Corps. Washington, D.C., Government Printing Office, 1964.

UNITED NATIONS, *United Nations Series on Community Development: Selective Book List*. New York: Department of Economic and Social Affairs, 1960.

A Working Bibliography on Community Development, Carl R. Jantzen and Iwao Ishino, December 1962. Institute for Community Development, Continuing Education Service, Michigan State University, East Lansing, Michigan.

MAGAZINES AND PERIODICALS IN COMMUNITY DEVELOPMENT AND RELATED FIELDS

Adult Education. Quarterly. Adult Education Association, 1225 19th Street, N.W., Washington, D.C. 20006.

Adult Leadership. Monthly. Same address as *Adult Education*.

AID Digest. Agency for International Development, Washington, D.C.

Community Development Bulletin. Quarterly. Community Development Clearing House, Institute of Education, University of London. Malet Street, W.C. 1, London, England. (scheduled to cease publication as of December 31, 1964)

Community Development Review. Agency for International Development, Washington, D.C.

Fundamental and Adult Education. Quarterly. Published in English, French, and Spanish. English edition, UNESCO Publications Center, 801 Third Avenue, New York, N.Y.

Human Organization. Society for Applied Anthropology, Rand Hall, Cornell University, Ithaca, N.Y.

International Development Review. Quarterly. Society for International Development, 1346 Connecticut Avenue, N.W., Washington, D.C.

International Review of Community Development. International Federation of Settlements and Neighborhood Centres, Piazza Cavalieri di Malta 2, Roma, Italy. Semi-annual, complete issue devoted to a single topic of interest in the community development field.

International Social Work. Quarterly. International Conference of Social Work, 345 East 46th Street, New York, N.Y.

Journal of Social Issues. Society for the Psychological Study of Social Issues, P.O. Box 1248, Ann Arbor, Mich.

Koinonia Magazine. Koinonia Foundation, Box 5744, Baltimore 8, Md.

322   *Appendix II*

Rural Sociology. Quarterly. Rural Sociological Society, Department
of Rural Sociology, Cornell University, Ithaca, N.Y. Frequent
articles of interest to the community development field.

Transaction. Bi-monthly. Published by the Community Leadership
Project, Washington University, St. Louis, Mo.

UNESCO Courier. UNESCO Publications Center, 801 Third Avenue,
New York, N.Y.

SOME STUDIES OF LOCAL DEVELOPMENT

* ABRAHAMSON, JULIA, *A Neighborhood Finds Itself.* New York: Harper and Row, Publishers, Inc., 1959. (book)

AMERICAN FRIENDS SERVICE COMMITTEE, "Barpali," a 20-minute
film concentrated on the "social and technical assistance program of the AFSC in one particular village in India." (film)

BIDDLE, WILLIAM W., *A Pattern of Fundamental Education: A Puerto
Rican Project Report.* Program of Community Dynamics, Earlham College, Richmond, Indiana. Annual Report #8, 1956.
(pamphlet)

———, *People Grow in Communities: A Case Study from a Small
Town.* Program of Community Dynamics, Earlham College,
Richmond, Indiana. Annual Report #9, 1957. (pamphlet)

* ——— AND LOUREIDE J. BIDDLE, *Community Dynamics Processes:
Two Case Studies of People in Development.* New York:
Schwarzhaupt Foundation, 1962. (pamphlet)

BINGHAM, JONATHAN B., *Shirt-Sleeve Diplomacy: Point Four in Action.* New York: The John Day Company, Inc., 1953. Examples
of Point Four programs in local communities. (book)

BRUYN, SEVERYN T., *Communities in Action.* New Haven, Conn.:
College and University Press, 1963. Community action in four
U.S. cities. (book)

COADY, M. M., *Masters of Their Own Destiny.* New York: Harper
and Row, Publishers, Inc., 1939. How people in a bleak area
of Nova Scotia "lifted themselves by the bootstraps," with the
stimulation of a local priest, the author. (book)

Community Development Review, Vol. 8, No. 1, March 1963, "An
Indian Community Development Project in Bolivia," Lorand
D. Schweng. (periodical)

Community Development Review, Number 6, September 1957. Entire issue: "The Case Study: Its Abuses and Uses," by Irwin T.
Sanders; also three specific case studies of community development overseas, in India, the Philippines, and Pakistan. (periodical)

Du Sautoy, Peter, "Case Studies from Ghana," 1962 and following. Department of Adult Education, University of Manchester, Manchester, England. (manuscript)

———, *The Organization of a Community Development Programme.* London: Oxford University Press, 1962. This book and du Sautoy's earlier *Community Development in Ghana* (Oxford University Press, 1958) give a detailed account of the community development program in that country. (books)

Franklin, Richard, "Another Cantebury Tale: A Case History in Community Development," *Adult Leadership,* September 1961. (article)

General Federation of Women's Clubs and the Sears Roebuck Foundation, *The Story of the 1962–1964 Community Improvement Program, "Won among Many."* Washington, D.C.: General Federation of Women's Clubs, 1964. (brochure)

Journal of Social Issues, Vol. XVI, No. 4, 1960, "Leadership and Participation in a Changing Rural Community." Edited by John Harding, Edward C. Devereux, Jr., and Urie Bronfenbrenner. (The "Springdale Story.") (periodical)

King, Clarence, *Working with People in Small Communities.* New York: Harper and Row, Publishers, Inc., 1958. Eleven case studies of development projects overseas. (book)

Lipman, Rabbi E. J., and Albert Vorspan, *Tale of Ten Cities.* New York: Union of Hebrew Congregations, 1962. Study of the relationship and interaction of the Protestants, Catholics, and Jews in ten American cities. (book)

* Loring, William C., Jr., Frank L. Sweetser, and Charles F. Ernst, *Community Organization for Citizen Participation in Urban Renewal.* Boston: Housing Association of Metropolitan Boston, 1957. Contains brief case outlines of various citizen and neighborhood groups formed under the Boston program discussed in the book. (book)

* McKee, Elmore, *The People Act.* New York: Harper and Row, Publishers, Inc., 1955. A series of case studies of people in action in various parts of the U.S. (book)

Mann, Peggy, "We Moved into the 'Worst Block in Town,'" *Redbook,* November 1963. (article)

* Mayer, Albert, and Associates, *Pilot Project, India.* Berkeley, Calif.: University of California Press, 1959. The story of the rural development project in Etawah, Uttar Pradesh, India. (book)

324 Appendix II

MOORE, HENRY E., *Nine Help Themselves*. University of Texas: Southwestern Cooperative Program in Educational Administration, 1955. (book)

MOTT, WENDALL, "A Village Builds a Road," *American Friend*, January 24, 1957. (article)

OGDEN, JEAN, *Five Community Development Stories Out of West Africa*, Case Studies Series B, Vol. 1, November 1962. Agency for International Development, Washington, D.C. (pamphlet)

———— AND JESS OGDEN, *Small Communities in Action*. New York: Harper and Row, Publishers, Inc., 1946; and *These Things We Tried*, Harper and Row, Publishers, Inc., 1947. Stories from the small community experience of the Ogden husband and wife community development team. (books)

POSTON, RICHARD W., "Community Education in Southern Illinois," in National Society for the Study of Education, *Community Education*. Chicago: University of Chicago Press, 1959.

ROSS, MURRAY G., *Case Histories in Community Organization*. New York: Harper and Row, Publishers, Inc., 1958. (book)

Southern Illinois University, "Battleground, U.S.A.," a 16 mm sound film produced by the Department of Community Development at Southern Illinois University. Shows how the community development staff moved into a community and set up a community development program. (film)

TEAF, HOWARD M., JR., AND PETER G. FRANCK, *Hands across Frontiers: Case Studies in Technical Cooperation*. The Hague: Netherlands Universities Foundation for International Cooperation, 1955. Distributed in the United States by Cornell University Press, Ithaca, New York. Outlines and describes various programs of technical assistance overseas, by the United States government and private organizations. Implications for community development work.

UNIVERSITY OF NEW ENGLAND, Armidale, N.S.W., Australia, *Kyogle: A Year's Work in Community Development*. Department of Adult Education, Pamphlet No. 3, June 1962. (pamphlet)

INDEX

Index